DATE DUE

MAR – 1 2004		
OCT – 1 2004		
OCT 1 6 2006		
MAR 0 2 2007		
OCT 1 0 2007		
SEP 25 2007		
SEP 3 0 2008		
SEP 2 6 2008		
FEB 18 2010		
MAR 2 6 2012		
GAYLORD		PRINTED IN U.S.A.

PETRARCH

PETRARCH

FROM A COPY BY MRS. ARTHUR LEMON OF THE PORTRAIT IN THE LAURENTIAN LIBRARY, FLORENCE

PETRARCH

HIS LIFE AND TIMES

BY

H. C. HOLLWAY-CALTHROP

LATE OF BALLIOL COLLEGE, OXFORD
BURSAR OF ETON COLLEGE

WITH TWENTY-FOUR ILLUSTRATIONS

NEW YORK
COOPER SQUARE PUBLISHERS, INC.
1972

Originally Published 1907
Published 1972 by Cooper Square Publishers, Inc.
59 Fourth Avenue, New York, N. Y. 10003
International Standard Book No. 0-8154-0406-9
Library of Congress Catalog Card No. 75-187413

Printed in the United States of America

TO

WILHELMINA

MY WIFE

THE publican, that man of sin,
To lure confiding drinkers in
And advertise his beer and wine,
Over his door displays a sign :

So to get readers for my book
And tempt them in its leaves to look,
I at its front and entry frame
A lure, the best I know—your name.

PREFACE

IN a short Life of Petrarch, which aims at interesting the reader in fourteenth-century history, and in one of its most fascinating personalities, there can be no room for the elaborate discussion of chronological and other "cruces." Students of the period know only too well how many, how intricate, and how exasperating these difficulties are; happily they are hardly ever of first-rate importance. In these pages I have done my best to ensure accuracy, and in no case have I put forward a statement without careful consideration of the evidence; but in no case, either, has space permitted me to give a full digest of such evidence. In trivial matters I have simply stated what seems to me the most probable version of the facts: in questions of more moment I have indicated the existence of a doubt and of possible alternative solutions. Usually, but not always, I have followed Fracassetti, to whom all students of Petrarch and his times owe a debt of deepest gratitude.

It is equally impossible within the limits of a Preface to give a list of the authorities on which any life of Petrarch must be based. Anyone who wishes to pursue the subject further may be referred to the first chapter of Dr. Koerting's *Petrarca's Leben und Werke* (Leipzig, 1878), where he will find an admirable digest of the chief materials available to that date; a foreign bookseller will keep him informed as to later publications. Here I may just mention that de Sade, Baldelli, Domenico Rossetti, Fracassetti, and Dr. Koerting are the modern writers to whom my obligations are greatest.

After all, however, Petrarch himself is far and away the most important authority for his own biography; the following narrative is substantially taken from his writings, and I think there are very few statements in it which do not find valid support —I dare not say complete proof—there.

My cordial thanks for helpful correspondence are due to Mr. Lionel Cust, to the Rev. E. H. R. Tatham, to Dr. Paget Toynbee and, above all, to Professor Ker, who has constantly encouraged my work on Petrarch, and has given this book the inestimable benefit of his supervision.

Equally cordial are my thanks to three younger friends, Mr. D. Home of Christ's College, Mr. F. W. Hunt of Oriel, and Mr. Dennis Robertson, K.S., of Eton, for the unstinted help with which they have supplemented the deficiencies of my eyesight by writing my MS., verifying my references, and correcting my proofs.

H. C. H.-C.

ETON COLLEGE
May, 1907

CONTENTS

CHAPTER I

EARLY YEARS, 1304–1326 . . . . PAGE 1

CHAPTER II

AVIGNON AND LAURA, 1326–1329 . . . 26

CHAPTER III

TRAVEL AND FRIENDSHIP, 1329–1336 . . . 43

CHAPTER IV

ROME AND VAUCLUSE, 1336–1340 . . . 72

CHAPTER V

THE CROWN OF SONG, 1340–1341 . . . 92

CHAPTER VI

PARMA, NAPLES, AND VAUCLUSE, 1341–1347 . . 102

CHAPTER VII

ROME AND RIENZI, 1347 122

CHAPTER VIII

THE GREAT PLAGUE AND THE DEATH OF LAURA, 1348–1349 135

CHAPTER IX

FLORENCE AND BOCCACCIO, 1350 . . . 146

ix

CHAPTER X

VAUCLUSE, 1351–1353 155

CHAPTER XI

MILAN AND THE VISCONTI, 1353–1354 . . . 174

CHAPTER XII

CHARLES IV AND PRAGUE, 1354–1357 . . . 187

CHAPTER XIII

DOMESTICA, 1357–1360 201

CHAPTER XIV

THE FOUNDER OF HUMANISM—PETRARCH'S WORK AND
ITS RESULT 215

CHAPTER XV

THE SORROWFUL YEARS OF THE SECOND PLAGUE—DEATHS
OF FRIENDS, 1360–1363 230

CHAPTER XVI

THE MASTER AND HIS PUPILS—VENICE, PADUA, AND
PAVIA, 1364–1367 244

CHAPTER XVII

THE POPE IN ROME, 1367–1370 270

CHAPTER XVIII

THE LAST YEARS, 1370–1374 285

CHAPTER XIX

CONCLUSION AND SUMMARY 303

INDEX 309

LIST OF ILLUSTRATIONS

PETRARCH; FROM A COPY BY MRS. ARTHUR LEMON OF THE
PORTRAIT IN THE LAURENTIAN LIBRARY, FLORENCE   *Frontispiece*

FACING PAGE

VIEW OF BOLOGNA   21

VIEW OF AVIGNON   28

LAURA; FROM A COPY BY MRS. ARTHUR LEMON OF THE PORTRAIT
IN THE LAURENTIAN LIBRARY, FLORENCE   .   .   . 32

THE PALACE OF THE POPES, AVIGNON   49

THE MONUMENT OF POPE JOHN XXII, AVIGNON   .   .   . 64

THE TOMBS OF THE SCALIGERI, VERONA   88

THE MONUMENT OF KING ROBERT OF NAPLES   .   .   . 94

POPE CLEMENT VI; FROM A PORTRAIT IN THE BRITISH MUSEUM 107

VIEW OF VAUCLUSE AND THE CASTLE OF THE BISHOP OF
CAVAILLON 119

RIENZI; FROM AN ITALIAN PRINT 125

LAURA; FROM A PRINT IN THE PADUAN 1819 EDITION OF THE
CANZONIERE   137

BOCCACCIO; FROM A PORTRAIT IN THE BRITISH MUSEUM .   . 148

THE TOMB OF JACOPO II DA CARRARA, WITH INSCRIPTION BY
PETRARCH 154

VAUCLUSE; THE SORGUE AND PETRARCH'S GARDEN .   .   . 163

THE EQUESTRIAN STATUE OF BERNABÒ VISCONTI   .   .   . 178

THE TOMB OF ANDREA DANDOLO, WITH INSCRIPTION BY PETRARCH 184

INNOCENT VI; FROM A PORTRAIT IN THE BRITISH MUSEUM   . 204

THE TOMB OF NICCOLÒ ACCIAIUOLI   214

PETRARCH'S HOUSE IN VENICE   241

THE CASTLE OF PAVIA 253

URBAN V; FROM A PORTRAIT IN THE BRITISH MUSEUM   .   . 272

PETRARCH'S HOUSE AT ARQUÀ   288

PETRARCH'S TOMB   303

PETRARCH AND HIS TIMES

CHAPTER I

EARLY YEARS

1304-1326

F RANCESCO PETRARCA, better known to English-speaking readers as Petrarch, was a wanderer from his birth. Owing to his father's banishment from Florence, he was "begotten and born in exile"; and throughout the seventy years of his life he never continued long in one stay. But the habitual stir and bustle of his existence contrast strongly with the quiet of some of its interludes. Few men can ever have had a more varied experience or a wider range of interests than this restless traveller, the companion of cardinals and princes, the friend of great statesmen, the ambassador from the Lords of Milan to an Emperor, who was also the hermit of Vaucluse, the poet of Laura, the lover of country life known to a circle of devoted friends as "Silvanus," the indefatigable student, the great scholar to whom, more than to any other man, we owe the Revival of Learning in Europe. His character was as rich in variety as the circumstances of his life. He cherished great ideals, and did more than a man may well dare to hope towards their realisation ; but he often erred in his application of them to the problems of practical life.   Intellectually the most gifted man of his age, he rendered incalculable service to the mental development of mankind; but he occasionally wasted his brilliant talent in trivial and unworthy controversy.   Fervent in piety, enthusiastic in friendship and in the pursuit of noble aims, he was not exempt from frailty, while the ardour of his temperament explains, and may be held to excuse, a certain want of balance in his character.   We see in him no mirror of perfection, but a man of high virtues and splendid gifts, of quick human sympathies and impulses, of a self-questioning spirit not at unity with itself, of provoking but not ignoble foibles, a man to admire, to pity, sometimes to quarrel with, to love always.

Petrarch came of an ancient and honourable, but not a noble, family.   For three generations at least his ancestors had been Notaries in the city of Florence.   His great-grandfather, Ser Garzo, was a man of saintly life and great repute for wisdom, the counsellor and referee not only of neighbours and intimate friends, but of politicians and men of letters.   He lived to the age of 104, and died at last on his birthday in the same room in which he had been born.   His son, Ser Parenzo, seems to have maintained the honourable traditions of the family without adding to its distinction ; but his son again, Ser Petracco, the father of Petrarch, was a man of extraordinary talent, combining a refined

taste in literature with ability of the highest order
in the hereditary profession of the law. Born probably in 1267, he rose rapidly in the service of the
State, and before he was thirty-five years of age
had held many important public positions; for
instance, he was Chancellor of the Commission for
Reforms, and in 1301 was a member of an important embassy to Pisa.

The highest dignities of the State seemed to lie
within the reasonable compass of his ambition, and
it must have been about this time that the happy
prospects of his life were crowned by his marriage
with the young and charming Eletta Canigiani.
But in the year 1302 he was arraigned before a
criminal court on a trumped-up charge of having
falsified a legal document, convicted in his absence,
and sentenced to a fine of 1000 lire or the loss of
his right hand. Banishment and the confiscation
of his property were the result of his refusal to surrender and take his sentence. Every one knew
that the charge was false, a pretext devised to give
some colour of justification to the banishment of a
political opponent, and that his real offence consisted in his adhesion to the party of the " White
Guelfs," of which the poet Dante was the most
illustrious member.

The cross-currents of mediæval politics in Italy
are numberless, and it is hard to steer an intelligible
course among them; every rule had almost as many
exceptions as examples, and every principle was
liable to violation to suit the convenience of its
nominal upholders. But speaking broadly, it may

be said that the Guelf championed civic independence under the hegemony of the Papacy, the
Ghibellin personal government under the sovereignty of the Emperor.   How far either Pope or
Emperor exercised an effective control within his
own   party   depended   mainly   on   his   personal
character and that of those with whom he had
to deal; the Angevin Kings of Naples and the
Republic of Florence were often more powerful
than the Pope, while on the Ghibellin side the
great Lords of Lombardy habitually acted as independent princes, and scarcely pretended to give
more than a nominal allegiance to the successors
of Frederick II.

In Florence the Guelf party had ruled supreme
for nearly forty years, and the political struggle
centred upon the efforts of the people to limit the
authority of the nobles.   Suddenly the Guelf party
was rent in twain by a feud which began, much as
our own Wars of the Roses are said to have begun,
in a domestic brawl.   The feud spread from Pistoia,
the city of its origin, to Florence, where the nobles,
seeing in it a chance of regaining the power and
privileges recently taken from them, espoused the
quarrel of the " Blacks," or extreme Guelfs, and
accused the " Whites," the more moderate faction,
of endangering the safety of the State by encouraging Ghibellinism.   With Florence thus divided
against herself, the right arm of the Church was
paralysed, a state of things so serious that even
Pope Boniface VIII was for once in his life disposed to moderate counsels, and nominated Charles

of Valois, brother of the King of France and cousin
of the King of Naples, to act as mediator between
the factions. There were old ties of friendship and
alliance between the Royal House of France and
the Republic of Florence, and the great body of the
people gladly welcomed the Prince, who swore to
respect their laws and liberties, and to deal justly
with all parties. By these promises he gained admission to the city, into which he made his solemn
entry on All Souls' Day, 1301. But he was no
sooner within the walls than he shamelessly violated
all his pledges, set at naught the Constitution of the
State, and openly encouraged the "Black" faction
to murder and rob their principal opponents. For
the violence of the "Black" Guelfs some excuse
may be found; Florence was surrounded by bitter
enemies, and the honest men of the party may
really have thought that the "Whites" had been
guilty of disloyalty to the Guelf cause, or of weakness in serving it, while the nobles had been exasperated by special legislation directed against
their order, and could hardly be expected to forego
an opportunity of revenge. But for Charles no
shadow of justification can be pleaded; he was
false to his commission, false to his plighted word,
false to the people who trusted him. His conduct
ranks among the meanest betrayals which history
records.

It was probably at this time that Ser Petracco
was forced to leave the city, though formal pro-
ceedings were not taken against him till many
months later, and the date of his "trial" and con-

demnation is October 2nd, 1302. His young wife
went with him into banishment, and they found a
refuge, together with many of their friends and
fellow-exiles, in the Ghibellin city of Arezzo, a
retreat especially convenient to Petracco, as his
hereditary property at Incisa lay on the direct
road to Florence, and only twelve miles across the
State boundary.

In 1303 he returned for a few weeks to Florence
as ambassador for his party. Boniface VIII was
dead, and Benedict XI made another attempt at
reconciling the Guelf factions. With this object he
sent as Legate to Tuscany the Cardinal Niccolò da
Prato, an honest man zealous for peace. On May
10th, 1303, the Florentines received the Cardinal
with open arms, gave him the temporary government of the city, and elected Priors devoted to his
interests, who issued safe-conducts to the envoys of
the White Guelfs.

All promised well; the people were earnest for
peace, the Cardinal was benevolent and sincere;
the "White" envoys seem to have been reasonable
in their demands. But the "Black" extremists
were resolved to prevent a peace which would ruin
their supremacy in the State, and they shrank from
nothing that might serve their object. By a clever
forgery of the Cardinal's hand and seal, they persuaded the people that he was summoning a Ghibellin army to Florence; the negotiations were
broken off; the envoys returned to report their
failure to their friends, and the Cardinal, suspected
by every one except those who had brought him

into suspicion, retired to his native Prato, and laid the territory of Florence under an interdict.

Peaceful means having failed, the "Whites" resolved on an attempt to redress their grievances by force. The Cardinal, in an evil hour for his reputation as a statesman, encouraged them in their design, and so played into the hands of the "Blacks" and confirmed the bulk of the people in their suspicions of him. Acting on his suggestion, the exiles mustered their forces and appeared before the walls of Florence on the morning of July 20th, 1304. But scattered as they had been among the cities of Tuscany and the Emilia, concerted action was difficult and secrecy impossible; some of their contingents arrived too late; they found their enemies forewarned; and after some fruitless skirmishing they were forced to retreat and disperse.

We do not know whether Petracco, who had played so prominent a part in the peace negotiations, shared the responsibility for this ill-judged and ill-executed appeal to arms; but he probably shared its dangers, and if so, he was away from home when his eldest son was born. "On Monday, July 20th, 1304," Petrarch tells us in one of his letters, "the very day on which the exiles were beaten back from the walls of Florence, just as the dawn began to brighten, I was born in the city of Arezzo, in Garden Street as it is called, with such travail of my mother and at such peril of her life, that not only the midwives, but even the physicians believed for some time that she was dead." The

street still keeps its old name of *Vicolo dell' Orto;*
the house which first sheltered the poet of Laura
and founder of Humanism still stands, and now bears
on its walls a marble tablet inscribed with Petrarch's
name, with three passages from his writings in
which he speaks of his birthplace, and with an
attestation of the transfer of the house in 1810 from
private to public ownership. The city has always
been proud of her accidental connection with
Petrarch, and he for his part was equally proud of
her as his birthplace. "Arezzo," he declared to an
Aretine friend, "has been far more generous to an
alien in blood than has Florence to her own son."
And more than four centuries after his death
Arezzo reaped a rich reward for her hospitality to
his parents, when Napoleon after Marengo, out of
reverence for the memory of Petrarch, exacted no
penalty for the stubborn resistance of the Aretines.

Intimately as his name has been associated with
that of Arezzo in the imagination of posterity, he
spent there only the first six months of his life. In
February, 1305, Eletta left Arezzo with her little
son, and went to live on Petracco's hereditary
property at Incisa. On the way the future poet
had a narrow escape from drowning : he was
carried "on the arm of a strong young fellow, as
Metabus carried Camilla, wrapped in a linen cloth
and slung from a knotted staff. While crossing the
Arno, the young man was thrown by a stumble of
his horse, and nearly perished in the rushing stream
through his efforts to save the burden entrusted to
him." No harm came of the accident, and the

party arrived safely at Incisa, where Petrarch was to spend the next seven years of his life.

Somehow or other this little country estate had escaped the decree of confiscation which deprived Ser Petracco of the rest of his property. The obvious theory that it belonged to Eletta's family and not to her husband's is disproved by documents; probably, therefore, Petracco was not its sole owner; he may have held it jointly with other relatives, or it may have been settled on his wife in return for the dowry which she brought him. Whatever the explanation, Eletta was able to live there unmolested, and Petracco, though banished and proscribed, could easily visit her by stealth. The rulers of a mediæval State cared chiefly about its cities and fortified places; so long as there were no conspiracies hatching, they would not be over-active in policing a little country village. Moreover, the great range of the Prato Magno, at the foot of which Incisa lies, offers many a lonely sheep-track by which an exile might travel unsuspected, and many a wooded nook where, sheltered by friends, he might find a hiding-place from any casual search-party. Petracco certainly did contrive to visit his wife, and in 1307 their second son, Gherardo, was born; a third boy, who died in infancy, must have been born much later, though the local inscriptions at Incisa claim him too as a native of the place, for Petrarch retained a vivid recollection of his love for this baby-brother and of his poignant sorrow at the child's death.

We have no details of the life at Incisa; but any

one who has lived the year through in Tuscany can imagine them for himself, for the essential features of Tuscan life are as little changed as the scenery itself. You may search Europe from end to end and find no more ideal spot than Incisa for a poet's upbringing. It is a bright little township on the left bank of the Arno, deriving its name from the gorge or cutting which the river has here made for itself through the rock. To the west are steep round-topped hills rich with vegetation ; to the east a lovely maze of low ridge and fertile valley lies between the channel of the Arno and the massive range of the Prato Magno. Then, as now, the corn grew between rows of pollards, mostly maple, over which twined the stems and tendrils of the vines ; then, as now, you might see by the summer moonlight, after the corn was reaped, the white or fawn-coloured oxen moving slowly between the trees, dragging through the stubble such a plough as that of which Cincinnatus held the stilts. Mingled with the vineyards are groves of olives ; above them on the slopes of the mountain grow the chestnuts, the meal of which is a staple food of the country-folk ; higher yet is a belt of pines and beeches ; and above all the immense expanse of short, crisp grass, sweet to crop and elastic to tread, from which the range takes its name of " the Great Meadow." The passion for Nature, which distinguishes Petrarch from his predecessors, was surely first aroused in him by the beauty of his childhood's home.

Nor was this his only debt to Incisa. From

every peasant he would hear those Tuscan songs which are distinguished above all popular poetry by grace of imagery and refinement of diction ; his quick, impressionable brain would receive from them its first idea of poetic expression ; here surely was the origin of that Italian spirit which in later years he breathed into the courtly forms of the Provençal lyric. A tablet marks the house, still standing on the steep hillside amid the ruins of an ancient castle, which tradition assigns as the home of Eletta and her children ; another tablet of very recent erection on the little town hall commemorates Petrarch's connection with the place ; it is a sound instinct which has led the composers of both inscriptions to emphasise the fact that here the future poet's childish lips first opened to the sweet accents of his mother-speech.

The current of Italian politics had borne him as a baby to Incisa ; the same stormy current swept him out of this quiet home seven years later, and carried him to have his first glimpse of the great world at Pisa. Henry of Luxemburg had been elected King of the Romans with the full consent of Pope Clement V, if not actually at his suggestion ; for the first time it seemed as if Emperor and Pope might work heartily together to reconcile the Italian factions. Never was man so well fitted as Henry for this honourable task. Men said of him that he was neither puffed up by victory nor cast down by defeat ; among the petty intrigues of German princes and Italian despots he walked serene, intent upon justice, so that he did indeed

deserve the magnificent eulogy of Dante, who assigned a seat in the highest heaven, in the very
Rose of the Blessed, to "the lofty Henry, who
should come to guide Italy aright before she was
ready." He failed, but his failure was more glorious
than the successes of meaner men. In the spring
of 1312, however, when he marched through Lombardy into Tuscany, the hopes of his friends ran
high. The Pope, though notoriously capable of
treachery, had not yet declared himself a traitor to
the Emperor of his choice, and if the Cæsar's
authority were backed by the Pope, Guelf and Ghibellin alike might be expected to bow before it.
The prospect was still fair when Henry took up
his quarters in Pisa, a stronghold of Ghibellinism loyal through all vicissitudes to its noblest
champion. Hither came Ser Petracco, with many
of his political friends, to meet the Emperor, and
hither, finding himself at last in a place of safety,
he summoned his wife and children to join him.
So it was in Pisa that the little Petrarch first beheld
the glories of a rich and artistic Italian city, at this
time the rival of Florence herself in the beauty of
her buildings. The cathedral and the baptistery
stood then as we see them to-day, only the bronze
doors and a few decorative details remaining to be
added at a later date; the leaning tower wanted
only the topmost tier of its arches; the cloister of
the Campo Santo was built, and the best artists of
Tuscany had begun to cover its walls with frescoes
of the rarest beauty. By the Arno stood the little
fishermen's chapel of the Spina, a gem in marble,

finished only a year or two before, and the quays
on either side were lined with a stately row of
palaces which Venice herself could not surpass for
many a day to come. To a quick-witted child of
precocious æsthetic sense Pisa must have seemed a
city of fairyland.

He stayed about a year within her walls, till the
defeat of Henry VII quenched the last spark of
genuine Imperialist enthusiasm in Italy. Henry
had been crowned in Rome, but in other respects
his expedition ended in failure. The Pope played
him false ; Naples and Florence met him with open
and successful opposition ; and after a fruitless campaign he died in August, 1313, at Buonconvento, a
little fortified town in the territory of Siena. It was
commonly believed that a priest had poisoned the
consecrated elements, but there is no evidence of foul
play, and the fatigues of an arduous campaign may
well have brought about Henry's death by natural
causes. Indeed, it is probable that many suspected
poisonings in the Middle Ages were really cases of
"something in—itis," which the medical men of the
day were incompetent to diagnose.

Henry was laid to rest in his faithful Pisa, where
his tomb, by the master hand of Giovanni Pisano,
may still be seen ; and in his grave were buried the
last hopes of the Florentine exiles, who must now
choose between a shameful recantation and perpetual banishment. Like Dante, Ser Petracco had
once already rejected the former alternative ; he
now decided to leave Italy altogether, and to settle
in Avignon, whither Clement V had transferred the

Papal See four years before. So the party left
Pisa, apparently in the autumn of 1313, and travelled
to Genoa, where they were to take ship for Marseilles. Never did Petrarch forget that wonderful
journey by the foot of the Carrara Mountains and
along the Eastern Riviera. Forty years later he
recalled with rapture the memory "as of a lovely
dream, liker to a heavenly than an earthly dwelling-
place, even such as the poets celebrate when they
sing of the Elysian fields." The pleasant hill-paths,
the bright ravines, the stately towers and palaces
enchanted him ; the hillsides seemed a vast garden
of cedar, vine, and olive ; and when at length he
entered Genoa, it seemed to him "a city of Kings,
the very temple of prosperity and threshold of
gladness."

Though short, his stay in Genoa was memorable
for the formation of the earliest and one of the most
intimate of his many friendships. He met here
Guido Settimo, a boy of his own age, who was to
be his fellow at school and college, his host at
Avignon and guest at Vaucluse, and of whom he
could write fifty years later that to see Guido, then
become Archbishop of Genoa, was much the same
as to see himself, since they had lived together
from childhood in perfect harmony of disposition
and everything else.

Guido's father, like Ser Petracco, was about to
settle at Avignon ; so at Genoa the two families
took ship together for Marseilles. A southerly
winter gale nearly wrecked them outside the
harbour, but they presently got safely to land, and

journeyed up the valley of the Rhone to Avignon.
Here they found themselves in a fresh difficulty :
"the place could barely accommodate the Roman
Pontiff and the Church, which had lately followed
him thither into exile, for it had in those days but a
small number of houses, so that it was overflowed
by this deluge of visitors." The fathers, accordingly,
decided to establish their families in the neighbouring town of Carpentras, "a little city in truth, but still
the chief place of a little province," where they found
suitable houses for themselves and a grammar school
for the education of their boys. Here Petrarch
spent four of the happiest years of his life. For
politicians, especially for those whose fortunes were
bound up with the Roman Curia, the times were
troublous. Pope Clement V died in this very town
of Carpentras, and the Conclave assembled there ;
but the Cardinals would not come to an agreement,
and the See remained vacant for two years. All
this mattered nothing to the two boys. "You remember those four years," Petrarch writes to Guido
in the letter already freely quoted; "what a delightful time it was, with perfect freedom from care, with
peace at home and liberty abroad, and with its
leisure hours spent amid the silence of the fields. I
am sure you share my feelings, and certainly I am
grateful to that season, or rather to the Author of
all seasons, who allowed me those years of absolute
calm, that undisturbed by any storm of trouble I
might drink in, so far as my poor wit allowed, the
sweet milk of boyish learning, to strengthen my
mind for digesting more solid nourishment."

The "sweet milk of boyish learning" was administered by Convennole of Prato, perhaps the
most celebrated schoolmaster of his day, and as
famous for the oddities of his character as for the
excellence of his teaching.   He was said to have
kept a school for fully sixty years, and his renown
was justified by the number of his pupils who afterwards attained to distinction in learning and politics
and to positions of eminence in the Church.   Among
them all Petrarch was his favourite ; this was so
notorious that in after-years Cardinal Giovanni
Colonna, who delighted in the old man's simplicity
and scholarship, used to tease him by asking :
" ' Tell me, master, among all your distinguished
pupils, whom you love, as I know, is there any
room in your heart for our Francesco?' And thereupon the old man's tears would rise so that he
would either be silent, or sometimes go away, or, if
he was able to speak, he would swear by everything
sacred that he loved none of them all so well."
There is good reason to think that he had been
Petrarch's tutor in Italy, and that he accompanied
the family to Avignon and Carpentras ; at all events,
he transferred his school thither, and there Petrarch
advanced under his tuition from childish lessons to
profounder studies in Latin grammar and literature, in rhetoric and in dialectic.   The last that we
hear of Convennole is a tragi-comic episode which
resulted in a serious literary loss.   In his old age
he fell into great poverty, and Ser Petracco helped
him liberally with money ; after the latter's death
he relied wholly on Petrarch, who gave him money

when he could, and when he had none, as was
often the case, procured him loans from richer
friends, or lent him something to pawn. One day
the old man's distress got the better of his honesty.
He borrowed two works of Cicero, the unique MS.
of the *De Gloria* and *The Laws*, together with some
other books, ostensibly for literary work of his own,
"for not a day passed without his planning out
some work with a high-sounding title, and writing a
preface for it, after which his fickle fancy would
straightway fly off to some totally different matter."
Presently his delay in returning the books led
Petrarch to suspect the truth, and he found that
Convennole had pawned them. He would have
redeemed them himself, and begged to be told the
pawnbroker's name; but the old man in an agony
of shame protested that he would do his duty, and
begged for time to redeem his honour. Petrarch
would insist no further; but Convennole's neces-
sities presently obliged him to return to Tuscany,
where he soon afterwards died, and Petrarch, who
was then at Vaucluse, heard nothing of his departure till the people of Prato sent to ask him to
write his epitaph. In spite of every effort, he could
never find a trace of his missing Cicero; "and so,"
he says, "I lost my books and my tutor at the
same time." Of *The Laws*, other copies were preserved, but the *De Gloria* has been a lost book
from that day.

It was while still a schoolboy at Carpentras, and
probably very early in his stay there, that Petrarch
first saw Vaucluse, the place which was afterwards

to be more closely associated with his name than any of his residences. Ser Petracco one day brought home Guido Settimo's uncle as his guest, and he, being a stranger to the neighbourhood, was anxious to see the celebrated source of the Sorgue. The two boys begged to be allowed to share the excursion, and as they were too small to ride on horseback alone, they were mounted each in front of a servant, and in this fashion Eletta, "the best of all mothers that ever I knew," as Petrarch calls her, who loved the little Guido almost as well as her own boys, was content to let them go. "And when we arrived at the source of the Sorgue," Petrarch continues, "I remember as though it had happened to-day how I was moved by the strange beauty of the spot, and how I spoke my boyish thoughts to myself as well as I could to this effect : Here is the place which best suits with my temper, and which, if ever I have the chance, I will prefer before great cities."

After four happy years at Carpentras the troubles of Petrarch's life began, when his father sent him to study law at the High School of Montpellier. Petrarch, now in his seventeenth year and a boy of precocious talent, already felt that literature was his vocation, and hitherto his father, a sound scholar with a finer literary judgment than most scholars of the day, had encouraged him in his tastes. "From my boyhood," he tells us, "at the age when others are gaping over Prosper and Æsop, I buckled to the books of Cicero, impelled both by natural instinct and by the advice of my father, who professed deep veneration for that author, and who

would easily have gained distinction as a man of
letters if his splendid talent had not been diverted by
the necessity of providing for his family. . . . At
that time I could not understand what I read, but
the sweetness of the language and majesty of the
cadences enchanted me, so that whatever else I
read or heard sounded harsh in my ears and quite
discordant. . . . And this daily increasing ardour
of mine was favoured by my father's admiration and
the sympathy which he showed for awhile with my
boyish study." Presently, however, Ser Petracco
changed his tone; his means had been seriously im-
paired by his political misfortunes; his son must
begin to think of a profession at which money could
be earned; what more natural than that he should
destine his brilliant boy for the traditional calling of
the family, in which he himself had won so considerable a reputation? It was well enough to unbend
the mind over the masterpieces of antiquity, but the
study of them must not interfere with the serious
business of life, and he began to bid the lad "forget
Cicero and set himself to the study of the laws of
borrowing and lending, of wills and their codicils,
of property in land and property in houses." One
day, finding that the young scholar could not be
persuaded to divorce himself from his classics,
Petracco took sterner measures. "I had got together," says Petrarch, "all the works of Cicero
that I could find, and had hidden them carefully
away for fear of the very thing that actually happened, when one day my father fished them out
and threw them into the fire before my very eyes,

to burn like the books of the heretics. At this I set up as terrible a howling as if I myself had been thrown upon the logs, whereupon my father, beholding my sorrow, plucked out two of the books just as the flames were on the point of reaching them, and holding Virgil in his right hand and Cicero's *Rhetoric* in his left, gave them with a smile, as an offering to my tears, saying, 'Keep the one for an occasional hour of recreation, and the other as a stimulus to your study of civil law.'"

Petrarch was a dutiful son, and for seven years applied himself diligently to the studies marked out for him by his father, and gave promise of great proficiency in them; but all the time his heart was elsewhere, and to the end of his life he regarded this period of legal study as "rather wasted than spent." Probably he underrated the benefit of it; an eager, fervent temper such as his needs discipline as well as instruction, and it may be that the steady grind at an uncongenial subject did much to develop his indefatigable industry, and to enable him to get the best results out of his genius when he came to apply it to the things for which he really cared.

At all events, he was happy at Montpellier, in spite of distasteful studies. The place was then "a most flourishing town, the sovereignty of which was vested in the King of Majorca with the exception of one corner belonging to the King of France, who . . . soon afterwards managed to get possession of all the rest. And what a peaceful calm prevailed there at that time, what wealth its merchants enjoyed, how full of scholars were the streets, and

VIEW OF BOLOGNA

Alinari

what a number of masters taught in the school!"
Above all, he still had Guido Settimo for his companion during the whole four years that he spent
there ; for Guido too was ordered to study the law,
and was happier than his friend in finding it congenial to his tastes and disposition.

Early in 1323 the two friends went to finish
their legal training at Bologna, whither Petrarch's
younger brother, Gherardo, either accompanied or
soon afterwards followed them. No young man
could be better qualified than Petrarch to enjoy the
pleasures and interests of university life ; with an
insatiable appetite for literature he combined a
capacity for friendship which assured him of the
full benefit of the social life of the place. In
Bologna, the premier University of Italy, he found
charming surroundings and pleasant companions, so
that "nowhere was life freer or more delightful,"
and his residence there seemed "not the least of
the benefits which God had given him." Only the
educational methods of the day seemed to him
radically wrong. " Philosophy," he protests, "is so
prostituted to the fancies of the vulgar, that it aims
only at hair-splitting on subtle distinctions and
quibbles of words. . . . Truth is utterly lost sight
of, sound practice is neglected, and the reality of
things is despised. . . . People concentrate their
whole attention on empty words."

For himself, he continued " to bend beneath
the weight of legal study" during the whole of his
residence at Bologna, his tutor being the Canonist
Giovanni Andrea, the most celebrated lawyer of the

time, "a chief glory of the city and University," where he held the Chair of Canon Law for forty-five years. Unhappily he was not satisfied with being first in his own profession, but assumed the airs of a dictator in literature and criticism too, a pose in which his ignorance and arrogance at once amazed and disgusted his more cultivated pupils. Yet tutor and pupil must have been on good terms on the whole, for they made an expedition together to Venice for the mere pleasure of seeing the place, and may probably have included visits to Pesaro and the country round Rimini in the same tour.

Petrarch appears to have had no other tutor while at Bologna, for the old tradition, which made him the pupil of Cino da Pistoia there, is certainly erroneous. The two poets admired each other; they exchanged poems during Cino's lifetime, and Petrarch wrote the beautiful sonnet *Piangete, Donne* as a lament for his death. Moreover, the young poet's genius was influenced for good by his study of the elder's art, and in this sense only he may be called a pupil of Cino. The latter was probably absent from Bologna during the whole of Petrarch's residence there.

The study of law and the companionship of his tutor were far from monopolising Petrarch's time at the University. His leisure hours were devoted to literature and to rambles round the city in company with his friends. One of these was a young poet, Tommaso Caloria of Messina, with whom Petrarch soon formed one of those close and ardent

friendships the record of which is the most delightful feature of his biography. Their tastes were congenial, their talents similar in kind if not in degree,
and Petrarch thought so highly of Tommaso's
genius as to name him among the poets in the
Triumph of Love. Something of this high estimate
may have been due to the partiality of friendship,
but Petrarch's critical instinct was not easily misled
even by the fervour of his affections.

With Tommaso, Guido, and other friends, Petrarch spent many a holiday in rambles through the
delightful country of the Emilia which lies round
Bologna. " I used to go with those of my own
age," he says, "and on festal days we would wander
to a great distance, so that the sun often set while
we were still in the country, and we did not get
back till the dead of night. But the city gates
stood open, or if by any chance they had been
shut, there was no wall to the town, but only a
brittle paling half rotten by age . . . so that you
could approach it from numberless points, and each
of us could make entry where it suited his convenience." We are accustomed to think of the
fourteenth century as a turbulent age, when might
was right, and a city's safety lay in the strength of
her walls and the courage of her people. It is a
little surprising, therefore, to read of this free, joyous
student life, and still more so to hear of a rotten
paling as the only rampart of an Italian town.

Before Petrarch had quite completed his twenty-
second year, he and Gherardo were summoned
home by the news of their father's death ; they left

Bologna on April 26th, 1326, and travelled with all speed to Avignon. Ser Petracco was not quite sixty years old, and his death must have come with the shock of a surprise to the family, for his health had been good, and so little had he felt the weight of years, that he threw the whole household into commotion in his indignation at finding the first white hair on his head when more than fifty years of age. This is the single humorous anecdote of him that has come down to us; for the rest he seems to have been an austere man, who failed to win the full confidence of his children, though he always commanded their deep respect. He had lived a hard life, which may well have deadened his sensibilities, and, after all, he was not more despotic than most parents, who claim to mould their children's lives without taking due account of peculiarities in their temperament. Intellectually he had much in common with his greater son, though he lacked the latter's delicate fancy and creative genius; morally the father was probably the stronger man of the two, but in the strength of his character there was an element of harshness, and the more finely strung nature of the son, with his keenness of human sympathy and his enthusiasm for noble ideals, appeals more successfully to the imagination and affection of mankind.

A still keener sorrow was in store for the brothers. Eletta, according to the received tradition, which is probably correct, died only a few weeks after her husband. Though Petrarch mentions her very seldom in his extant writings, there is enough to show the depth and enthusiasm of his love for her. His allusion to her as "the best of all mothers that ever he knew" has been already quoted, and the Latin poem in which he laments her death overflows with tenderness.   He calls her

> Elect of God no less in deed than name;

speaks of her as possessing

> Nobility to wake the Muses' choir,
> Supreme affection, majesty of soul;

and declares that

> The good will aye revere thee; I must weep
> Thy loss for aye! Not verily that Death
> Brings aught of terrible to thee, we grieve;
> But that thou, sweetest mother, leavest us,
> Me and my brother, wearied, where the ways
> Of Life divide, midst of a stormy world.

Throughout his life her memory remained fresh in his heart, and when a little granddaughter was born to him in his old age, he had the child christened by the cherished name of Eletta.

CHAPTER II

AVIGNON AND LAURA

1326-1329

SER PETRACCO had done much to retrieve his fortune; two years previously he had been able to provide a suitable dowry for his natural daughter Selvaggia on her marriage with a gentleman of Florence, and at his death he left a substantial amount of property. But not a penny of this inheritance ever reached its lawful owners; the executors contrived to convey it all to their own uses. "The plague of faithless guardians," Petrarch wrote many years afterwards to his brother, "pursued us from our boyhood. Thanks to our bad luck or our simplicity, we seemed a couple of solitary lads not given to making close scrutiny and easy to fleece. 'Tis an old truism that *opportunity makes the thief;* and this opportunity made us poor instead of rich, or rather—let us recognise the bounty of God—it made us men of leisure instead of men of affairs, unburdened instead of heavily laden." The only fragment of his inheritance that Petrarch ever received was "a volume of Cicero so exquisite that you could hardly find its equal, which my father used to cherish as his darling treasure, and which escaped the hands of his executors not because they wished to save it for me, but because they were busy plundering what they considered the more valuable portions of my inheritance." Unhappily this beautiful MS. was pawned together with the *De Gloria* by old Convennole, and so Petrarch lost the last vestige of his father's property.

Being now his own master, he determined to be not a lawyer, but a scholar and a poet. He made his choice deliberately, and he never regretted it; his instinct told him truly that the advancement of learning was his vocation, and never was any man's choice of work more fully justified by the event. It is hardly possible to exaggerate the effect of that choice on the revival of learning in Europe.

But a scholar in the early fourteenth century could not live by his pen. At Florence and Bologna the men of letters were mostly lawyers; elsewhere, and especially at the Papal Court, they were nearly always Churchmen. Petrarch's course was obvious; he immediately took the minor orders, which were sufficient to give him a *locus standi* and hopes of preferment in the Church without fettering his liberty of action, but he delayed till long afterwards his ordination as priest, which was a far graver matter, and might possibly have hindered rather than helped him in his early career. It has sometimes been urged as a reproach against him that he entered the Church without any vocation to the ministry; and his defenders have replied that in so doing he only followed the custom of the age, that the minor orders imply no stringent obligation and require no special vocation, and that in spite of

occasional human frailties he was one of the most
devout-minded men of his time, with strong religious tendencies even in the early youth which he
spent, to use his own words, "in subjection to his
vanities." All these answers are valid, but to say
the truth they are all superfluous. The Church of
the Middle Ages took thought for men's intellects
as well as for their souls; she was organised for
mental culture as well as for spiritual devotion; and
the scholar found his natural place in her ranks side
by side with the preacher and the theologian.

Circumstances equally dictated his choice of
a residence. He hated Avignon: he declaims
with quite comic vehemence against its very soil
and climate, calling it "the melancholy Avignon,
built upon a rugged rock, on the banks of the
windiest of rivers." Much more violent are his
denunciations of its politics and its morals. Avignon, as the seat of the Papal Court, was treasonably
usurping the sovereign rights of Rome; she was
the Babylon of a captivity worse than the Jewish,
because voluntary and base; Babylon is his habitual
name for her, and under this opprobrious nickname
he denounces alike the perfidy of her rulers and the
wickedness of her inhabitants. And the society in
which the gay licence of Provence met the darker
corruptions of an unscrupulous priesthood furnished
only too much matter for his diatribes. Yet nowhere else could he think of establishing himself.
His father had formed influential connections at the
Papal Court, and he himself was beginning to be
known in the city; in no other place could a brilliant

VIEW OF AVIGNON

Brun

young Churchman begin his career with such hope of speedy preferment; most important of all, the intellectual opportunities and interests of Avignon were unrivalled in Europe. That it was the native home of the Provençal school of poetry, which had reached its zenith more than a century before, was the least of its merits. As the seat of the Papacy it was a cosmopolitan city, the centre of European politics, the goal of envoys from every court, of scholars from every university, and the resort of the greatest artists in Italy, summoned thither to decorate the palace of the Popes. It was here that Petrarch met his friend Simone Martini, commonly called Memmi, of Siena, who is said to have painted the beautiful portraits of him and Laura preserved in the Laurentian Library at Florence, and to have introduced portraits of them into his great fresco in the Spaniards' Chapel there. The latter portraits, if really the work of Martini, which is doubtful, must have been painted from memory, for Petrarch was never in Florence during the painting of this fresco, and Laura was never there at all; and they show much less individuality of feature and expression than the former pair. The Laurentian portrait of Laura may possibly have been the one which Petrarch commissioned Memmi to paint for him, and for which he thanked him in two sonnets couched in terms of warm affection and high esteem.

This society of artists, scholars, statesmen, and men of the world was an ideal environment for a young man eager to acquire and diffuse knowledge, eager also for personal renown; and the astonishing speed with which Petrarch's celebrity as a poet spread through Europe must have been mainly due to the men of all countries who learned to appreciate him at Avignon.   He himself admitted that no-where else, as things stood, could he have found such opportunities as were open to him at Avignon; only he held that things ought to have been other-wise, and these opportunities should have been open to him not at Avignon, but in Rome.

However great may have been his disgust at the fouler corruptions of Avignonese society, he took his full share of its pleasures and gaieties.   He was at this time a young man of engaging appearance, comely if not strikingly handsome, with a high colour and a complexion rather fair than dark ; his eyes were animated in expression and remarkably keen of sight—in the Laurentian library portrait they are rather small, but very clear and beautiful—he was of middle height, and his limbs, though not very strong, were well knit and agile.   In early and middle life his health was robust, and he was extremely temperate in his habits, "drinking noth-ing but water throughout his childhood and down to the close of the period of youth."   From the Laurentian portrait we see further that he had an intellectual face, with a rather low but very massive forehead, a large, straight nose, delicately arched eyebrows, high and well-modelled cheekbones, and a beautiful mouth with lips that shut at once firmly and smilingly.   By the time that he sat for this picture his chin had grown double, but still kept the appearance of having been finely cut in younger days. He was well qualified for the part of a dandy, and played it with his brother's support to admiration. "You remember," he writes twenty years later, "the quite superfluous gloss of our exquisite raiment, and our daintiness in putting it on and off, a troublesome business which we performed morning and evening; you remember too our terror lest a single hair should get out of place, or a breath of wind ruffle the arrangement of our curls, and how we swerved from every horse that met or passed us, lest a speck of dust should mar the shine of our scented cloaks, or a touch should disarrange the folds in which we had laid them. . . . And what shall I say of our shoes? What a cruel, unremitting warfare they waged with our feet, which they were supposed to protect! They would soon have made mine quite useless, if I had not taken warning by the straits to which I was pushed, and preferred giving a little offence to other folk's eyes before crushing my own muscles and joints. And what of our curling-tongs and the dressing of our hair? How often the toil of it delayed our sleep at night and cut it short in the morning! Could any pirate have tortured us more cruelly than we tortured ourselves by twisting cords round our heads? We twisted them so tight indeed at night, that in the morning our mirror showed us crimson furrows across our foreheads, and in our anxiety to show off our hair we had to make it hide our faces."

But though he ruffled it with the best of the

dandies, so that all Avignon pointed him out as a
model of elegance, he never allowed frivolity to
distract him from scholarship. He was bent on
acquiring knowledge, and he found friends, some of
them much older than himself, who were able and
willing to help him. One of them was Giovanni
of Florence, one of the Pope's writers, an old man
well qualified by character, learning, and experience
to be an adviser of youth. To him Petrarch confided his hopes and his difficulties, and in return the
old man spoke to him of the true method and right
aim of study, bidding him not to be cast down by
an apparent check in his pursuit of learning, seeing
that the recognition of our ignorance is the first
step to knowledge. In the last year of his life
Petrarch was asked to advise a young man who
feared that he had come to a standstill in his work,
and answered that he could do no better than repeat
to him the counsel which he had himself received
from Giovanni of Florence.

Another friend by whose affectionate help and
advice he profited much was the lawyer Raimondo
Soranzio, "a venerable and noble old man," who
gloriously sacrificed all hope of preferment by with-
standing the Pope himself in a good cause. He
possessed a fine library of the classics, though he
himself cared little about any of them except Livy,
and he generously allowed Petrarch the free use of
his books; indeed, it was he who lent him the *De
Gloria*, of which the melancholy history has already
been told.

So far Petrarch's life had been a happy one; he

LAURA

FROM A COPY BY MRS. ARTHUR LEMON OF THE PORTRAIT IN THE LAURENTIAN LIBRARY,
FLORENCE

had met with misfortunes, it is true, but they were
not of such a kind as could daunt a high-spirited
youth, and many an ambitious young man of letters
would gladly compound for them all on condition
of having Petrarch's advantages.   But now, in
the twenty-third year of his age and less than a
year after his return to Avignon, the great crisis of
his life came upon him, bringing him twenty-one
years of deep unhappiness, hardly compensated by
the enduring renown which was its fruit.   On
the 6th April, 1327, at the hour of Prime, he first
saw Laura in the Church of St. Claire, and was
overwhelmed at once with the love of which he
tells us : " In my youth I bore the stress of a
passion most violent, though honourable and the
single one of my life ; and I should have borne it
even longer than I did, had not Death, opportune
in spite of its bitterness, quenched the flame just as
it was beginning to grow less intense." It is to the
vicissitudes of this deep and enduring passion that
we owe the poems by which their author holds his
high rank among the masters of song.

Who was Laura? Frankly, we do not know.
In all probability Petrarch purposely destroyed all
marks of identification ; if this was his intention,
his success was complete, and the riddle will probably never be answered with certainty. So careful
was the lover to guard his lady's secret, that even
in his lifetime his friends would tease him by pretending to believe that he was in love with no
woman at all, but only with the laurel crown of
poetry, which he symbolised under the name of

Laura; and this allegorical theory has never been quite without adherents. Happily no reasonable person, acquainted with all the evidence and with Petrarch's methods of thought and expression, can doubt its falsity. That in answer to a friend's banter he protested the reality of his passion counts for little; of course he would have done that whether he were maintaining a fact or a fiction. But the manner of his protestation, with its revelation of a spirit vexed by fluctuating emotions and conflicting desires, carries conviction. Much more conclusive, however, indeed absolutely conclusive, are the references to Laura in his Dialogues *De Contemptu Mundi*, and the two pathetic entries on the fly-leaf of his Virgil. The Dialogues, which he called his *Secretum*, were written for himself alone; under the form of a dialogue with Saint Augustine they constitute a private record of his inmost thoughts and feelings. He never published them; it is doubtful whether even his most intimate friends were ever allowed to read them; their very existence was certainly unknown till after his death to the great body of his admirers. Yet it is precisely in this private record that we find the most valuable information as to his love for Laura and its effect on his character and his work. And on the fly-leaf of his Virgil, the book which he carried everywhere with him, now preserved in the Ambrosian Library at Milan, he noted down, again for his own eye only, among the most solemn events of his life, the dates of his first meeting with Laura and of her death. This is conclusive; for on no

conceivable theory can Petrarch, writing for himself
only, have set down the date of Laura's death in 1348,
if she was but the symbol of his laurel crown, which
he gained in 1341, and which showed no sign of
fading during his lifetime. But if the support of
circumstantial evidence is wanted, there is plenty to
be had. The *Canzoniere*, for instance, describes
in minutest detail every feature of the beloved
lady's face except her nose; it is hard to imagine a
poet spending so much pains on the unsubstantial
features of an allegorical picture; it is quite incon-
ceivable that, describing all the rest, he should
forget the most prominent of them all; had Laura
been a mere allegory, we should have had either no
portrait or a complete one. Nor is it conceivable
that Petrarch would have spoken of a fictitious
passion in the terms of strong abhorrence which,
under occasional impulses of ascetic fervour, he
applied to his earthly love. The strength of a
reaction is a sure gauge of the strength of the action
which preceded it, and the intemperate fervour of
Petrarch the ascetic bears witness to the intensity
of the emotions of Petrarch the lover and the poet.

Laura was a real woman, and Petrarch was
desperately her lover; so much may safely be asserted, so much and no more. We do not even
know that her real name was Laura; here may well
be the grain of truth from which the whole allegorical myth sprung; nothing is more likely than
that Petrarch, who constantly gave nicknames of
affection to his friends, should have called the lady
whom he loved by a name that associated her in his

fancy and in the ears of the world with his life's ambition. Was she married or single? Again we do not know. The received opinion follows the conjecture of the Abbé de Sade, and identifies her with his ancestress, Laura de Noves, wife of Count Hugo de Sade, a nobleman of Avignon. But the evidence for her marriage rests mainly on a questionable interpretation of a single Latin contraction, while the general tone of the *Canzoniere* supports the theory that she was unmarried. If this was the case, Petrarch may well have called his love for her an "honourable" passion, not merely in the sense in which Provençal courts of love adjudged honourable the devotion of a troubadour to his lady, but in the more modern and domestic sense that he hoped to win her in marriage; for a dispensation from the minor orders could easily be obtained, though the story of Pope Clement VI having offered him a dispensation from priest's orders must be dismissed as an idle tale.

Another theory, much in vogue just now, represents her as a simple village maiden, possibly of gentle birth and able to read the Italian poems of her lover, but innocent of the turmoil of city society, living and dying at the foot of a hill a few miles out of Vaucluse, and buried within the precincts of the valley. It is a pretty theory; unfortunately it raises more difficulties than it solves, and contradicts more facts than it explains. The riddle is still unread.

Whoever she was, there is no exaggerating the effects of her influence on her lover. His love for her was the critical experience of his life, and under its stimulus his whole nature leaped into fuller and more vigorous life. Laura gave him little encouragement and no hope that she would ever return his love; great was his joy when he received so much as a smile or a kindly glance from her whose perfections he was making celebrated through the length and breadth of Europe. Once, when he so far presumed upon her mood of unwonted kindliness as to talk to her openly of love, she bade him know that she was not such an one as he seemed to think her. Her coldness purified his passion; in spite of himself he revered a chastity so uncommon in the society in which he lived. He suffered, but his moral nature gained strength and elevation from the suffering. "Through love of her," he wrote in his *Secretum*, "I attained to love of God"; and again, "It is to her that I owe what little merit you see in me, and I should never have gained such name and fame as I have, save for the nobility of feeling with which she cultivated the sparse seeds of virtue planted by nature in my breast. It was she who reclaimed my youthful spirit from all baseness."

No less remarkable was the quickening of his intellectual powers. He had been "devoted to the study of poetry long before he saw Laura," and his earlier verses had won him no little repute among men of taste and learning. Yet of these *Juvenilia* he has allowed not a line to come down to us. He coveted high renown; he wished to live by his best work alone; and when at a later date he came to

arrange his papers for eventual publication, he carefully destroyed everything which his maturer judgment pronounced incapable of sustaining his reputation.   He then threw into the fire " a thousand or
more letters and poems," among which, as de Sade
ingeniously conjectures, were probably included all
the letters containing references to Laura and to
the incidents of his intercourse with her ; and the
earlier Italian poems doubtless formed part of the
same literary holocaust.   These must have had
considerable merits, for no mere rubbish could have
obtained a vogue in such a society as that of Avignon ; but we may be sure that Petrarch would not
have destroyed them if they had been on a level
with his later work.   It is safe to conclude that, till
his meeting with Laura, he had shown little more
than the promise of poetical excellence.   Now, however, under the stimulus of love, he suddenly leaped
to eminence as one of the master poets of the
world.   Two characteristics especially distinguish
the *Canzoniere* from the work of other poets : the
uniform excellence of its workmanship, and the
minuteness with which it portrays the subtlest
phases of emotion.   The four parts of which it is
composed differ widely in tone and feeling ; individual poems in each part differ equally widely in
the interest of their subject-matter ; but in beauty
of form, in delicacy of expression, in perfection of
melody, there is no distinction between its earlier
and later poems ; the earliest-written sonnet of the
series—the sonnet numbered XVI in the ordinary
editions—is, technically speaking, a model which no

writer of sonnets has surpassed. Partly this uniformity of skill must have been due to subsequent polishing, for Petrarch had the habit of keeping his works by him and constantly making alterations and improvements in them ; but it is only work of fine quality which can be brought to perfection by revision, and Petrarch's sudden leap to excellence must have been mainly due to the influence of his love.

Even more remarkable is the other distinguishing characteristic of the *Canzoniere*. Petrarch has been well called "the poet of the heart of man"; human sentiment is his theme, and from the abundance of his own experience he draws the picture of all its phases. When he writes of the external world, he deals in generalities, for its aspects are matters of secondary interest to him ; it is on the delineation of feeling, from the fervour of indomitable passion to the airiest trick of graceful fancy, that he lavishes his unrivalled powers of analysis and expression.

It is not possible within the limits of a short biography to attempt either a detailed criticism of the *Canzoniere*, or a minute estimate of the influences which helped to fashion it, and of its own influence on the development of European literature. Briefly it may be said that, while in matters of form and phrase Petrarch's debt to the Provençals is great, the temper and spirit of the poems are entirely Italian. The "courtly" forms of Provençal lyric lay ready to his hand ; so did a stock of phrases which for three centuries had been the common property of poets. Of these he availed himself so freely that critics to whom form seems the all-important thing in literature may with some justification go near to accuse him of plagiarism. But those who judge poetry by its spirit will rightly maintain that the *Canzoniere* breathes of Italy. Cino's influence counted for more in the making of it than that of all Provence; yet even Cino and the Tuscans did not contribute very much to its essential character. It is the mirror of its author's soul, and that soul was Italian.

This intensely personal character of the *Canzoniere* explains its failure as a model. Itself perhaps the most exquisite book of poetry ever published, it gave rise to one of the feeblest and most tedious schools of verse that have afflicted the world. The Petrarchists could imitate their master's tricks of diction and refine wearisomely upon his "conceits"; but they could not catch his spirit, and the breath of life was not in them.

A brief description of the scheme and contents of the *Canzoniere* may be of service to those who wish to make closer acquaintance with it. The collection, as set in order by Petrarch himself, consists of four parts: (1) Sonnets and Songs during the life of Madonna Laura; (2) Sonnets and Songs after her death; (3) Triumphs "in vita ed in morte"; and (4) Poems on various occasions. The contents of Parts I and II are sufficiently described by their titles. Part I consists of 207 sonnets, 17 odes, 8 "sestine," 6 "ballate," and 4 madrigals, in all 242 poems, composed between the 6th April, 1327, the day on which Petrarch first saw Laura, and the 6th April, 1348, the day of her death. Part II is much shorter; it contains 90 sonnets, 8 odes, 1 "sestina," and 1 "ballata," exactly 100 poems in all, composed after Laura's death, and probably before 1361, the third critical date in Petrarch's life, after which he seems to have written little, if any, Italian poetry. Part III contains the *Triumphs*, of which the scope and object are well set forth by Marsand as follow : "The poet's aim in composing these *Triumphs* is the same which he proposed to himself in the *Canzoniere*, namely, to return in thought from time to time now to the beginning, now to the progress, and now to the end of his passion, taking by the way frequent opportunities of rendering praise and honour to the single and exalted object of his love. To reach this aim he devised a description of man in his various conditions of life, wherein he might naturally find occasion to speak of himself and of his Laura. Man in his first stage of youth is the slave of appetites, which may all be included under the generic name of *Love* or *Self-Love*. But as he gains understanding, he sees the impropriety of such a condition, so that he strives advisedly against those appetites and overcomes them by means of *Chastity*, that is, by denying himself the opportunity of satisfying them. Amid these struggles and victories *Death* overtakes him, and makes victors and vanquished equal by taking them all out of the world. Nevertheless, it has no power to destroy the memory of a man, who by illustrious and honourable deeds seeks to survive his own death.

Such a man truly lives through a long course of ages by means of his *Fame*. But *Time* at length obliterates all memory of him, and he finds in the last resort that his only sure hope of living for ever is by joy in God, and by partaking with God in His blessed *Eternity*. Thus Love triumphs over Man, Chastity over Love, and Death over both alike; Fame triumphs over Death, Time over Fame, and Eternity over Time."

Part IV consists of twenty sonnets and four odes written on various occasions, mostly of public interest, and contains some of the noblest passages ever inspired in the soul of a poet by the fervour of idealistic patriotism. Many of these will be noticed in connection with the events to which they refer ; here it is enough to say that if every other scrap of Petrarch's work had perished, the odes *Spirto Gentil* and *Italia Mia* would of themselves establish his claim to rank with the greatest masters of lyric song.

CHAPTER III

TRAVEL AND FRIENDSHIP

1329-1336

WE have no record of the two years following the first meeting with Laura; they were probably spent in Avignon, and we may confidently ascribe to them the earliest of the extant poems. But not even love and poetry could distract Petrarch from scholarship, and in the summer of 1329 he undertook the first of many journeys in which he combined the delights of travel and sight-seeing with a diligent hunt for forgotten manuscripts of the classics. This passion for travel for the love of sight-seeing is one of the many minor traits in Petrarch's character which mark him as belonging rather to the modern than the mediæval age; throughout the Middle Ages men travelled far and wide on errands of war, of diplomacy, of commerce, and of religion; but Petrarch may fairly be called the first of the tourists. Still keener was his passion for book-hunting, and the two went well together. "Whenever I took a far journey," he tells us, "I would turn aside to any old monasteries that I chanced to see in the distance, saying: 'Who knows whether some scrap of the writings I covet may not lie here?' Thus about the twenty-fifth year of my age, in the course of a hurried journey among the Belgians and Swiss, I came to Liège, and hearing that there was a good quantity of books there, I stayed and detained my companions while I copied out one of Cicero's speeches with my own hand and another by the hand of a friend, which I afterwards published throughout Italy. And to give you a laugh, I may tell you that in this fine barbaric city it was a hard matter to find a drop of ink, and what we did get was exactly the colour of saffron."

Meanwhile stirring events had happened in Italy. Lewis of Bavaria, elected King of the Romans, had invaded the land, and he had been crowned Emperor in Rome, first by the Bishops of Venice and Ellera, and then again by an Anti-Pope whom he had set up in the Chair of St. Peter. As the death of Henry VII quenched the last spark of genuine Ghibellin sentiment in Italy, so the expedition of "the Bavarian," as the old chroniclers call him in scorn and hatred, marks the acknowledged end of the old divisions. From the day when Ghibellin Pisa and Milan had once acted in concert if not in alliance with Guelfic Florence and Angevin Naples to oppose the invader, the old names had become mere badges, still worn perhaps for custom and tradition's sake, but seen of all men to be empty of significance. The old rivalries were still too keen, the old feuds too bitter, to permit of lasting union ; the ancient enmities broke out afresh as soon as the Bavarian had recrossed the Alps. But their mere suspension marks a new phase of national feeling.

When Milan and Florence had engaged in hostilities against a common enemy, and that enemy a foreigner, Italian unity had ceased to be a mere dream. Its realisation might be the work of centuries, but it had at least become a possible aspiration of practical politicians.

Prominent among the Ghibellin families who now rallied to the Papacy was the Roman House of Colonna, and it was a young Churchman of this House who accomplished an act of daring which placed Pope John XXII deep in his debt. To the pretensions of Lewis and his Anti-Pope John replied by a Bull of Excommunication against them both; this Bull, if it was to produce its full dramatic effect, must be openly published in Rome itself; yet its publication was no easy matter, for the Bavarian held the city, and a troublesome Papalist ran no small risk of his life. The risk was accepted by Giacomo Colonna, youngest son of old Stefano, the head of the House, who, accompanied by four masked companions, publicly read the Bull of Excommunication and nailed it to the door of the Church of San Marcello. This was the signal for a popular outbreak, which presently forced the Emperor to quit Rome and begin the retreat which ended in his expulsion from Italy. So conspicuous a service merited a signal reward, and Giacomo, though under the canonical age, received the bishopric of Lombez, a village near the source of the Garonne at the foot of the Pyrenees.

Two years later, in the summer of 1330, the young Bishop went to take possession of his see, and with him went Petrarch, whom he had known by sight only as a fellow-student at Bologna. It was after his Roman adventure that he sought Petrarch out and began an acquaintance which soon ripened into a devoted friendship.

To the sojourn at Lombez Petrarch ever afterwards looked back as one of the most delightful episodes in his life, "a summer of almost heavenly bliss," of which the mere remembrance made him happy. His devotion to his patron was deep and sincere; Giacomo's brilliant wit and sound learning were doubly attractive in a man who, though a priest, had shown the qualities of a soldier and a courtier; the delicacy of his nature made the name "patron" synonymous with "friend," and with this charm of intellect and character he combined an earnest sense of duty which made him throw himself into the affairs of his petty diocese as energetically as into the great drama of European politics.

Two other lifelong friendships were the fruit of this happy visit. Lello Stefani, the "Lælius" of the letters, was a Roman of noble rank though not ancient descent, a man of letters, a soldier, and a statesman, attached to the House of Colonna not only by hereditary ties, but by bonds of affection so strong that not even political differences in that age of bitter feuds could strain them. Very happily chosen was the name of "Lælius," suggested no doubt by its likeness to "Lello," and approved as reminiscent of the Lælii and the Scipios. "That name of note among old-world friends still endures as a name of good omen to friendships," wrote

Petrarch; "and this third Lælius is my second self, nay, rather one and the same with me."

Dearer even than Lælius, dearest indeed of all Petrarch's friends, was the young Flemish musician Lewis, known to the poet and his circle as their Socrates. "Thou alone, my Socrates," writes Petrarch twenty years later, "wert given to me not, as the rest of my friends, by the land of Italy, but by Annea Campineæ, so that the poverty of thy fatherland might be exalted in the richness of thy talent, and Nature assert her prerogative of fashioning great souls from any soil and under every sky. Therefore to my profit she bore thee, a man of such parts, and brought thee forth at the very time when I was being born afar off in another sphere of the world; and although thy birth made thee a foreigner, yet art thou become more than half Italian by the courtesy of thy spirit, by the intimacies of thy life, and especially by thy love for me. Marvellous that in men born so far apart there should be such neighbourhood of souls, such unity of wills, as have now in our case been attested by the witness of twenty years! From the earnestness of thy character and from thy sweet pleasantness we chose thee thy surname; and while thy supremacy in the art of music might have persuaded us to call thee *Aristoxenus*, the better judgment of thy friends prevailed in naming thee our *Socrates*." A volume might be filled with quotations from Petrarch, illustrating the depth and the ardour of this flawless friendship: to Socrates he writes every passing thought with that perfect confidence which reveals the small things of life as readily as the great, which is not afraid of giving undue importance to trifles nor shy of opening the heart on matters of the gravest moment, but utters whatever is uppermost in the mind without reserve and without disguise, in the happy certainty that whatever interests or affects the speaker will equally interest and affect the hearer. Petrarch was a good lover and a good hater; in all his friendships we are charmed by his loyalty, his ardour, and his most delightful partiality; but in the friendship with Socrates we find in addition a tenderness of sentiment, a lover-like self-abandonment, which distinguishes it in kind and in quality from all the rest.

In mid-autumn the whole party returned to Avignon, and Petrarch took up his residence in the house of Giacomo's elder brother, the Cardinal Giovanni Colonna. He himself would have preferred to remain with his first patron, but Giacomo judged more wisely of his friend's interest: his own career, brilliantly as it had opened, was still in the making; it would be affected by the accidents of Roman and Papal politics, and he could not therefore give Petrarch either a settled home or the certainty of leisure for his work. On the other hand, the Cardinal's position was assured: three years earlier, while still a young man under thirty, he had received the highest dignity of the Church short of the Papacy itself, and the great influence which any Cardinal of his House would inevitably possess was heightened in his case by the elevation

THE PALACE OF THE POPES, AVIGNON

of his character, by his blameless life, and by his reputation for independence in speech and action. Moreover, his house at Avignon was the centre of learned and polite society. He prized his position as a patron of letters, and would fully appreciate the fact of which Petrarch himself seemed charmingly unconscious, that his protégé's reputation as a scholar and a poet would add to the distinction of his household, and amply repay him for his hospitality.

For the next sixteen years their personal relations were of the pleasantest, and even after Petrarch's political adhesion to Rienzi had made it impossible for him to be the intimate associate of a Colonna, he still wrote to the Cardinal in terms of unabated respect and gratitude. Probably he never felt for him quite the same ardour of brotherly love which Giacomo had inspired in him. But he revered him as "a man of the utmost goodness and innocence of heart, far beyond the wont of cardinals." He was attached to him by ties of intellectual sympathy and community of tastes, and the friendship between them was so close that Petrarch could declare that in the Cardinal's household he "lived many years, not as under a master, but as under a father; nay, rather as with a most loving brother, or still more truly as with himself, and in his own house." A little incident which happened while Petrarch was an inmate of the house throws so interesting a light, alike on the personal relations between the two men and on domestic discipline in the fourteenth century, that it is worth quoting at length in spite of its triviality. "You may remember," Petrarch wrote some years later to the Cardinal, "how there was once a serious quarrel among some of your people, and blows were struck, at which you were so justly incensed that you sat down as it were on a judgment-seat, and calling your household together, administered an oath to each one of them, binding them to speak the truth. Even your brother Agapito, Bishop of Luni, had sworn, and I was just stretching out my hand, when in the full tide of your anger you drew back the Gospels, and in the hearing of them all declared that you were satisfied with my simple word. And to make it clear that you never regretted your action, and that the kindness of it was not unpremeditated, whenever similar incidents occurred, as they often did, you never allowed me to be sworn, though all the rest were bound by oath."

In the Cardinal's house Petrarch had the happiness of still living with Socrates, and for a time with Lælius too ; he also found installed there two friends, the soldier Mainardo Accursio of Florence, and the Churchman Luca Cristiano of Piacenza, with whom he lived thenceforward on terms of closest intimacy. He had certainly known Luca and possibly Mainardo also at Bologna, but it was at Avignon that the acquaintance ripened into so affectionate a friendship that Petrarch could write of it to Socrates : "The four of us had but one mind. . . . Where could you find a kindlier spirit than our Luca or a more genial comrade than Mainardo ? The former, indeed, was so formed in mind as to be not only the sweetest and brightest of housemates, but also the sharer and companion of our studies; while the latter, though unpractised in matters of this sort, was abundantly furnished with the qualities which are the object of such studies, to wit with courtesy, faith, liberality, and constancy of mind. In a word, though untrained in the liberal arts, he had learned to be a good man and a good friend, and it was better for us to have one such in our band, than for us all to be devoted to scholarship and negligent of everything else." Mainardo has generally been identified with the Olympius of the letters, but some recent critics ascribe the name to Luca; the point is a doubtful one, and the safe course is to speak of both friends by their real names. Both of them, Petrarch declares, knew every thought of his heart as he knew theirs, and many years later he gave a practical proof of his affection for Luca by resigning a canonry at Modena in his favour.

Petrarch was fortunate too in his relations with the whole Colonna family. Stefano the Elder, at this time on a visit to his son the Cardinal, treated him from the first like one of his own sons. There must have been a peculiarly winning charm in the poet's character, which throughout his life made him the friend and confidant rather than the dependent of his patrons. In his presence the sternest character grew gentle, and the stiffest neck bowed willingly to the yoke of affection, so that to him Azzo da Correggio was sincere and Bernabò Visconti courteous. And old Stefano, the man of antique mould, who "looked like Julius Cæsar or Africanus come back in the flesh, but for his great age," who was "the bravest and stoutest man of our time in confronting a foe, though so loving to his family that he seemed wrapped up in their life," Stefano, whose fierce triumphs and bitter sufferings in his struggle with Boniface VIII seemed to have hardened body and soul in him to iron, became all gentleness in his intercourse with Petrarch, confided to him with tears the forebodings of his heart as to the fate that awaited his family, and granted to his intercession what he had refused to many other friends, the pardon of one of his sons with whom he had had a bitter quarrel. Such confidence and kindness from one so stern and unbending to most men made a deep impression on Petrarch, whose sensibility was a prominent element in his disposition, and he always speaks of Stefano as "a man of unique character, to be regarded with mingled awe and admiration."

Much more familiar was his intercourse with Stefano's brother, Giovanni Colonna di San Vito; he too had played a brave part in the struggle with Boniface VIII, but he was not cast in his brother's iron mould; exile and hardship and the gout had done much to break his spirit, and he was now an amiable but rather querulous old man, who conceived an extraordinary affection for Petrarch, and treated him like a friend of his own age. For his diversion Petrarch wrote a comedy, which he afterwards burnt, and after Giovanni's departure from Avignon at the end of 1331 wrote him several letters, as well as a humorous fable called *The Spider and the Gout.*

Cardinal Colonna's house was Petrarch's home for nearly seven years, and here he had opportunities of meeting the many distinguished men from all parts of Europe, who came on errands of business or of diplomacy to the Papal Court. Among others he became acquainted with the celebrated Richard de Bury, Bishop of Durham in 1333, and soon afterwards Chancellor and Lord High Treasurer of England, who was entrusted by Edward III with no less than three diplomatic missions to the Pope. On either the first or the second of these Petrarch met him, and had a discussion with him on the site of the Island of Thule. He describes the author of *Philobiblon* as a man of brilliant talents and good knowledge of letters, from his youth up curious to an incredible degree in abstruse questions, and already possessed of one of the finest libraries in the world; a description which tallies well enough with the received estimate of Richard as a brilliant dilettante and amateur of literature, rather than a profound and serious scholar.

To this period undoubtedly belong a great many of the Italian poems, and from them we may infer that Laura was resident in Avignon, and that her poet had frequent opportunities of meeting her. To this period also belongs the Latin poetical letter to Enea Tolomei of Siena, called forth by King John of Bohemia's visit to Avignon and subsequent descent into Italy. John had first invaded Italy in 1330 as the ally of Lewis of Bavaria, but the latter, suspecting him of fighting for his own hand, had picked a quarrel with him and instigated a rising against him in Bohemia. John left his son Charles, a lad of sixteen, in nominal command of his Italian army, hastened home, and soon restored order in his own kingdom. Then, being still eager to further his Italian projects, he turned to Philip of France, and so began the alliance which eventually brought him to his death at Crécy. Philip, ever ready to fish in troubled waters and sure that in the event of success he would get the lion's share of the plunder, agreed to help John with a large force; and to give some colour of justification to their enterprise, these royal filibusters agreed that John should go to Avignon and obtain the Pope's sanction. Once more Italian patriotism was roused against the foreigner, once more old enemies sank their differences and formed a temporary league against the Franco-Bohemian invaders; and Petrarch, burning with indignant zeal, wrote that letter to Tolomei which is the Latin counterpart of the noble ode *Italia Mia*, written long afterwards at a time of even sorer trouble to Italy. In both poems we feel the purity and strength of his love for Italy and the loftiness of his political idealism, and, what is perhaps even more remarkable, in the Latin letter we find Petrarch the enthusiast, the poet, some would say the visionary, going straight to the heart of the matter and laying his finger unerringly on the real practical cause of the mischief. Others might be misled by appearances— even so shrewd a writer as the chronicler Giovanni

Villani speaks of John as Italy's chief enemy—but Petrarch, though as yet little versed in practical politics, detects Philip as the real culprit, and, neglecting the Bohemians, directs the whole force of his invective against the French.

The Italian league was soon successful. John lost Pavia to Azzo Visconti, and the French army was soon afterwards annihilated before Ferrara, so that by the month of October, 1333, the King was forced to return to Bohemia, and in the words of an old writer, "the fame of him vanished like smoke from the plains of Lombardy." Meanwhile Petrarch had set out on a journey to Paris. Probably the Pope's action in secretly encouraging the invasion of Italy, while pretending to discourage it, had intensified his dislike of the Papal Court, and the unsuccessful course of his love for Laura may have made him restless and dissatisfied. He was certainly eager for sight-seeing, and persuaded the Cardinal, though with some difficulty, to let him go on a foreign tour. In Paris he sought out the Augustinian friar Dionigi of Borgo San Sepolcro, who was lecturing at the University on Philosophy and Theology. Dionigi was a man of deep piety and unusual learning, a theologian of scholarly sympathies, and a friend to whom Petrarch could confide all the troubles of his heart. Probably he took him for his confessor; certainly he sought his advice about his love for Laura. Dionigi showed keen insight into the character of his penitent. He judged that spiritual zeal would be for him the best antidote to an earthly passion, and showed an even

more remarkable grasp of his moral and intellectual
temperament by directing his attention not to the
more ascetic of the fathers, but to the liberal and
cultured Augustine.   Petrarch already knew and
possessed the *De Civitate Dei ;* Dionigi now gave
him a copy of the *Confessions,* which Petrarch ever
afterwards carried about with him in all his journeys.
Predisposed as he was to admire St. Augustine, it
is nevertheless from his intimacy with Fra Dionigi
that we must date the passionate enthusiasm of hero-
worship which henceforward inspired him with the
same feeling for Augustine as his spiritual guide
that he already felt for Cicero as his master in
literature.   From this intimacy too dates the development in Petrarch of a devotional impulse
which henceforth shared the empire of his soul with
his zeal for learning.   He has now two ideals, those
of the scholar and of the saint, and occasionally,
though not very often, the two ideals clash in
violent spiritual conflict.   In such moments of agony
—for to Petrarch's sensitive nature the strife was
nothing less than agony—he is possessed with
ascetic fervour, and for a moment condemns all
earthly aims as vanity and vexation of spirit ; but
this was not his normal temper ; it was only at rare
and brief intervals that he lost sight of the nobler
conception of the scholar who is also a saint.

"You tell me," he writes in answer to a bantering accusation from Giacomo Colonna, "that I do
but affect a reverence for Augustine and his works,
while really I have never torn myself away from
the poets and philosophers.   And why, pray, should

I tear myself away from those to whom you can see that Augustine himself clung close?" Again he asserts that Cicero's writings, "though diverse from Christianity, are never adverse to it," and that the great classical authors are full of sentiments in harmony with the Christian spirit. And when Boccaccio was momentarily thrown off his balance by a supposed revelation commanding him to re-nounce poetry and scholarship, Petrarch could reassure him by a letter containing some of the noblest passages ever written on the right relation of literature to religion. And the point which chiefly attracts him in the *De Civitate Dei* is that Augustine "could base it on a great foundation of philosophers and poets, and adorn it with all the colours of the orators and historians."

Far more violent and far more constant was the struggle between spiritual devotion and earthly love. The latter was, indeed, too strong a feeling to be overcome by any concurrent emotion, but henceforth at least "it no longer held sole possession of the spirit's chamber, but found there another sentiment fighting and striving against it." It is just this strife of conflicting emotions that calls forth our liveliest sympathy. Doubtless the steadfast man who marches to his end with never a stumble by the way is a heroic figure, but our tears flow and our hearts are wrung rather for the sensitive soul responsive to every impression, and battered by the storm of opposing passions, which nevertheless through error and through pain achieves its escape as through Vanity Fair and the Valley of the Shadow of

Death to the Delectable Mountains and the peace of Beulah.

In Paris he "spent a long time, exploring it thoroughly from a wish to see everything, and to discover whether all its reputed glories were real or imaginary, and, when daylight often failed, making use of the night as well." Next he visited Ghent, "which, like Paris, boasts of Julius Cæsar as its founder, and all the other peoples of Flanders and Brabant, whose trade is the preparation of wool and weaving." Thence he went to Liège, "a place noted for its clergy," which he had already visited four years previously, and to Aix-la-Chapelle, where some priests of the cathedral showed him in MS. a legend of Charlemagne and the foundation of the city. From Aix, after taking the baths, "which are warm like those of Baiæ," he went to Cologne, "situated on the left bank of the Rhine, a place which may well be proud of its position, its river, and its people. Marvellous was it in a barbaric land to find so advanced a civilization, so beautiful a city, such dignity in the men, and such comeliness in the women." By good luck he arrived on St. John's Eve, and witnessed a picturesque local ceremony performed on that day. And, by a further stroke of good fortune, which shows how widely his fame as a poet was already spread, he found friends in the place, with whom he could converse in Latin, and who could give him an explanation of what he saw. About sunset "the whole bank of the river was covered with a brilliant and vast concourse of women. Good heavens! What beauty

of form, feature, and dress! One whose heart was
not already engaged might well have been smitten
with love. I stood on a spot of rising ground,
from which I could attend to all that was going on.
There was a wonderful throng without any disturbance; and each in her turn the women, some of
whom were girdled with sweet-scented herbs,
hastened to turn their sleeves above the elbow and
wash their white hands and arms in the current,
murmuring some soft words in their foreign tongue.
. . . Understanding nothing of the ceremony, I
asked one of my friends in a quotation from Virgil—

> ' What means this concourse at the river's bank?
> What seek the souls here gathered?'

And he answered that this was a very old national
custom, the women, especially among the common
people, believing that all the impending misfortune
of a whole year is washed away by this day's
ablution, and that henceforth better fortune succeeds.
At which I smiled and said, ' O too happy dwellers
by the Rhine, if all your miseries are purged by
him! Neither Po nor Tiber has ever availed to
wash away ours. You pass on your evils down the
Rhine to the Britons, and willingly would we send
ours to the Africans and Illyrians; but our streams,
it would seem, are too sluggish.' At this they all
laughed, and at last, late in the evening, we left the
riverside."

At Cologne he was greatly interested in "the
illustrious monuments of Roman greatness," and in
the association of the place with Agrippa and
Augustus. He saw "the Capitol, the image of

ours, except that in place of the Senate, which
there debated questions of peace and war, here a
mixed choir of comely lads and maidens sings
nightly praises to God"; he also saw "the beautiful,
though yet unfinished, church in the midst of the
town, which they rightly call their high church,
and in which lie the bodies of the Magi Kings,
brought by three stages from East to West."   On
the last day of June he left Cologne, and gave proof
of his courage, not to say rashness, by venturing to
travel alone, unarmed, and in time of war through
the forest of the Ardennes, which he found "a
dismal and weird country," but which inspired him
to write the beautiful sonnet *Per mezz' i boschi.*
At length, "after compassing many a large tract of
country," he came on the 8th of August to Lyons,
"another noble colony of the Romans, and a little
older than Cologne"; and to his transports at the
sight of the Rhone we owe the sonnet *Mille piagge.*
Here he fell in with one of Cardinal Colonna's
servants, who gave him news which decided him to
rest a few days in Lyons, and then go quietly on to
Avignon by boat.

Giacomo Colonna had for some time past been
planning a visit to Rome, and had promised to take
Petrarch with him.   To see Rome, and especially
to see it in his friend's company, was one of the
poet's dearest wishes, and he was hurrying back to
Avignon in the hope that they might make the
journey together in the course of the autumn, when
he heard from the Cardinal's servant that Giacomo
and Lælius had already started without waiting, as

had been expressly agreed, for his return.   Bitterly
disappointed, he wrote to Giacomo to reproach him
for his breach of faith, the cause of which he could
not conjecture.   But on arriving at Avignon, he
learnt that family affairs of great importance had
required the Bishop's immediate presence in Rome.
Some years previously the perpetual quarrels of
the Colonna and the Orsini families had been suspended by a truce, the term of which expired this
summer.   The Pope, unable to bring about a lasting reconciliation, issued a Bull on the 3rd of June
prolonging this truce for a year, but it was already
too late.   In May the Orsini, headed by Bertoldo,
the bravest and most popular of their chiefs,
entrapped Stefano Colonna the Younger into an
ambush, where they attacked him with greatly
superior forces.   But Stefano and his party, though
outnumbered and taken by surprise, fought so
gallantly that they won a complete victory, routing
the Orsini and killing Bertoldo and his cousin
Francesco.   Such at least was the story as told
and believed in Cardinal Colonna's household, and
the Pope's subsequent action seems to confirm its
truth, in spite of Villani's assertion that Stefano
Colonna was the author of the ambush.   Often as
the rival houses had engaged in similar affrays, this
was the first occasion on which any of their chiefs
had been killed, and the affair created an immense
sensation in Rome and Avignon.   The Orsini,
aided by their relative Cardinal Poggetto, the Papal
Legate, were eager to avenge their defeat, and it
was to counteract their schemes that Giacomo

started in such haste for Rome. Probably through his influence and that of Cardinal Giovanni, the Pope was persuaded to administer a severe rebuke to his Legate, and the House of Colonna maintained for the time its superiority over its rivals. Petrarch, who as yet knew nothing of Roman politics but what he heard from his patrons, of course shared their gratification, and addressed a stirring sonnet to Stefano the Younger, exhorting him to avoid the error of Hannibal, who conquered at Cannæ, but failed to follow up his victory. With this sonnet, which was written in Italian that the Colonna men-at-arms might understand it, he sent a Latin letter to Stefano to the same effect, and also composed a Latin poem made up of original lines and quotations placed alternately, which, however, he destroyed on finding that others had anticipated him in this queer method of composition.

Much as he rejoiced in the victory of his patrons, he was still more elated by the news, which he also heard on reaching Avignon, that King Philip of France had engaged to lead a new Crusade, and that the Pope had announced his intention of bringing back the Papacy to Italy. To him, as to all devout men of his age, it seemed a shameful and horrible thing that the holy places should be in the possession of unbelievers, and that Christian princes and states should turn their arms one against another, instead of combining to rescue the cradle of the faith from Saracen domination. In spite of the failure of all previous Crusades, he seems to have had no doubt that success was now

possible and even easy, if only the effort were
sincerely made; and the hope inspired him to
address to Giacomo Colonna the ode *O aspettata
in Ciel*, in which he exhorts the Bishop to employ
his great influence and his unrivalled eloquence in
rousing the sons of Italy to take their part in the
glorious enterprise. John XXII's proposal to return
to Rome, which he regarded as the only rightful
seat of the Papacy, stirred him to yet higher enthusiasm. Thus it seemed to him that Christendom
now bade fair to escape from two of the chief evils
that afflicted the age, and the double hope is finely
expressed in the sonnet *Il successor di Carlo*, in
which he urges the Princes of Italy to assist King
and Pope in their endeavours. Philip, who but a
few months since seemed to be Italy's worst enemy,
can now be honoured with the title of "successor to
Charlemagne"; and when "the Vicar of Christ,
returning to his nest, sees first Bologna and then
our noble Rome," Italy, the gentle lamb, will rise
and smite the fierce wolves that have torn her. So
perish all who sow dissension betwixt hearts that
love should bind! Disappointment soon succeeded
to hope; King Philip took the cross indeed, but
with it received from the Pope the right to levy
a tithe on the revenues of the Gallican Church, and
with the grant in his hands he soon dropped the
pretext of crusading zeal on which he had obtained
it. The Pope kept up appearances a little longer,
and the Cardinal Legate was ordered to build a
palace at Bologna for his reception on his way to
Rome. Presently, however, the palace took the

form of a fortress commanding the city, and the Pope too had got what he wanted by his pretext.

He died in the following year at the age of ninety-one; he had been Pope eighteen years, and had amassed eighteen million lire in specie, as well as plate, gems, and ornaments to the value of seven millions more. He was not a great or a good Pope, and as a theologian he nearly split the Church by propounding an unorthodox opinion on the Beatific Vision. But he must have had some good qualities of head and heart, for though he remained at Avignon, he was shrewd enough to appreciate the value of the Roman tradition, and he won the friendship of so upright a man as Cardinal Colonna, who, as Petrarch tells us, loved the man though not his errors. The Conclave which followed was a hotbed of intrigue; the French party was the strongest, but the Italians, though unable to carry a candidate of their own, could prevent any one whom they disliked from obtaining the requisite two-thirds majority. To gain time, the Frenchmen put forward Cardinal Fournier, the least influential member of the College; but when the scrutiny was taken, it was found that every one had voted for Fournier in the belief that only a few others would do so, and he was declared unanimously elected. The new Pope himself was more astonished than any one at the result, and is said to have exclaimed, "Your choice has fallen on an ass." He took the name of Benedict XII. The election of a Frenchman was, of course, distasteful to Petrarch, but it was not long before Benedict showed him marks of personal friendship and

THE MONUMENT OF POPE JOHN XXII, AVIGNON

esteem : he allowed Petrarch to address him in a poetical Latin letter urging the return of the Papacy to Rome, and though he never yielded either to this or to subsequent appeals of the same kind, he was certainly not displeased at them, for he presently conferred on their author his first ecclesiastical preferment, a canonry at Lombez.

Soon afterwards began Petrarch's friendship with Azzo da Correggio, one of those friendships with Italian despots which have puzzled some of his admirers and scandalised many of his critics. How, it is asked, could Petrarch, with the praises of virtue and fidelity always on his lips, seek the society and extol the merits of men steeped in crime, to whom treachery and assassination were mere moves in a game of political intrigue, and whose reputation for cruelty and lust is the blackest spot in the record of the Italian people ? With many members of these ruling families Petrarch lived on terms of intimate acquaintance ; to three of them, namely, to Azzo da Correggio and to Jacopo and Francesco da Carrara, he was bound by ties of warmest friendship. How was this possible ? The easy explanation and the false one is that Petrarch was a hypocrite and a sycophant. The truth is less easily stated, and to men of our age and country will never be fully comprehensible. In the first place, it must be remembered that until the researches of comparatively recent historians shed a flood of light on the period from the thirteenth to the sixteenth centuries, history had given a one-sided account of these Italian despots.

The world was so shocked at their unspeakable crimes that it forgot their equally extraordinary merits. Numbers of them were men of the most brilliant intellectual gifts, lovers of literature, appreciative patrons of art, gallant in war, splendid and usually generous in peace. They were, to use a modern catchword, strenuous men in every department of life. Thorough was their motto, efficiency their ideal; if morality could be banished from the world, they might be taken as types of complete manhood. The man who saw only their good side might well be carried away by enthusiasm for their excellencies, and it is unquestionable that something in Petrarch led them to show him as much as possible of their best and as little as possible of their worst side. Of their base intrigues and unscrupulous treacheries he evidently accepted the version which they themselves gave him; and if this says little for his faculty of impartial discernment, such blindness to the faults of a friend is at worst the weakness of an over-trustful nature. However incomplete the explanation, to those who have entered into Petrarch's character the facts are indisputable, that he was not a hypocrite, and that he was the friend of Azzo.

Their friendship began at Avignon, but was the consequence of a faction-fight at Parma: the family of Correggio, acting as henchmen of the Lords of Verona, had driven the Rossi out of Parma; the latter came to plead their cause before the Pope, and were opposed by Azzo da Correggio and Gulielmo da Pastrengo, an accomplished scholar and lawyer of Verona. Azzo and Gulielmo engaged Petrarch as their advocate in the Papal consistory, and the poet won his case in this, the only lawsuit in which there is any record of his having appeared. His success got him the temporary goodwill of Mastino della Scala, at that time Lord of Verona, and the enmity of Ugolino de' Rossi, Archbishop of Parma ; it is more important that he was henceforth on terms of warm friendship with both Azzo and Gulielmo.

To the following year belongs an incident trivial in itself, but interesting as showing a little trait in which Petrarch anticipated the modern spirit. Accompanied by his brother Gherardo and a couple of servants, he made the ascent of Mont Ventoux, "a steep and almost inaccessible mass of crags," and one of the highest peaks in Provence. He was fascinated by the wild beauty and majestic solitude of peak and ravine, which were foolishness to the classical and a terror to the mediæval world ; and however small an achievement the ascent of Mont Ventoux may appear to a member of the Alpine Club, it entitles Petrarch to be called the first of the climbers. Among the ridges of the hills the brothers found an old shepherd, who tried hard to dissuade them from the ascent, saying that "fifty years ago he had been led by the same impetuous eagerness of youth to climb the peak, but had got nothing by it save toil and regret and the tearing of his flesh and clothes by the rocks and brambles ; and never either before or since had any one been known to dare the like." The brothers, how-

ever, persevered, and the old man, finding remonstrance of no avail, showed them a steep track
among the rocks, still giving them many warnings,
which he kept shouting at them after they had gone
forward. "We left with him," says Petrarch in a
letter to Fra Dionigi, "so much of our dress and
other things as was likely to be in our way, and so,
girded just for the mere ascent, we set ourselves
eagerly to our climb. But, as always happens, the
strenuous effort was very soon followed by fatigue ;
so after going a little way we rested on one of the
rocks.

"Thence we started again, but at a slower pace,
and I especially began to prosecute mountain climbing at a more moderate speed. My brother pursued his upward path by the shortest way over the
very ridges of the mountain ; but I was less hardy
and inclined to the lower paths, and when he called
after me and pointed to the more direct way, I
answered that I hoped to find the ascent of the
other side easier, and was not afraid of taking a
longer route if it offered a gentler slope. This I
put forward as an excuse for my laziness ; and while
the others had already arrived on high ground, I
kept wandering along the hollows, though no easier
ascent appeared anywhere, but the way grew longer
and my vain toil heavier. Presently I grew heartily
tired and sick of this aimless wandering, and determined to go straight up the heights. There, tired
and distressed, I came up with my brother, who
was waiting for me and had refreshed himself with
a long rest, and for a little time we went on to-

gether.   But we had hardly left that ridge behind,
when behold! I forgot my former circuit, and again
fell upon the lower paths; so I once more wandered
along the hollows, seeking a long and easy way,
but finding only long trouble.   I tried, forsooth, to
put off the trouble of climbing; but no human
device can do away with the nature of things, and
no material body can rise higher by descending.
Why make a long story?   Three or four times in
a few hours the same thing occurred to me, to my
own vexation and my brother's amusement."   So
he sat down in a hollow and moralised on the far-
off altitude of the life of blessedness and the
strenuous climbing needed to attain to it; and
"these thoughts wonderfully strengthened both body
and mind in me to undergo the rest of the ascent.
Would that I might accomplish in spirit that other
journey, for which I sigh day and night, even as,
overcoming at length all difficulties, I accomplished
this of to-day with my bodily feet! . . . There is
one peak higher than the rest, which the rustics
call 'the little boy,' for what reason I know not,
unless it be from sheer contradiction, as I suspect
is the case with sundry other names; for it looks
truly like the father of all the neighbouring mountains.   On its top is a little piece of level ground,
on which we at length rested our weary limbs. . . .
Here I stood amazed . . . the clouds were under
our feet . . . and I looked in the direction of Italy,
to which my heart is most inclined. . . . Then a
fresh train of thought occurred to me, and I remembered that to-day was the tenth anniversary of

my leaving Bologna. . . . Oh! the changes of those years! . . . I no longer love what I used to love; nay, that is not true; I do love still, but with more modesty and a deeper melancholy. Yes, I still love, but unwillingly, in spite of myself, in sorrow and tribulation of heart. . . . Then I began to think that in ten years more I might at least hope to be fit to encounter death with a quiet mind. . . . And passing at last from thoughts of myself . . . I began to admire the view, from the hills of the province of Lyons on the right to the bay of Marseilles on the left, with the Rhone flowing close under us. While looking at each object in the landscape, and now considering the earthly scene and again passing to matters of a higher nature, it occurred to me to look at the *Confessions* of Augustine which you gave me, and which I keep and always carry about with me in memory alike of the author and the giver. I opened the little volume of tiny compass but infinite sweetness, intending to read the first passage that might offer; for what could I find there but words of piety and devotion? It chanced, however, that I hit upon the tenth book of the work. My brother stood listening, waiting to hear a sentence from Augustine by my mouth; and God is my witness, as well as he who was standing by, that my eyes first lit on the passage where it is written: 'And men go about to marvel at the heights of the mountains, at the huge waves of the sea, at the broad estuaries of the rivers, at the circuit of the ocean, and at the revolutions of the stars, and forsake their own souls.' I stood

amazed, and begging my brother, who was eager
to hear the passage, not to trouble me, I shut the
book, angry with myself for having even now been
marvelling at earthly things, when I ought long
since to have learnt even from the philosophers of
the Gentiles that there is nothing marvellous in
comparison with the soul, and when it is great all
things are small beside it. . . . Then I felt that I
had seen enough of the mountain, and turned my
mind's eye back upon myself; and from that time
no one heard me speak till we reached the bottom.
For that passage had brought me occupation
enough; nor could I believe that I had lighted on
it by mere chance, but I fancied that what I had
read there was a special message to my own heart.
. . . Amid the reflections thus engendered . . . I
returned in the depth of night and by moonlight to
the rustic inn, whence I had started before dawn,
and where I am writing you this hurried letter
while the servants are preparing supper. . . . You
see then, my loving father, that I would hide nothing
from your sight, but am diligent in making known
to you not only the general course of my life, but
the separate thoughts of my heart. Pray, I entreat
you, for those thoughts, that though they have long
been wandering and unstable, they may stand firm
at the last, and after fruitless tossing on many a sea,
may return to the one good true and sure foundation of the soul."

CHAPTER IV

ROME AND VAUCLUSE

1336-1340

TEN full years had passed since Petrarch, summoned back from Bologna by the news of his father's death, had quitted Italy, the land of his devoted attachment; and it does not appear that he had yet had an opportunity of revisiting her. Three years earlier, as we have seen, he had hoped to go to Rome with Giacomo Colonna, but the latter's hurried return thither after the affray with the Orsini had baulked him of the expected visit. In December of this year a bantering invitation from Giacomo gave him another opportunity which he eagerly seized. "With joy and laughter" he read in this letter that his friend esteemed him already, in spite of his youth, the cleverest deceiver in the world. "You try to deceive Heaven itself," the Bishop seems to have said, "by feigning devotion to Saint Augustine; you do deceive the world and get yourself immense credit by feigning a passion for 'Laura,' when the crown of 'laurel' is the real object of your heart's desire; and you very nearly succeeded in deceiving me by feigning a burning desire to come and visit me in Rome." To this agreeable jesting, which forms the chief support of the allegorical theory of Petrarch's love, the poet

replied by protesting the genuineness of his double
devotion. "Would to God," he cries, "that your
banter were true, and my passion a feint and not
a madness! . . . But you know well that it is so
violent as to have affected my bodily health and
complexion. . . . I can only hope that the sore
will come to a head in time, and that I may find the
truth of Cicero's saying that 'one day brings a
wound and another day healing.' Against this
fiction, as you call it, of Laura, perhaps that other
fiction of Augustine may help me, for by much
grave reading and meditation I may grow old before
my time. . . . But as to yourself and Rome . . .
answer me seriously; put out of sight the longing
to see your face, which I have borne now for over
three years, thinking daily, 'lo! to-morrow he will
come,' or 'lo! in a day or two I shall start'; take
no account of the heavy burden of my troubles
which I can scarce be content to share with any one
but you; grant that I have cooled in my desire to
see your most illustrious father, your noble brothers,
and your honourable sisters; still, what do you
think I would not give to see the walls and hills of
the city, and, as Virgil says, 'the Tuscan Tiber and
the palaces of Rome'? No one can imagine how
I long to look upon that city, deserted and the mere
image of old Rome though it be, which I have
never yet seen! . . . I remember how Seneca
exults in writing to Lucilius from the very villa of
Scipio Africanus, and thinks it no small matter to
have seen the place where that great man spent his
exile, and where he laid his bones, which his father-

land could not afterwards obtain. If such were the feelings of a Spaniard, what, think you, must I feel, who am Italian born? For here is no question of the villa of Liternum or the tomb of Scipio, but of the city of Rome, where Scipio was born and nurtured, where he won equal glory as victor and as accused, and where not only he, but numberless other men lived, whose fame shall endure for ever."

To him a journey to Rome was indeed a pilgrimage not of religion only, but of politics and culture also. In the continuity of her history he saw an epitome of human development; many before him had been moved by the recollection of her ancient glories; and the theory of her claim to be the seat alike of Papacy and Empire had been formulated by Dante in a treatise which may be called the political testament of the Middle Ages; but Petrarch is the first to read her history as a whole and to regard its changing periods as mere phases in one deathless career. She is to him the sacred city not merely of Christendom, but of humanity.

The Cardinal's permission for the journey was obtained, and Petrarch immediately started for Marseilles, where he took ship for Cività Vecchia. Off Elba he encountered a storm, but arrived safely in port, probably about the middle of January. Here he found it impossible to go on to Rome without an escort, for the Orsini had collected a strong force with which they held the approaches to the city. For the present therefore he remained in Capranica (Mons Caprarum), a hill-fortress some thirty miles from Rome, where he was welcomed

by Orso, Count of Anguillara, who had married
Agnese Colonna, one of Stefano the Elder's many
daughters. Thence he sent a courier to inform
Giacomo of his arrival, and also wrote a full account
of his surroundings to Cardinal Giovanni. " I have
lighted on a place in the Roman territory," he
says, "which would suit my troubled feelings admir-
ably if my mind were not in haste to be elsewhere.
Known formerly as the Mount of Goats . . . it
became gradually peopled by men, who built a
citadel on the highest mound, round which have
clustered as many houses as the narrow limits of
the hill allowed. Though unknown to fame, it is
surrounded by famous places ; on one side is Mount
Soracte, well known as the dwelling-place of Silvester, but also made illustrious before Silvester's
time by the songs of the poets ; on another side are
the lake and hill of Ciminus, mentioned by Virgil ;
and there is Sutrium only two miles away, the
favoured haunt of Ceres and, as the legend runs, a
colony of Saturn. Not far from the walls they
show a field in which they say the first crop of corn
in Italy was sown by a foreign king and reaped
with the sickle; which marvellous benefit so softened
the rude spirit of the people, that this foreigner was
by their favour chosen king during his life and
worshipped after his death, for after reigning to
a good old age, he was represented as a god with a
sickle in his hand. The air here seems most
healthy, and there are beautiful views from the
surrounding hills. . . . Peace alone is wanting to
complete the prosperity of the country. . . . For

what do you think? The shepherd arms himself for his woodland watch, from fear rather of robbers than of wolves; the ploughman dons a breastplate and takes a spear to do the office of a goad in prodding the flank of a troublesome ox; the fowler throws a shield over his nets; the fisherman too hangs his hooks with their beguiling bait from the tempered blade of a sword; and, ridiculous as you will think it, when a man goes to draw water from the well, he lowers a rusty helmet at the end of his dirty rope. In a word, there is nothing done here without arms. All night long the watchmen howl upon the walls and voices call to arms; what cries are these to take the place of the sounds I have been wont to draw from the melodious strings! Among the dwellers in these lands nothing looks secure; there is not a word of peace nor a feeling of their common humanity, only war and hatred and all things after the likeness of the works of devils. In this place, illustrious father, half willingly and half unwillingly I have now spent sixteen days; and so powerful is habit, that while all others rush to the citadel at the clang of arms and braying of trumpets, I may often be seen wandering over the hills, diligently thinking over something to win me the favour of posterity. All are astonished to see me at my ease, fearless and unarmed; while I am astonished to see them all fearful, anxious, and armed: such differences are there in the ways of men! If haply I were asked whether I wish to go hence, I should find it hard to answer; 'twere well to be gone, and yet 'tis pleasant to stay."

Orso, "the Bear who is gentler than any lamb," and
Agnes, "one of those women who are best praised
by silent admiration," entertained Petrarch till
Giacomo could join him, which he did on January
26th, riding unmolested from Rome with his eldest
brother Stefano the Younger and only a hundred
horsemen, although five hundred of the Orsini beset
the road. The party probably stayed in Capranica
for some days. Sonnet XXXIV, *Perch' io t' abbia
guardato*, was certainly written there, and others of
the extant poems probably owe their origin to those
"wanderings among the hills" of which Petrarch
speaks to the Cardinal. Presently they moved on
to Rome, where he was received as one of themselves by the whole family, especially by old
Giovanni di San Vito, who made himself his constant companion and guide through the city. Even
in this day of her humiliation the glories of Rome
paralysed for awhile his powers of composition.
"What must you expect me to write from the
city," he says, "after the long letters I sent you
from the hills! You may well be looking for an
outpouring of eloquence now that I have arrived in
Rome. Well, I have found a vast theme, which
may serve perhaps for future writing; but just now
I dare not attempt anything, for I am overwhelmed
by the miracle of the mighty things around me,
and sink under the weight of astonishment. But
one thing I must tell you, that my experience is
contrary to what you expected. For I remember
that you used to dissuade me from coming hither,
chiefly on the ground that my enthusiasm would

cool at the sight of the city laid in ruins, and ill-
answering to its fame and to the idea which I had
formed of it from books.   And I too, though burning with eagerness, was not unwilling to wait, fear-
ing lest the image which I had formed in my mind
should suffer loss by actual sight and by the presence which is ever the foe of great reputations.
This time, however, wonderful to say, nothing has
been lowered and everything has been heightened
by it.   In truth, Rome is greater and her remains
are greater than I thought, and my wonder is now
not that she conquered the world, but that she did
not conquer it sooner." Some years later he
reminds Giovanni di San Vito of their delightful
excursions together.   "We used to stroll side by
side in the mighty city," he writes, "and not only
in it, but around it as well, and every step brought
some suggestion to stir the mind and loose the
tongue."   The two were often accompanied by
Paolo Annibaldi, this year joint Senator of Rome
with Stefano the Younger, the head of a House
allied to that of Colonna by ties of marriage
and friendship.   Paolo's "extraordinary worth and
humanity" had made Petrarch his dear friend:
unlike most of the Roman nobles, he cared for the
artistic and historical monuments of the city and
sorrowed over her ruin.   His death in the year
1355, while still in the flower of his age, was a
veritable tragedy; one of his sons was killed in a
faction-fight, and he fell dead in an access of grief
across the mutilated body of his boy.

Strongly as Petrarch had always felt the claims of

Rome to be the seat of Empire and Papacy, he was now more than ever disposed to assert her rights. Accordingly he wrote once more to Benedict XII, resuming the subject of his former poem, but speaking now in his own person, and asserting the superiority of Rome over all other countries. Benedict had now settled the theological question of the Beatific Vision, and so, Petrarch suggested, had time to take measures for resuming his proper position as husband of Rome and father of all Italy. But probably the Pope had never really intended to return; certainly, even if he had been sincere in expressing his wish to do so, the intrigues of the French party among the Cardinals were successful in detaining him at Avignon, and so thoroughly had he become convinced of the necessity of remaining there, that he was now laying the foundations of the papal palace designed to form a permanent residence for himself and his successors.

We do not know how long Petrarch stayed in Rome, but he must have left soon after Easter if he found time during this summer for the extended travels which seem clearly indicated in a poetical letter addressed to Giacomo Colonna. These travels can hardly be assigned to any other date. He returned to Avignon on August 16th; at some time in the interval he paid a visit to Lombez to take up his canonry there, and in the course of these four or five months he appears also to have made a sea trip to Morocco and to have visited the English Channel. He speaks expressly of having

seen "the mountain hardened by Medusa's eye" in
the country of the Moors, by which he must mean
some part of the chain of Mount Atlas; and thence,
he says, he went northward, and came "where the
swollen wave of the British sea wears away with
flow and ebb of tide the shores that stand doubtful
which shall receive its stroke." The chronology
is extremely difficult, and some critics take the short
way of treating the whole letter as mere rhetoric.
But the travels indicated were not quite impossible
of accomplishment in the four and a half months
available for them, and to regard inconvenient
allusions as worthless evidence on the ground that
they occur in a poem is to ignore difficulties, not to
solve them.

Avignon on his return appeared to him more
detestable than ever; during his absence, if we may
trust another of his Latin poetical letters, he had
enjoyed intervals of respite from the violence of his
passion for Laura, but the sight of her rekindled
that passion in all its fury. We may suppose too
that his hatred of Avignon as the usurper of the
rights of Rome was intensified by his visit to the
Eternal City. For "on my return thence," he tells
us, " I could not endure the disgust and hatred of
things in general, but above all of that most wearisome city, naturally implanted in my mind, and so
I looked about for some better retreat, as it were a
harbour of refuge, and found the valley, a very
small one, but solitary and pleasant, which is called
The Closed Valley, fifteen miles distant from Avignon, where rises the king of all river sources, the

Sorgue. Captivated by the charm of the place, I transferred thither my books and myself." He bought a small house at Vaucluse with a strip of riverside meadow adjoining it, and so installed himself in the one of his many residences which is best entitled to be called his home, and has been most closely associated by posterity with his name and fame.

Many reasons make the date of his settling at Vaucluse one of the most important in his life. Hitherto he had been entirely dependent upon his patrons; now, though still looking to them for preferment, he had a home of his own in which he could order his life after his own fashion. Here he was free from the agitation which the sight of Laura never failed to renew in his spirit—he intimates repeatedly that to avoid her was his main object in going to Vaucluse—and here he could indulge that love of scenery, that passion for nature and solitude, which was so rare among the men of his day, and contrasts so strongly with his own interest in man as "the proper study of mankind." Here too he had abundant leisure for literary work; he was free from the bustle and distractions of town life, and he made such good use of his time that "nearly everything which he ever wrote was either finished, begun, or planned here." But though enjoying the leisure and quiet of almost complete solitude, he was not cut off from his friends or from society. Socrates and Lælius came often to see him; the Cardinal's house at Avignon was open to him whenever he chose to go there; and visitors

from every part of Europe, attracted by his fame,
sought him out in his retreat. "While I was living
in France in the period of my youth," he says, "I
was surprised to see sundry noble and talented men
come from the further provinces of France, as well
as from Italy, with no other design than that of seeing me and holding conversation with me; among
whom was Peter of Poitiers, of honourable memory,
a man illustrious alike for piety and for learning.
And you will wonder the more when I tell you that
some of these visitors sent me magnificent presents
in advance, and then came in the wake of their gifts,
as though they would smooth the way and open the
gates by their liberality. . . . By word and deed
they proclaimed that they came to Avignon solely
to see me, so that if I was not in the city, they
would take no heed of anything there, but hastened
on to the source of the Sorgue, where I generally
spent the summer." Such homage was very gratifying to Petrarch; the love of fame was strong in
him; he shared and fostered that eager pursuit of
personal glory which marked the Italians of the
Renaissance. He made some parade of despising
the opinions of "the vulgar," but in his heart he
liked even popular applause, and he could not fail
to be elated by the unstinted homage paid to his
genius by men qualified to appreciate it. It is
pleasant to add that when embarrassed by the difficulty of disposing of these admirers' gifts without
offence to the givers, he solved the problem with
characteristic generosity by sharing them with his
friends.

At Vaucluse he had the happiness of finding a neighbour who soon became one of his most intimate friends. Philip de Cabassoles was a member of a noble Provençal family connected by long-standing ties of marriage and friendship with the House of Anjou, and especially with the Neapolitan branch of it. King Robert of Naples indeed, who as Count of Provence was his sovereign, held him in such esteem that by his will he appointed him a member of the Neapolitan Council of Regency during the minority of his granddaughter Joanna. Philip's personal qualities justified the unanimous good opinion of his contemporaries. He had already won a reputation for brilliant intellectual attainments ; he was an eager student and an enthusiastic patron of letters ; in private life he was the most loyal of friends ; and when the time came in 1343 for him to take up the ungrateful task of statesmanship at Naples, he struggled gallantly though ineffectually to uphold public order and political probity amid the welter of factious intrigue which followed the Wise King's death. Long before the canonical age he had been appointed by John XXII to the bishopric of Cavaillon, "a little town," as Petrarch describes it, "about two leagues from Vaucluse, which as being the seat of a bishopric is dignified with the name of city, but which has no quality of a city except the title and its antiquity." Vaucluse lay within the diocese of Cavaillon, and one of the Bishop's official residences was a castle perched on the crags which overhang the valley. Here Petrarch paid his respects to Philip, who was a year his junior in age, and the two men, mutually attracted by each other's great qualities, contracted an intimacy, which soon ripened into one of the closest and most valuable of Petrarch's friendships. Philip "loved him not only with a Bishop's love, as Ambrose loved Augustine, but with that of a brother," and his affection was repaid in full. The friends spent hours in each other's society, entering each other's houses unannounced, and using each other's books as a common possession. To Philip Petrarch dedicated the *De Vita Solitaria*, and he was one of the very few friends ever permitted to see the poet's compositions in the rough.

Another motive, of which Petrarch preserved no record, may have contributed to his wish for partial retirement from Avignon. In this year (1337), an illegitimate son was born to him. Of his fault much has been said: in some it has aroused genuine indignation, in others a base satisfaction at the lapses of a devout and passionate soul; of his punishment and repentance those know best who have studied his writings most closely and read his character most accurately. To a man of his physical habit temptation came with its fullest force; is it not punishment enough that to a man of his spiritual temperament penitence was an agony of the soul? We do not know who was Giovanni's mother; there is reason to suppose that she was a person of humble origin, and that she was also the mother of his daughter Francesca, born to him six years later; we do know that after the birth of the latter child, while Petrarch was still under forty, he regained control of his passions, and that his subsequent life was free from stain. He was punished also, as we shall see later, by the conduct of the boy, conduct which was probably aggravated by the father's injudicious handling of a stubborn and perverse disposition, and by mutual misunderstanding due to the inherent difficulty of their relations. Petrarch's very conscientiousness made the mischief worse; he felt himself deeply responsible for Giovanni's character and education; though he did not call the boy by the name of son, he procured him letters of legitimacy, and never hesitated to acknowledge his own fault, if the acknowledgment was necessary for Giovanni's preferment. He spent infinite pains, too, on training the boy in liberal learning; in return he unhappily demanded a pliancy foreign to Giovanni's nature, and any father who would learn how to deter a son from the path in which he wishes him to walk has only to study the history of Petrarch and Giovanni. It is the melancholy story of two persons connected by no tie except that of natural kinship, which, if it does not inspire community of tastes and mutual affection, will surely aggravate and embitter the disagreement of their tempers. Doubtless the boy was most to blame; he was constitutionally idle, perverse, and sullen. But it is evident enough that his faults were enhanced by the mismanagement of his father. To those whose character commanded his sympathy Petrarch was the best of friends and the most genial of instructors, but he had neither patience nor tact enough to overcome the difficulties of a

natural antipathy.   Above all things, idleness and
sullenness were hateful to him ; so when Giovanni
was idle, he lectured him and teased him with
instances of exemplary diligence, or tried to rouse
him out of the sulks by sermonising, or, worst of
all, by sarcasm and ridicule.   Conscientiously he
tried to do his duty ; but the more he tried the
worse he blundered, and it is hardly surprising that
the boy showed his worst side to his father, while
some of Petrarch's friends discerned in him through
all his faults a promise of better things.

On April 17th, 1338, during a visit to Avignon,
he had the inestimable joy of recovering the beautiful MS. of Virgil which had been one of the treasures of his father's library, and had been stolen
from him in 1326.   We do not know the circumstances in which he regained possession of it, further
than that his own note on the fly-leaf speaks of its
"restitution," which seems to point to a voluntary
act on the part of its unlawful possessor.   Precious
as is the codex itself, this fly-leaf is more precious
still, for on it in Petrarch's beautiful handwriting
(a kind of delicate black-letter, which cannot have
been taken by Aldus, as tradition asserts, for the
model of his cursive type) are recorded the dates of
his first meeting with Laura and of her death,
together with the deaths of his son Giovanni, of
Socrates, and of many other friends.   Surely a more
pathetic document was never penned in the whole
course of literary history.   From the date of its
recovery this cherished volume accompanied its
owner everywhere ; and on its fly-leaf, the page

which his eye would see oftener than any other, he
"set down a record of the cruel events, not without
a bitter sweetness in the remembrance of them."
Some time after Petrarch's death the book became
the property of Gian-Galeazzo Visconti, and was
kept at Pavia till the submission of that city to the
French King's troops in 1499, when Antonio Pirro
saved it from the plunderers; from him it passed
through several hands till it was bought by Cardinal
Borromeo, who presented it to the Ambrosian
Library at Milan.   Napoleon stole it, but in 1815
it was restored to Milan, and is still one of the chief
treasures of the library.

About this time Petrarch came in contact with
Humbert II, the last Dauphin of Vienne.   The impending outbreak of war between France and
England placed this Prince in a position of em-
barrassment, for he owed homage both to the
Emperor and to the King of France.   The former
summoned him to help his ally, King Edward III,
the latter to join the French force against the English.   The Dauphin's chief anxiety seems to have
been to keep out of the fighting; an old chronicler
describes him as having the air and manners of a
woman; and his double allegiance furnished a not
unwelcome pretext.   Instead of joining either party,
he established himself at Avignon, where the Pope
had assigned him a house, and employed himself
in prosecuting a lawsuit with the Archbishop of
Vienne.   Cardinal Colonna got Petrarch to write
him a letter exhorting him to take up arms for
Philip, but the peaceful disposition of the Dauphin

was proof against the poet's eloquence.   He stayed
at Pont du Sorgue and prosecuted his lawsuit.   It
was probably with him that Petrarch and his brother
Gherardo made an expedition to the Ste. Beaume,
or cave of St. Mary Magdalene, near Marseilles.
A man "whose high position far transcended his
prudence," Petrarch tells us, a great personage whose
society was not at all pleasing to him, frequently
pressed him to accompany him on this expedition.
Petrarch as constantly refused till Cardinal Colonna
backed the great man's request; the poet then
yielded, and some devotional Latin verses of
mediocre quality were the fruit of his visit to this
sacred but fearsome cavern.   For his brother
Gherardo the journey proved more notable: he
took advantage of it to visit for the first time the
Carthusian monastery of Montrieu, in which some
years later he was to take the vows.

About this time also Petrarch had the happiness
of renewing his friendship with Azzo da Correggio
and Gulielmo da Pastrengo.   Their mission to
Avignon was the result of one of those family feuds
ending in murder so frequent in the history of the
Italian despots.   Mastino della Scala had taken
possession of Lucca in defiance of the treaty rights
of the Florentines; his cousin Bartolommeo, Bishop
of Verona, was accused, truly or falsely, of a conspiracy to murder him and hand over Lucca to the
allied troops of Florence and Venice.   Azzo da
Correggio was the accuser, and on August 6th,
1338, Mastino, probably accompanied by Azzo, met
the Bishop on the steps of the cathedral and

Drucker

THE TOMBS OF THE SCALIGERI, VERONA

stabbed him to death.   Then he sent off Azzo in hot haste as his ambassador to the Pope to obtain absolution, and associated Gulielmo and another lawyer with him as his advocates.

They reached Avignon in September, and Petrarch, hearing of their arrival, came over from Vaucluse to see them.   But hardly had he reached Avignon when a frenzy of emotion overmastered him ; the sight of the city brought back the wild tumult of his passions ; he could not stay, but fled back to Vaucluse, and a day or two afterwards wrote to tell Gulielmo the cause of his absence. The violent mood soon passed, no doubt, and he renewed the habit of which he speaks in this letter, of "revisiting this ill-omened city and returning voluntarily into the snare to which no hook of necessity drew him."   The ambassadors stayed a whole year at Avignon, and the friends met frequently both there and at Vaucluse.   In September, 1339, the Pope formally absolved Mastino, and the envoys returned to Italy.

The year 1339 is notable too for Petrarch's first meeting with the Abbot Barlaam, under whom three years later he made an ineffectual attempt at learning Greek.   Barlaam was a native of Calabria, but had lived most of his life in Salonika and Constantinople, where he was Abbot of the monastery of St. Gregory.   He is described by Boccaccio as a man of diminutive stature but huge learning ; as a theological disputant he had made bitter enemies at Constantinople, but just now he was in high favour with the Court, and the Emperor Andronicus had sent him to Avignon on one of those futile missions which had for pretext the reunion of the Churches, and for real object an inquiry whether the West could be cajoled into helping the East with men or money.

Petrarch has left some delightful accounts of his life at Vaucluse, but most of these refer to the second and third periods of his sojourn there, and will be noticed later. There is evidence enough, however, to show that this first period too was one of intense literary activity, pursued in a life of rustic frugality. "Long would be the story," he writes, "if I went on to tell what I did there through many and many a year. This is the sum of it, that almost every one of the poor works which have come from my pen was either completed, begun, or planned there. . . . The very aspect of the place suggested to me that I should attempt my bucolic poetry, a woodland work, and the two books upon the life of solitude . . . and as I wandered among those hills on a certain Friday in Holy Week I hit upon the thought, which proved a fruitful one, of writing a poem in heroic verse about the great Scipio Africanus the Elder, whose name, I know not why, had been dear to me from my boyhood." In addition to all these compositions, there is good reason to think that his earlier years at Vaucluse saw at least the beginning of his greatest prose work, the *Lives of Illustrious Men;* and if he wanted a change from original composition, there were always his classical manuscripts lying ready to his hand for the careful annotation which reveals to us the wide range and the thoroughness of his reading.

As evidence of his manner of life, take the following delightful note in which he invites Cardinal Colonna to sup with him : " You will come a long-hoped-for guest to supper, and will remember that we have no market of dainties here. A poet's banquet awaits you, and that not of Juvenal's or Flaccus' kind, but the pastoral sort that Virgil describes : 'mellow apples, soft chestnuts, and rich store of milky curd.' The rest is harder fare : a coarse, stiff loaf, a chance hare, or a migratory crane—and that very seldom ; or perhaps you will find the chine of a strong-flavoured boar. Why make a long story? You know the roughness of both place and fare, and so I bid you come with shoes not only on your feet, but, as the parasite in Plautus wittily says, on your teeth too."

CHAPTER V

THE CROWN OF SONG

1340–1341

PETRARCH had not yet reached his thirty-seventh birthday when he won the object of his highest ambition—the Crown of Song. The bestowal of this laurel wreath was an ancient custom last observed in Rome in the case of the poet Statius, who received the bays from Domitian as the prize of a contest of "music and gymnastic." Though twelve centuries had elapsed since that event, the memory of the custom still survived: Dante had coveted the crown in vain, and Petrarch from his earliest manhood made no secret of his eager desire to win it. He was attracted by its historical connection with old Rome, by the picturesque nature of the ceremony, above all by the public recognition of the recipient's mastery in the art of poetry. He was no dilettante scribbler, no amateur of letters desirous of the palm without the dust; he was willing, nay eager, to live laborious days, and to spend himself and his substance in the pursuit of learning. But he cared dearly too for the reward so hardly earned; he longed for the applause of men qualified to appreciate him; he was athirst for fame. Even his thirst must have been assuaged when on one and the same day, September 1st, 1340, he received letters from Rome and from Paris offering him the object of his desire. He wrote that very evening to Cardinal Colonna asking his advice as to which invitation he should accept. "I am at the parting of two roads," he said to the Cardinal, "and I stand hesitating and knowing not which I had better take; it is a short story, but wonderful enough. To-day about nine o'clock I received a letter from the Senate summoning me in pressing terms and with much persuasion to Rome to receive the crown of song. To-day also, about four o'clock, a message reached me with a letter on the same subject from the illustrious Robert, Chancellor of the University of Paris, my fellow-citizen, and a firm friend to me and my fortunes. He urges me with carefully chosen reasons to go to Paris. Who could ever have suspected, I ask you, that such a thing would happen among these rocks and hills? In fact, the thing is so incredible that I send you both the letters with the seals uninjured. The one summons came in the morning, the other in the evening; and you will see how weighty are the arguments which appeal to me on either side. Now since joy suits ill with deliberation, I own that I am as much perplexed in mind as joyful at my good fortune. On one side is the attraction of novelty, on the other veneration for antiquity; on the one my friend, on the other my country. One thing indeed weighs heavily in the latter scale, that the King of Sicily is in Italy, whom of all men I can most readily accept as judge of my ability. You see now all the waves that toss my thoughts; you, who have not scorned to put your hand to their helm, will direct by your counsel the stormy passage of my mind."

Petrarch would hardly have asked the Cardinal's advice if he had not been sure of the answer. To balance the claims of Rome and Paris was a pretty literary exercise; but in his judgment Paris kicked the beam. Rome was for him the world's capital, whose offer of the crown proclaimed him the world's poet; in Rome he meant to be crowned, and to Rome Cardinal Colonna advised him to go.

On the way he would visit Naples. Robert the Wise, titular King of Jerusalem and the Two Sicilies, had long been one of his heroes. He wrote of him as "that consummate king and philosopher, equally illustrious in letters and in dominion, unique among the kings of our day as a friend of knowledge and of virtue." And Robert deserved high praise. He had his faults, though Petrarch did not see them. He reminds us a little of our British Solomon, who stands at the close of the Renaissance as Robert stands at its opening, a king eager to be reputed wise, whose statesmanship was too often mere statecraft, and whose learning bore the taint of pedantry. But the comparison with James is grievously unjust to Robert; his faults, if like in kind, were less in degree, and he had what the Stuart lacked—the saving grace of magnanimity. There was nothing petty about him. His title "King of Jerusalem" was a mere reminiscence of an episode in history; of the Two Sicilies the island

THE MONUMENT OF KING ROBERT OF NAPLES

kingdom had passed under the sway of the
Aragonese; but the realm of Naples throve under
his rule, and carried weight in European politics
out of all proportion to its natural resources. As
a skilful diplomatist and a prudent ruler Robert
earned his surname of "the Wise."

He earned it still better as a friend of learning;
the greatest of his services to his age and country
lay in his treatment of artists and men of letters.
The brilliant and versatile Emperor Frederick II
had lived with poets as comrades, not as depen-
dents; Robert followed this forgotten example, and
made it the fashion. He received Petrarch not as
a client, but as a friend; under colour of "examin-
ing" him, he organised a public display of the
poet's prowess, and lavished on him every possible
token of friendship and esteem. By this reception
of Petrarch, Robert enthroned intellect in the face
of Europe.

Petrarch's journey from Provence, his stay in
Naples, and his coronation in Rome occupied nearly
two months; there is some conflict of evidence as
to the exact dates of his movements, and even as to
the day of the coronation, but the following narrative gives what seems to be the most probable
account. Accompanied by Azzo da Correggio, he
left Avignon on February 16th, 1341, and took
ship at Marseilles. The friends reached Naples
early in March, and remained there as the guests of
King Robert till the beginning of April. Day after
day Petrarch and the King had long conferences,
at which they discussed poetry, history, and philo-

sophy; personal intercourse heightened their mutual
admiration, and the poet's enthusiasm knew no
bounds when Robert declared to him that he valued
learning and letters above the crown of Naples
itself. Then came the examination alluded to
above, surely the longest vivâ voce on record, when
Robert assembled his whole Court, and for two
days and a half propounded question after question
in every known branch of learning. All these the
poet seems to have answered to the satisfaction of
his audience, and on the third day Robert solemnly
pronounced him worthy of the laurel crown, and
offered to confer it on him with his own hand in
Naples. But Petrarch was loyal to Rome; only in
the Capitol would he receive the supreme distinction; and Robert respected a preference of which he
fully understood the motive. It was only his age,
he declared, and not his royal rank, that prevented
him from going himself to Rome for the occasion.
Feeling himself unequal to the journey, he appointed
the accomplished knight Giovanni Barili, a favourite
officer of his household, to act as his deputy, wrote
letters testifying to Petrarch's worthiness to receive
the laurel, and gave him his own purple robe to
wear at the ceremony.

With Barili Petrarch formed a lasting friendship,
and to this Neapolitan visit he owed also a still
closer intimacy with Marco Barbato, the Chancellor
of the kingdom, a native of Ovid's birthplace
Sulmo, himself a man of letters and a poet, "excellent in talent, and still more excellent in life."
The warmth of Petrarch's friendship for Barbato

is testified by a number of letters couched in terms of confidence and affection, and by the dedication to him of the Latin poetical letters. Yet they met only twice in twenty-two years; and from 1343 to Barbato's death in 1363 their intercourse was carried on entirely by correspondence. Their friendship furnishes an interesting example of a sympathy which twenty years of absence could not weaken.

On April 2nd Barili and his attendants left Naples, and either then or two days later Petrarch and Azzo set out in turn by a different route for Rome. They arrived safely on Good Friday, the 6th, and were received by Orso and the members of the Colonna family present in the city; but when they inquired for Barili, no news of him could be heard. Hastily they sent out a courier to scour the country; but Easter Eve passed without tidings of the King's envoy, who had in fact fallen into the hands of banditti near Anagni, and was detained their prisoner for several days. The coronation could not be deferred beyond Easter Sunday, for on the close of that day Orso's senatorship came to an end, and it was essential that Petrarch should be crowned while the Chief Magistracy was still held by one of his friends. Early on Easter morning, therefore, April 8th, trumpeters summoned the populace to the Capitol. The novelty of the spectacle, resumed after an interval of centuries, the splendour and pomp of the pageant, probably also the newly awakened zeal for art and letters, drew a vast crowd of onlookers, whose enthusiastic

applause drowned, at least for the moment, the
voices of envy and detraction. Here, in Rome,
they were met to do honour to the poet and scholar
whose enthusiasm for their city was to be the keynote of the new learning, who was to revive and
popularise the memories of her glorious past, and to
claim anew for her, in these days of her desertion by
Pope and Emperor, the indefeasible right to rule
the world.

Of the ceremony itself we have few details ; but
from what we know we can infer that it was worthy
of the occasion. Twelve boys, richly dressed in
scarlet, led the way ; they were all fifteen years of
age, and were chosen from twelve of the noblest
Roman families. After them, clad in green and
crowned with flowers, came six of the principal
nobles of the city, Petrarch's old friend Paolo Annibaldi being one of them ; and in the midst of this
distinguished escort walked Petrarch himself, wear-
ing the purple robe of the King of Naples. After
him came the Senator escorted by the chief func-
tionaries of the city, and we may be sure that a
procession in which the leading men of Rome and
their sons took part was not lacking in either the
number of its attendants or the brilliance of its
pageantry. When they reached the top of the
Capitoline Hill a herald summoned Petrarch to
speak. He saluted the people, and, taking a verse
of Virgil for his text, gave an elaborate discourse
on the difficulties, delights, and rewards of poetry,
concluding with a prayer that the Senator, as repre-
sentative of the Roman people, would be pleased to

bestow on him the crown of which the King of "Sicily" had judged him worthy. Then he knelt down before Orso, who placed the laurel crown on his head and declared aloud that he gave it him as the reward of distinguished merit. After this Petrarch recited a sonnet, which has not been preserved, in remembrance of the heroes of old Rome, and the veteran Stefano Colonna spoke a glowing eulogy of the newly crowned poet.

This ended the ceremony on the Capitol. It seems to have been purely civic in its character, for no hint is given of any ecclesiastical rite or function in connection with it. But Petrarch was of all men least likely to forget the claims of religion; very great as might be his elation at the recognition of his genius and his work, he remembered in the hour of his triumph to give God the glory. The procession reformed and escorted him to St. Peter's, where he publicly gave thanks for the honour conferred on him, and left his laurel crown to hang among the votive offerings of the cathedral. The day ended with a banquet in his honour, and the presentation to him by Orso of a diploma testifying to his excellence in the arts of poetry and history, authorising him to teach and dispute in public and to publish books at his pleasure, and conferring upon him the citizenship of Rome in recognition of his loyal devotion to her interests.

Thus ended a day notable not only in the life of its hero, but in the history of letters. It is probably true that Petrarch owed this conspicuous honour as much to the partiality of his friends as to the general recognition of his services. The best of his work was still to be done; he himself in old age, looking back on this most brilliant day of his life, admitted with evident sincerity that the leaves of his laurel crown were immature, and that a not unnatural result of its reception was to bring upon him much envy and ill-will. It was by his Italian poetry that he was chiefly known as yet, and we have seen that his Italian poetry, exquisite and in some respects unique as are its qualities, had little effect in the really important work of his life, the revival of learning. In connection with that work, it is true that he had already gained a European reputation as an earnest and indefatigable student, bent on accumulating knowledge, and eager to diffuse it; but he had as yet published little or nothing to justify in the face of the world the high esteem of his admirers. Still, when every allowance has been made for personal influence, and every possible point conceded to those who were already carping at the honour conferred on him, the fact remains that his coronation marks the awakening of general interest in learning, the end of an age in which letters were the exclusive possession of a few, and the advent of a time when even those who did not themselves possess scholarship would owe the tone of their thought and the tenor of their daily life to the spirit born of the New Learning. This is Petrarch's pre-eminent claim to the grati- tude of humanity. He was hardly a better Latinist than John of Salisbury; he knew less Greek than Robert Grosseteste; but to his efforts, and not to those of any predecessor, we owe it that the culture of the Renaissance became a living force in the development of Europe. In this sense, our modern life may be said to date from the ceremony on the Capitol.

CHAPTER VI

PARMA, NAPLES, AND VAUCLUSE

PETRARCH had contemplated a stay of some
few days in Rome ; in the event his visit was
prolonged a day beyond his intention. Soon after
leaving the gates he encountered one of those
hordes of banditti which infested the Romagna, and
was forced to return to the city. He started again
the next day with a stronger escort, and reached
Pisa by the end of April. Three weeks later he
rejoined Azzo and took part in his triumphal entry
into Parma. For the past two years the Correggi
had been busy with another move in that game of
intrigue of which the Lordship of Parma was the
stake. When in need of an ally against the Rossi,
they played the jackal, as we have seen, to Mastino
della Scala ; but the Lord of Verona took something more than the lion's share of the prey, and the
Correggi were not the men to be content with bare
bones. Azzo's journeys to Avignon and Naples,
which coincided so happily with Petrarch's movements, were undertaken to obtain Pope Benedict's
and King Robert's consent to a plan for getting
Luchino Visconti of Milan to help in expelling
Mastino's troops from Parma and transferring the

sovereignty of the city to Azzo and his brothers.
The Visconti were ever ready to fish in troubled
waters, and Luchino willingly promised assistance,
in return for which the Correggi secretly undertook
to hand over the sovereignty to him after four
years' enjoyment of it. It is not quite clear, nor
does it much matter, how far Benedict and Robert
were aware of this secret stipulation : it seems un-
likely that they would have sanctioned a plan for
the aggrandisement of their worst enemy ; on the
other hand, they must have known the Visconti
character too well to suspect Luchino of giving anything for nothing. Probably they knew of the agreement, and trusted Azzo, the arch-intriguer, to break
his promise when the time should come for perform-
ing it. Be this as it may, the bargain was struck ;
Luchino sent troops from Milan ; on May 21st the
Veronese garrison was expelled, and on the 23rd
the brothers da Correggio, accompanied by Petrarch,
made their state entry into Parma amid a great
popular demonstration of joy and welcome. Probably the Veronese domination had really been
oppressive, and the bulk of the people may have
hailed the Correggi as genuine liberators ; while
those who had been too often deluded by promises
of freedom to put any further trust in princes may
have thought that, tyrant for tyrant, their own
nobles were at any rate less objectionable than a
stranger. And for a year or two things went well
in Parma ; while Azzo and his brothers remained
of one mind, they employed their brilliant talents in
the work of government, and really did much to

lighten the burdens and improve the administration
of the State.

Everything therefore promised well for the
happiness of Petrarch's first sojourn in Parma,
which was to last about a year. But not even
Azzo's companionship could keep him permanently
in the town; mountain and woodland called him
with an irresistible charm; and on the great spurs
of the Apennines above Reggio, where the River
Enza flows down from Canossa to the plain, he
found a pleasant summer refuge from the heat and
dust of the city. Either in the little village of
Ciano or in a neighbouring castle owned by the
Correggi, he spent a great part of the summer; and
here one day, as he wandered in the wood which
then bore the name of Silva Plana, he suddenly bethought him of the poem begun some years ago in
the solitude of Vaucluse. Eagerly he resumed the
interrupted work, composing a few lines on the
spot, and going on with it every day till his return
to Parma. Arrived there, he hired a quiet and
secluded little house and garden, situated on the
outskirts of the city, which pleased him so well that
he bought it a few years later. Here he applied
himself to his *Africa* with such vigour that in an
incredibly short time the nine books of the poem
were complete.

Doubtless his coronation acted as a sharp stimulus
to his powers; the excitement of so unique an
honour, and the desire to justify to himself and to
the world the renown which he enjoyed, might well
have stirred a less sensitive and less impetuous

nature to extraordinary efforts. Certain it is that the years immediately following the coronation were years of incessant literary work; and it is to the period between 1341 and 1361 that we owe the great bulk of the compositions which may be called the first-fruits of Humanism. Some estimate of the literary value and effect of these compositions will be attempted in a later chapter; here it is sufficient to note that the crowning honour of Petrarch's life produced in him not a sense of satiety or content-ment with repose, but, on the contrary, a livelier and keener ambition, a noble eagerness to deserve the fame which the world had already awarded him. Those who cannot see beneath the superficial flaws of a character may speak contemptuously of his vanity, his affectations, and his greed of fame; far other is the estimate of those who have read his heart and know the high idealism, the insatiable appetite for toil, and the profound sense of devotion to his calling, which lay beneath these insignificant and not unlovable foibles.

A remarkable and touching illustration of his celebrity is furnished by the visit of an old blind grammarian, a native of Perugia, who kept a school at Pontremoli, and who made his way at this time to Parma solely for the pleasure of spending a few hours in the company of the poet, of whose corona-tion he had heard, and from whose scholarship he anticipated, what indeed it was chiefly instrumental in producing, a great awakening of the mind of Europe.

Over this bright life of honoured work, pursued

alternately in happy solitude and in the still happier
companionship of friends, there soon came a cloud
of heavy sorrow; during this summer Petrarch
heard of the death of the friend of his under-
graduate days, the poet Tommaso Caloria of
Messina; and in the month of September he had
to bear a still more lamentable loss. News had
reached him that Giacomo Colonna was ill at
Lombez; and one night he dreamed that he saw
him walking alone and hurriedly on the bank of a
little stream in his garden at Parma; he hastened
to meet him, and poured out question after question
as to how he came there, and whence and whither
he was going; Giacomo, he thought, smiled brightly
as of old, and said, "Do you remember how you
hated the storms in the Pyrenees when you lived
with me on the Garonne? I am now worn out by
them, and am going away from them to Rome,
never to return." Petrarch in his dream would
have joined himself to his friend, but Giacomo
waved him affectionately away, and then in a more
decided tone said, "Stop, I will not have you this
time for a companion." Then Petrarch noticed the
bloodless pallor of his face and knew that he was
dead, and woke with his own cry of grief and
horror still ringing in his ears. Nearly a month later
came messengers from Provence with the tidings
that Giacomo had died at the very time when
Petrarch had thus seen him in a dream.

The new year (1342) brought him yet a third
bereavement by the death at Naples of Fra Dionigi
da Borgo San Sepolcro, for whom King Robert

CLEMENS VI.
mouicens. creat. die
dit an. 10. mens. 7.
br. an. 1352. Vac.

Petrus Rogerius, Le:
7. Maij an. 1342. Se:
Obijt die 6. Decem:
Sed. dies ii.

CLEMENT VI
FROM A PORTRAIT IN THE BRITISH MUSEUM

had three years previously obtained the bishopric of Monopoli. Fra Dionigi's influence was the strongest ever brought to bear on Petrarch's mind and character; as we have seen, he knew how to foster his penitent's religious enthusiasm without impairing his zeal for secular learning, and to his wise advice it must be largely due that Petrarch neither sacrified his intellect on the altar of fanaticism, nor forgot the Christian faith in reviving Augustan culture.

In the spring of this year, "sorely against the grain," he bade farewell to Italy and returned to Avignon. We know neither the precise date nor the compelling cause of his return, but it has been plausibly conjectured that Cardinal Colonna summoned him back, and that the summons may have had some connection with the Pope's last illness. Benedict XII died on April 25th, and on May 7th Pierre Roger was elected to succeed him and took the name of Clement VI. The election was a victory for the French party, but the new Pope was no bitter partisan; his official name was not ill-chosen as an index to his character; he was a "douce" man, self-indulgent to the point of laxity, incapable of saying No to friend or nephew, but incapable also of rancour, amiable in disposition, cultivated in mind, and if not quite a scholar, at least an intelligent amateur of scholarship. Petrarch speaks of him as "an accomplished man of letters, but overwhelmed with business, and therefore a devourer of digests." Their first meeting may have occurred in connection with an embassy from Rome,

which will be more fully noticed in the next chapter;
however this may be, the new Pope soon proved
himself a good friend to Petrarch. "Clement added
to my fortunes," the latter tells us ; and we shall
see that the addition consisted of no less than four
benefices conferred on himself and one on his son,
besides an informal offer of the papal secretaryship,
which was declined. To the first of these benefices,
the priory of St. Nicolas of Miliarino, in the diocese
of Pisa, Petrarch was appointed on October 6th,
1342.

But it is characteristic of him that the first use he
made of Clement's favour was to obtain preferment
for a friend. Barlaam, the "little man of huge
learning," had come back as a theological refugee to
Avignon. He was a poor Latinist, being a native
of Calabria, where to this day the peasants speak a
patois as much Greek as Latin in its origin.
Petrarch knew no Greek at all, and was acutely
conscious of this defect in his training. The two
friends started a course of mutual instruction ; but
before Petrarch had time to make any appreciable
progress, the bishopric of Geraci, in Calabria, fell
vacant, and he persuaded the Pope to bestow it on
Barlaam ; and so, in his own words, "deprived himself of the leader under whom he had begun
campaigning with no small hope of success."

It is too much to say with one of his biographers
that this lost opportunity prevented him from found-
ing the Renaissance on a Greek instead of a Latin
basis : his predilection for all things Roman would,
we may be sure, have prevented him from giving

the preference to Greek literature, however deeply
he might have felt its charm; but it is permissible to
suppose that, if he and Boccaccio had been as proficient in Greek scholarship as they were enthusiastic
for it, the full glory of the Renaissance might have
been antedated by a generation.

Greek, then, had to be given up; but with
Petrarch the surrender of one study meant closer
application to others; he was incapable of idleness,
and the winter months, spent mostly at Vaucluse,
but with frequent visits to Avignon, were a time of
incessant mental activity. Many of the Italian
poems are referable to this period, and he was probably working also on the *Lives of Illustrious Men*.
But above all this sojourn at Vaucluse is notable
for the writing of the three dialogues *On Despising
the World*, which to those who feel the charm of
Petrarch's nature and the intense humanity of his
character are the most fascinating of all his writings.
He called them his *Secretum;* in the form of dialogues
between Saint Augustine and himself he took the
Saint, as it were, for his confessor, and laid bare to
him his inmost heart. The dialogues give as faithful a portrait as a man may hope to paint of his
own personality; the light of them penetrates the
veil and makes visible to us the mechanism of the
soul. We see the Humanist, self-conscious, self-
questioning, taking himself, as it were, for audience,
and expressing even his solitary musings through
ordered forms of rhetoric; but beneath this surface
aspect we see even more clearly the passionate soul,
earnest in thought, sincere in faith, nobly tenacious

of its ideals; and through all the rhetoric of balanced
question and answer rings the note of genuine
emotion.   Very likely Petrarch may have foreseen
the probability that these dialogues would be published after his death ; very likely he may even have
found pleasure in the idea that posterity would one
day look deep into his heart.   None the less in
writing them he meant to be his own sole and
sincere confidant during his lifetime ; they were
truly his *Secretum;* and the elaboration of their style
is due less to their author's habitual craving to
deserve and win renown, than to his instinctive
feeling that the deep matters of the soul demand
the utmost pains that the artist can bestow on their
interpretation.

The interest of the *Secretum* quickens to pathos
when we find that its composition synchronises with
Petrarch's last battle and final victory over his
natural frailty.   In the spring of 1343 his daughter
Francesca was born ; thenceforward, as he tells us,
while still in the full vigour of manhood, be became
master of his passions, and lived free from the sin
which he had always loathed.   He bestowed the same
conscientious care on Francesca's nurture as on
Giovanni's, and with far happier results; gifted with
an amiable disposition, and trained apparently by
judicious guardians, the girl grew up to be the chief
solace and delight of her father's latter years.

From his quiet scholar's life at Vaucluse Petrarch
was presently recalled to the world of politics and
intrigue by the lamentable course of events at
Naples.   King Robert died full of years and of

honour in January, 1343, and immediately his kingdom sank into indescribable anarchy and corruption.
It was as if the Wise King, like the physician in
Poe's horrible story of arrested decomposition, had
been able to galvanise the dead body-politic, but
only with the result that, as soon as his controlling
power was withdrawn, the accumulated foulness of
years became manifest in an instant.   Robert's heir
was his granddaughter Joanna, a girl of sixteen,
married in her childhood to her cousin Prince
Andrew of Hungary, who was only a year her
senior.   Once again a parallel suggests itself between the House of Stuart and the Angevin House
of the Two Sicilies.   In Naples, as in Scotland, we
have a young queen of wilful temper and un-
governed passions ; a consort of mean abilities and
dissolute inclinations ; presently a murder, of which
the husband is the victim, and the wife is commonly
believed to be an accomplice, if not the instigator.
Certain it is that she made indecent haste to marry
her paramour, whose brother was the actual murderer.   The tragedy, in the earlier as in the later
case, took time to work out, and Petrarch could
have no more than a vague suspicion of doom impending over his old patron's family when he paid
his second visit to the city ; but already there was
more than enough to disgust him as a man and
distress him as an Italian patriot.

The voyage began with an omen of misfortune.
Starting by sea, he was shipwrecked off Nice, and
seems to have continued his journey by land.   On
October 4th he reached Rome ; on the 6th he went

with Stefano Colonna the Elder to Præneste, as the guest of Stefano's grandson Giovanni ; on the 12th he arrived at Naples. The primary object of his mission was to treat for the release from prison of some turbulent friends of the Colonna family, who had got the worst of a conspiracy ; but as the Pope's envoy he would naturally be expected to report on the situation, and two letters to Cardinal Colonna paint a gloomy picture. Power was in the hands of an unscrupulous Hungarian friar, a man of abandoned life and filthy habits, who by the irony of chance bore the name of Robert, as if to point the contrast with the Wise King whose heritage he misruled. Supported by a cabal of intriguers male and female, "this fierce inhuman beast oppresses the lowly, spurns justice, and pollutes all authority human and divine." Foreseeing something of what might happen after his death, King Robert had appointed Philip de Cabassoles head of a Council of Regency, which should hold office till Queen Joanna completed her twenty-fifth year ; he now "alone embraces the side of forlorn justice ; but what can one lamb do amid such a pack of wolves?" Property and life were alike insecure ; the very Council "must end its sittings at the approach of evening, for the turbulent young nobles make the streets quite unsafe after dark. And what wonder if they are unruly and society corrupt, when the public authorities actually countenance all the horrors of gladiatorial games? This disgusting exhibition takes place in open day before the Court and populace, in this city of Italy, with more than barbaric ferocity." Knowing nothing of what he was to see, Petrarch was taken to a spectacle attended by the sovereigns in state; suddenly to his horror he saw a beautiful youth, killed for pastime, expiring at his feet, and putting spurs to his horse fled at full gallop from the place.

His mission was a failure; he argued the prisoners' case before the Council, and on one occasion came very near succeeding; but the Council broke up without coming to a decision. Indirect influence seemed equally unsuccessful: "the elder Queen pities, but declares herself powerless; Cleopatra and her Ptolemy might take compassion if their Photinus and Achillas gave them leave." Eventually the men were set at liberty, but not till after Petrarch had left the city, and then only through the young Queen's personal intercession.

"Cleopatra" honoured her grandfather's friend personally, and appointed him her chaplain; but this was poor compensation for the misery of witnessing the ruin of Naples. A far greater consolation was the companionship of his friends Barbato and Barili, whose society he enjoyed throughout his two months' stay, and with whom he made long and delightful excursions in the surrounding country.

From the horrors of Naples, of which an appalling storm in the bay was perhaps the least, Petrarch fled away in December to Parma. Here too he was in a focus of intrigue; but the city was now his Italian home, where he could live his own life and pursue his studies at his pleasure. Moreover, the intrigues here, however much fighting they might entail, were conducted according to the usages of polite society, and the arch-intriguer was his friend.

The chronology of the next two years is so difficult, that even Fracassetti, the indefatigable editor and annotator of the *Letters*, has made mutually inconsistent statements with regard to it; the following version is given with some diffidence as best fitting in with the known facts and dates.

Petrarch reached Parma about Christmas, 1343, and stayed there till February, 1345 ; of his doings there we have no record. The times were troublous; the brothers da Correggio were quarrelling; and Azzo, rather than surrender the sovereignty as promised to Luchino Visconti, sold it to the Marquis of Ferrara. Thereupon Milan and Mantua formed a league, and in November, 1344, their allied forces laid siege to Parma. For three months Petrarch endured the disquiet and discomfort of life in a beleagured town; then "a great longing for his transalpine Helicon came upon him, since his Italian Helicon was ablaze with war," and he determined to break out at all hazards. About sunset on February 24th he and a few companions sallied forth unarmed from the city ; about midnight they were near Reggio, a stronghold of the enemy. Here they fell in with armed banditti, who threatened their lives ; unable to resist, they fled at top speed in different directions through the darkness. Petrarch was just congratulating himself on his escape, when his horse fell at some obstacle, and he was thrown heavily to the ground, half stunned, and so badly bruised on one arm that it was some days before he could put his hand to his mouth. As soon as possible he recovered his horse, and presently found a few of his companions; the rest had ridden back to Parma. The night was pitch dark, and rain and hail fell in torrents, so that the little party were forced to take shelter under their horses' bellies. When the dawn came, they travelled by by-ways to Scandiano, a friendly town, where they learned that a body of the enemy had been lying in wait to intercept them, and had only just gone back to quarters. Here Petrarch's arm was bandaged, and they went on to Modena, and thence, on the following day, to Bologna.

Soon afterwards he made his way to Verona, and here he was compensated for all recent perils and discomforts by one of the biggest literary "finds" ever vouchsafed to a book-hunter's diligence. In a church library he came across a manuscript of Cicero's letters. It has generally been supposed that the treasure-trove comprised both the *Familiar Letters* and those to Atticus, but there is some reason to think that only the latter were found on this occasion. However that may be, here was a discovery for which, even had it stood alone, the world must have hailed Petrarch its benefactor, and seldom has Fortune played so happy a stroke as that by which she gave to Cicero's most ardent and most distinguished pupil the supreme delight of being the first to see his master in the intimacy of private converse. The fact that Cicero had published letters was well known, and scholars had made eager but hitherto fruitless search for the precious manuscripts. Now at last the author to whom they all looked as "father and chief of oratory and style" stood revealed also as the brightest of correspondents, the wittiest of gossips, the most human of friends; and Petrarch noted with special delight that Cicero, like himself, could communicate every passing thought and share every momentary doubt with the friend who had won his heart. He lost not a moment in making a copy of the treasure with his own hands; and the discovery also inspired him with the idea of writing the first of his two letters to Cicero, by which he set the fashion of embodying historical criticism in the form of letters to dead authors.

Petrarch seems to have spent the whole summer in Verona, in happy companionship with Gulielmo da Pastrengo, and with Azzo da Correggio, who had fled thither on the failure of his plot in Parma. During his stay here he probably sent for his son Giovanni, now a boy of eight years old, and placed him under the charge of Rinaldo da Villafranca, a well-known professor of grammar in Verona. In the autumn he left Verona for Avignon, and Gulielmo accompanied him on his journey as far as Peschiera, on the Brescian border. A letter from Gulielmo, interesting because so few of the letters written to Petrarch by his friends have been preserved, tells of their journey to the little frontier town; the night spent almost wholly in talk, the start before sunrise, and the affectionate parting, on a knoll overlooking the Lago di Garda.

Nothing further is known of Petrarch's journey back to Avignon or of the date of his arrival, except that he was certainly there by the middle of December; he may quite possibly have arrived a month or two earlier.

The next two years were spent principally at Vaucluse. As on former occasions, his life there was diversified by frequent visits to Avignon, and there are many signs that he was fully in touch with the life of the Papal Court, and with the course of events in Provence and in Italy. With Clement VI he stood higher in favour than ever; in either 1346 or 1347 the Pope offered him the post of Papal Secretary and Protonotary, and though Petrarch wisely declined an honour which would have taken him from his proper business of scholarship to overwhelm him with the uncongenial burdens of official correspondence and court intrigues, the refusal in no way diminished Clement's anxiety to promote his interests; in October, 1346, he conferred on him a canonry at Parma, and in 1348 gave him the higher dignity of Archdeacon there. Once again it is pleasant to find that Petrarch's first thought on receiving an accession of wealth was to offer help to a friend. It must have been about the time of his nomination to the canonry that he wrote to an unknown correspondent: "I heard something the other day from one who knew about the state of your money chest, and I have determined to be so bold as to come to its assistance. Here then is an offering—I will not say from the surplusage of my fortune, for that would sound unpleasantly like bragging, nor does the mere phrase 'Fortune's bounty' quite express my meaning, so I will say that I have sent you a trifle from the bounties which Fortune has deigned to heap on me, who busy not myself with such things, beyond all expectation or wish of mine; and however small the gift, I doubt not but that you will deign to accept it, and in this little thing, as in a tiny mirror, you will see the sender's great affection, and will weigh the magnitude of his goodwill against the littleness of his gift."

Petrarch, then, maintained his place in the Pope's favour and his connection with friends at Avignon; but residence in the city was as distasteful to him as ever, and Vaucluse was his home for the next two years. There is an undated letter to Guido Settimo, almost certainly written at this time, in which he speaks of himself as still suffering from the smart of his old wound, and praying, as yet unsuccessfully, for deliverance. The allusion is unmistakable; time had done something to mitigate the violence of his passion, but his love for Laura was still the dominant sentiment of his heart. Vaucluse gave him peace; here he found full opportunity for quiet study of books and of nature, with just so much companionship of intimate friends as might serve to keep his faculties alert and his affections keen. Never surely has a storm-tossed soul taken refuge in a more perfect haven. Visit the spot to-day, and you find a busy little township clustered round a few mills whose wheels are driven by the Sorgue. But it is easy to ignore the modern buildings, to dot the lower slopes in fancy with patches of woodland, and to picture the place

Brun

VIEW OF VAUCLUSE AND THE CASTLE OF THE BISHOP OF CAVAILLON

as Petrarch knew it. There has been no appreciable change in the apparently perfect circle of steep hills crested with limestone crags, in the great silent pool where the river rises under the shadow of a cliff 350 feet high; or in the long rock-strewn falls through which it rushes noisily to the valley-level. The very fig tree growing between the rocks at the head of the cataract may be the descendant of one from which Petrarch could offer Cardinal Colonna a dish of figs drawn, like his jug of drinking water, from mid-stream. The little church may have stood on its present site; the Bishop of Cavaillon's castle, now a picturesque ruin, was then an almost impregnable fortress crowning a steep hill 600 feet high; only there was no thriving French village, but at most a few peasants' cottages dotted about the valley, with Petrarch's own house standing probably on the site now occupied by one of the mills, with his meadow bordering the stream, and his two gardens, the upper one on the slope by the cataract, the lower one originally perhaps a peninsula jutting into the river-bed, and by him converted into an island by the cutting of a little channel now utilised as a mill-race.

Here in the years 1346 and 1347 Petrarch "waged war with the nymphs of the Sorgue, seeking to annex enough of their domain to build a habitation for the Muses." Gardening gave him recreation; for work we know with certainty that this is the date of his treatise in two books *On the Solitary Life*, which he dedicated to the Bishop of Cavaillon. Philip watched over the composition of the treatise, though it was not till many years later that Petrarch sent him a copy of the finished work. And in 1347 a visit to his brother Gherardo at his monastery furnished him with the subject of his essay *On the Repose of Men vowed to Religion.*

It was to the troubles of Naples that Petrarch owed the pleasure of the Bishop's society. Andrew of Hungary had been murdered in September, 1345; Queen Joanna speedily married the murderer's brother, her cousin, Prince Lewis of Tarentum; King Lewis of Hungary led an expedition into Italy to avenge his brother's death; and Philip, sick of his position as nominal head of an ineffective Regency, left Naples in disgust, and came back to his diocese and to his castle above Vaucluse. Petrarch's grief at the ruin of Naples, poured out in a letter of lamentation to Barbato, was deep and sincere; but in intercourse with Philip he found perhaps an adequate compensation for his distress.

In January, 1347, he had the exquisite pleasure of taking Socrates to pay a visit to the Bishop at Cavaillon; the charming little letter in which he accepted the latter's invitation deserves to be translated in full. It runs thus :—

" I will come to you at the time when I know you will be glad to see me, and I will bring with me our Socrates, who is your most devoted admirer. We will come the day after to-morrow; and we will not shrink from the sight of a city, though we shall be dressed in rough country clothes. For we fled hither two days since, hurriedly and as at a bound, from the restless tumult of the town, like ship-

wrecked sailors making for shore, planning for ourselves a time of unharried quiet, and in the dress
which seemed most appropriate for the country in
winter. You bid us betake ourselves just as we are
to your city; we will obey all the more willingly as
we are drawn by eager longing for your company. Nor will we care greatly how our outer man
looks in your eyes, to whom we both wish and
believe that our souls stand visible and undraped.
One thing, most loving father, you will not deny
to the wishes of your friends: if you wish to have
us often as your guests, you will let us share no
special banquet of dainties, but your usual meal.
Farewell."

CHAPTER VII

ROME AND RIENZI

1347

PETRARCH'S life was full of startling contrasts and sharp surprises; but in all his career's vicissitudes no external event ever stirred his emotions quite so violently as the Roman crisis of 1347. The gardener of Vaucluse, the philosophical essayist on saints and hermits, the poet of a tranquillised but constant devotion, became in an instant the fervid politician, the people's champion, the prophet of a revolution. The society in which he lived was hostile to his ideals; he cared not whom he offended by his advocacy of them; his patron and lifelong friend was of the opposite faction; even gratitude and friendship must give place to the patriot's zeal; blows were being struck for Rome, and with all his soul Petrarch believed that the cause of Rome was the cause of God.

Fully to comprehend the high hopes excited in him by Rienzi, the hot enthusiasm with which he championed the Tribune in the face of a sceptical and unfriendly world, and the bitterness of his disappointment when the cynics were justified of their unbelief, and the gallant enterprise failed like any base intrigue of faction, we must realise

how all his ideals of government and all his
hopes of progress were based and centred in the
eagerly desired restoration of Roman supremacy.
From his father he inherited the political creed of
the White Guelfs expounded by Dante in the *De
Monarchiâ*. Pope and Emperor were alike the
consecrated vice-gerents of God on earth ; each in
his allotted sphere must rule the spiritual and
temporal world in conformity with the Divine Will ;
both were " Holy Roman," and both, as Petrarch
insisted more fervently than any of his predecessors,
must regard Rome as their capital city, and must
have a special care of Italy, " the Garden of the
Empire." Their authority over distant provinces
might be delegated to vicars and vassals ; but Italy
was their home, the motherland of the imperial
race, in whose chief city resided, dormant perhaps
but indefeasible, the right to rule the world ; and
both Pope and Emperor were bound to make the
government of Italy their chief and personal care.
In all this there was nothing peculiar to Petrarch ;
the Emperors claimed to be the legitimate successors of the Cæsars ; the Popes appealed to the
Donation of Constantine as their title to exclusive
sovereignty in Rome ; the claims of both were theoretically reconciled by the White Guelf creed. Nor
was Petrarch's personal enthusiasm for Rome a new
sentiment in the world ; the tradition of her greatness and the aspiration for its revival had never
quite died away, and a generation before Petrarch
wrote his first letter to Benedict XII, Giovanni
Villani had been inspired by the sight of the

Eternal City and the memory of her past glories
to set to work on his incomparable Florentine
Chronicle.   What differentiates Petrarch's enthusiasm for Rome from the sentiments of any predecessor is his conception of the continuity of her
history.   He regards its periods not as separate
episodes connected only by an accidental tie of
locality, but as successive stages in an ordered
development, phases bright or dark in one deathless
career, destined to lead, through whatever difficulties and trials, to the glorious consummation of
invincible empire.   Looking thus upon her history
as a whole, political forms and ordinances became
to him mere secondary matters; the Pope and the
Emperor themselves were but instruments designed
to secure the supremacy of the Roman people, the
people for whom Romulus built his sacred wall,
whose supremacy Scipio assured by his victory over
Carthage, for whose safety Cicero unmasked the
conspiracy of Catiline.   If only either Pope or
Emperor would devote himself to the service of the
Roman people, Petrarch would be a good Papalist,
a loyal Imperialist.   Alas! both were sadly neglect-
ful of their high mission; both were thinking only
of their own petty interests; neither of them would
live in Rome or work for her.   Suddenly, like
thunder from a clear sky, came the astounding news
that Rome had found her champion; that a man of
obscure origin but of lofty aims had made his
appeal to the noblest of her traditions; that he had
set himself to revive the great age of her history,
the age when the people was really sovereign, and

G. Guadagnini inc.

RIENZI

FROM AN ITALIAN PRINT

had taken for himself the title of Tribune as an earnest that he would be as the Gracchi, that he would stand for the people and break the yoke of their oppressors from off their necks. Petrarch's course lay before him clear and unmistakable: Rienzi was trying to realise his own ideals; at any sacrifice of private interests, even of private friend-ships, he must go with the champion of the Roman people.

Niccola di Lorenzo Gabrini, known to his own generation as Cola di Rienzo, and to ours by the further modification "Rienzi," was the son of a Roman innkeeper, who, finding the boy possessed of unusual talent, sent him to a school of grammar and rhetoric. Fired with enthusiasm for the classics, Rienzi completed his own education by diligent study of the ancient monuments and inscriptions, which lay neglected in the modern city. For a livelihood he adopted the profession of notary, but his leisure was spent in studying the history of old Rome, and in dreaming how her glories might be revived. He was by temperament a dreamer; a domestic tragedy made him a man of action. His brother was killed in a tumult; the political idealist was thenceforth the avenger of blood. He would exalt Rome by breaking the power of the barons who misgoverned her. He had self-restraint enough to await his opportunity. Meanwhile his talents, and especially his splendid gift of oratory, made him a conspicuous figure in Rome. Soon after Clement VI's accession—there is some doubt as to the exact date, but it was either in the summer of 1342 or early in 1343—he went to Avignon as chief spokesman of an embassy sent by the magistracy and people of Rome to the Pope. Here he must have met Petrarch, here in all probability their friendship began. There is even a tradition, unsupported by evidence, that the poet was associated with Rienzi as spokesman of the embassy; however this may be, it is safe to assume that Rome's youngest burgess, fresh from his coronation on the Capitol, must have used his influence at court in favour of his fellow-citizens. There is indeed a passage at the end of Petrarch's magnificent ode *Spirto Gentil*, from which some biographers have inferred either that the two men had never met previously to the composition of the ode, or that it must have been addressed not to Rienzi, but to some other eminent citizen of Rome. But the passage in question easily admits of an interpretation consistent with the narrative here given; the rest of the ode tallies perfectly with Rienzi and the events of 1347, and with no other person or events of the period; and the tone of Petrarch's earlier letters to the Tribune implies a friendship founded on personal acquaintance, as well as on community of ideas. It is equally safe to assume that intercourse with Petrarch acted as a keen stimulus to Rienzi. He came to Avignon as a man honoured in his own city, but unknown beyond it, nursing in his mind great hopes, which so far he had found no opportunity of communicating to others. Here he discovered that those hopes were shared by one who could make Europe ring with the praise of them, a man not only famous as the first poet and scholar of his age, but sought out by princes to be their friend and counsellor, and standing high in the favour of Pope Clement himself.

The embassy had little if any tangible result; but Rienzi's eloquent exposition of the troubles and needs of Rome is said to have made a favourable impression on the Pope, and this may help to explain the benevolent attitude of his Vicar four years later. Of the urgent need for reform there could be no doubt. Since the Pope's departure Rome had had no settled government; a series of faction-fights had constituted her history, the will of the temporary victors her law. Municipal affairs were supposed to be administered by the popularly elected heads of the thirteen city wards; but these Caporioni, as they were called, had no force at their back, and their office was an empty survival from a former Constitution. The machinery of government was in the hands of the Senator, a chief magistrate nominated annually by the Pope from the ranks of the nobles. If the Senator was a strong man in alliance with the barons of the predominant faction, he was feared and obeyed; but officially he was hardly more powerful than the Caporioni. He could never be impartial, for he was never independent. The House of Colonna, the House of the Orsini, these were by turns the effective rulers of Rome, and their government was sheer brigandage.

Rienzi, on his return home, set himself to evolve civil order out of this anarchy. He presently began

a series of harangues to the people, which involved
him in frequent quarrels with the nobles. Gradually he advanced in popular favour; many of the
lesser barons, jealous of the great Houses which
overshadowed them, witnessed without displeasure,
or were even inclined to further the rise of a new
power in the State; and it was long before the pride
of the Colonna allowed them to see in their unex-
pected antagonist anything but an object of ridicule
and insult. But Rienzi's leaven worked, and
choosing his opportunities with rare skill, he first
promulgated a set of laws for the reform of the
Government, and then persuaded the people to
assign to him the task of enforcing them. Alarmed
at last, but even now unable to measure the strength
of his despised opponent, Stefano Colonna hurried
back to Rome. The new ruler ordered him to quit
the city, and he had not provided himself with force
enough even to contest the mandate; he had to
obey, and the more prominent of the nobles either
accompanied, or soon afterwards followed him
into banishment. An abortive conspiracy only
served to increase Rienzi's power; his enemies were
forced to swear allegiance to the new institutions.
The reformer had conquered; for the first time
since the battle of Philippi, liberty was a word of
meaning in Rome. In the ecstasy of material
triumph, Rienzi was still mindful of the greatness of
his ideal; invested with absolute power, he took
for himself the title identified in the history of old
Rome with the championship of popular freedom,
and with consummate tact associated the Vicar

Apostolic with himself in the revived dignity. The two were acclaimed joint Tribunes and Liberators of the Roman people.

The astonishing tidings reached Avignon in the early summer of 1347; they were soon confirmed by a formal letter from Rienzi himself. Clement and some few members of the Sacred College may possibly have been statesmen enough to realise that the Papacy must ultimately succeed to any power wrested from the barons. The attitude assumed by the Vicar Apostolic in Rome, and the fact that Petrarch seems never for an instant to have lost favour with the Pope, are indications that the Tribune's success may have been not altogether unwelcome in the highest quarters. But among the Roman prelates, and especially in Cardinal Colonna's household, the news was received with consternation. Rienzi and all his works were denounced with unmeasured violence; and only one solitary voice was raised in defence of the reformer. That voice was Petrarch's. Immediately on hearing of Rienzi's accession to power, he wrote to him and to the Roman people a letter of praise, encouragement, and exhortation, which he knew would be circulated through the length and breadth of Italy; and he followed this up with other similar letters, with a Latin eclogue, and with the stately Italian ode already mentioned. To his fervid imagination, it seemed that "the ancient strife was being fought again," that the nobles were playing the part of the worst of the old patricians, and that the destruction of a power, the more intolerable because its possessors were aliens in blood, was the necessary preliminary to a reign of justice.

Estrangement from Cardinal Colonna was the inevitable result of Petrarch's championship of Rienzi; it was not in human nature that a patron should tolerate a client who openly advocated the ruin of his family, and it must be confessed that Petrarch was not happy in his manner of dealing with the breach. The eclogue *Divortium*, written on the subject of his parting with the Cardinal, though not ungraceful, strikes the reader as artificial even beyond the wont of this kind of allegory. Moreover, it tells less than half the truth. Dislike of Avignon, longing for Italy, a desire for a life of independence, are all indicated, and these were genuine motives as far as they went. But no hint is given of Petrarch's adhesion to Rienzi, which was the really determining cause of the separation. Worse still is the letter of condolence written from Parma some months after the battle of November 20th, in which the Colonna family was almost annihilated. It opens, indeed, with a sincere and touching acknowledgment of the writer's debt to the Cardinal, but all the rest is sorry reading. The laboured excuses for the delay in writing it, and the cold, stilted terms of its yet more laboured consolations, contrasting so strikingly with the passionate outburst of Petrarch's emotion when his heart was really wounded, suggest an inevitable task, undertaken with reluctance and somewhat ungraciously performed. Undoubtedly the very ardour of Petrarch's patriotism made him appear more callous than he really was; a man of less impassioned sincerity would have found it easier to veil his governing sentiment. And two things are very noticeable in the history of Petrarch's treatment of the Colonna disaster: first, that to the end of his life he never for an instant doubted the political necessity of breaking their power; and secondly, that in spite of this conviction, he never ceased to speak of them, as distinguished from the other Roman nobles, in terms of deep personal regard. His relations with his old friend and patron had become hopeless, and for this very reason he did himself less than justice in the attempt to continue them.

Avignon was now more than ever a place of torment to him, and even Vaucluse lay too near the hateful city to be tolerable as a residence. He resolved that he would go to Italy and take his stand by the Tribune's side. Rienzi seemed more firmly seated in power than ever; the fame of his great enterprise had spread far and wide; he had formally announced his assumption of power to the sovereign princes of Europe, and they in return had sent ambassadors of the highest rank to greet and congratulate him. On the very day when Petrarch set out from Avignon the great slaughter of the Colonna, which left old Stefano the survivor of all his sons except the Cardinal, and of nearly all his grandsons, might have seemed to have rid the Tribune of his most dangerous antagonists. But to those who could see beneath the surface, the canker of decay was already visible. On

November 22nd Petrarch, travelling southward, met a courier with letters from Lælius, which must of course have been sent from Rome before the 20th ; these gave news of Rienzi's doings which caused him the utmost alarm. He decided to suspend his journey and await events at Genoa. Letters written on the journey to Lælius and to Socrates expressed his dismay and apprehension, and on the 29th he wrote in the strongest terms of anxiety, warning, and entreaty to Rienzi himself. " I hear," he said, " that you no longer cherish the whole people, as you used to do, but only the basest faction of them." He implored Rienzi not to be the destroyer of his own work, but to stand firm on the lofty ground which he had taken, and to re-member that great efforts are needed to sustain a great reputation. Let him be mindful of his duty to be the servant of the State, not her tyrant.

Petrarch's grief at the impending ruin of his country was made, if possible, more poignant by his sense of the falseness of his own position. He had trumpeted Rienzi as the saviour of his country, the hero who had done at a stroke the duty which a long line of emperors had consistently neglected. For his sake he had broken old friendships, and exposed himself to the charge of callous ingratitude, the most odious accusation that could be brought against a man of his temperament. " A most fright-ful storm of obloquy," he foresaw, must break upon him, if Rienzi faltered in the great work, and with denunciation of the turncoat would be mingled bitter ridicule of the dupe. Petrarch was a self-conscious man, whose vanity would embitter such a trouble, though it would not turn him from his duty. The agony of his anxiety for his country and the alarm with which he viewed his own prospects are voiced in the despairing cry of his letter to Lælius: "I recognise my country's doom; wherever I turn, I find cause and matter for grief. With Rome torn and wounded, what must be the condition of Italy? With Italy maimed, what must my life be?"

One ray of hope crossed his mind: Lælius was an old and intimate friend of the Colonna; might not partisanship have led him into exaggeration of the Tribune's failings? Alas! his tidings were only too true. Rienzi's head was turned by the suddenness and completeness of his success. His cool judgment gave place to capricious obstinacy; he intrigued with the various parties among his opponents so clumsily that he united them all against him. He quarrelled with the Pope's Vicar, and cited Pope and Emperor to his tribunal; at the same time his pretensions disgusted the mob as much as his high position excited their envy. Centuries of misrule had left the Roman people ill-fitted for self-government; patience could hardly be expected of them. After all, was not Rienzi their creature? By what title, then, could he claim to be their despot? It is easy to tax the Roman people with fickleness; in fairness it should be remembered that they did not desert Rienzi till he himself had given unmistakable signs that his lofty patriotism had degenerated into a personal and rather tawdry ambition.   He rose to power as a great idealist, he fell like any faction-mongering Italian despot, and his fall was even more sudden than his rise.   Hardly had he celebrated an insolent triumph over the slaughtered Colonna, when Nemesis came upon him.   The mob rose against him in tumult, and to save his life he had to lurk for some days in a hiding-place in the city, and then flee in disguise to Naples.   The pitiful meanness of the catastrophe embittered his friends' grief at the failure of their hopes.   " At least," said Petrarch, " he could have died gloriously in the Capitol which he had freed."

CHAPTER VIII

THE GREAT PLAGUE AND THE DEATH OF LAURA

1348-1349

THE condition of Italy in 1348 seemed desperate indeed. For five years the Great Company, a body of soldier-adventurers disbanded by the Pisans at the close of a war with Florence, had subjected her to a war of brigandage; Naples lay at the mercy of the Hungarian invader; Lombardy and the Emilia groaned under the misrule of unscrupulous tyrants; and the only hopeful attempt ever made to restore the liberties and reassert the supremacy of Rome had just ended in ignominious failure. Finally, as if man had not done enough to devastate the "Garden of the Empire," she was now to suffer first a destructive earthquake, and then the ravages of that appalling scourge of God, the Great Pestilence. Boccaccio in his introduction to the *Decameron* has left a description of this awful visitation, which ranks among the masterpieces of literature. Perhaps the most striking impression derived from reading it is the feeling that communities and individuals alike lost their sense of responsibility; that the ordinary rules of life were abrogated, and the moral code superseded by the law that each man made for himself. Petrarch, too, speaks in a letter to Socrates of the unprecedented havoc wrought by the plague : " of empty houses, deserted cities, the fields untilled, their space seeming narrowed by the strewn corpses, everywhere the vastness of a terrible silence." He suffered his full share of the general misery : blow after blow fell upon him, crushing his spirit and crippling his power of work ; for a year and a half, he declared, in the letter just quoted, he could neither do nor say anything of worth. That is not literally exact: even at this season of abject sorrow he produced a few pieces of interesting work, including the poetical letter to Virgil written at Mantua ; but as compared with any other epoch of his life, the years 1348 and 1349 may be accounted a barren period. He was miserable and restless. Parma was his home, but he could not stay long at a time even in his " Cisalpine Helicon." We find him often at Verona, then wandering from one Lombard city to another, and beginning the connection with Padua, which was destined to become so intimate in the near future. At the end of January, 1348, he was at Verona ; on March 13th he returned to Parma, and brought with him the boy Giovanni, whose education he now entrusted to the grammarian Ghilberto Baiani. Giovanni probably lived at home, attending Ghilberto's school as a day-boy, and father and son were both the unhappier for an association which should have brought solace to the one and a new interest in life to both.

The first bereavement of which Petrarch received

LAURA

FROM A PRINT IN THE PADUAN 1819 EDITION OF THE CANZONIERE

certain tidings in this year of mourning was the death of his cousin and friend, Francesco degli Albizzi, a sorrow which he felt the more acutely as Francesco was struck down while on his way to pay him an eagerly expected visit. But already, if we may treat the uncorroborated evidence of passages in his Italian poems as sufficient authority for a fact, he had felt the presage of a far heavier loss, which must change the face of the world for him henceforward. On April 6th, the twenty-first anniversary of his first meeting with Laura, while resident at Verona, he felt a sudden presentiment of her death, and on May 19th a letter from Socrates reached him at Parma telling him that she had indeed died at the very moment of the mysterious warning. The fly-leaf of his Virgil contains this entry :—

"Laura, a shining example of virtue in herself, and for many years made known to fame by my poems, first came visibly before my eyes in the season of my early youth, in the year of our Lord 1327, on the 6th day of the month of April, in the Church of St. Clara of Avignon, in the morning. And in the same city, on the same 6th day of the same month of April, at the same hour of Prime, but in the year 1348, the bright light of her life was taken away from the light of this earth, when I chanced to be dwelling at Verona in unhappy ignorance of my doom. The sorrowful report came to me, however, in a letter from my Lewis, which reached me at Parma on the morning of the 19th day of May in the same year. Her most chaste and most beautiful body was laid to rest in the habitation of the Minor Friars at evening on the very day of her death. Her soul, I am persuaded, has returned, in the words that Seneca uses of Africanus, to the heaven which was its home.   I have thought good to write this note, with a kind of bitter sweetness, as a painful reminder of my sorrow, and have chosen this place for it, as one which comes constantly under my eyes, reckoning as I do that there ought to be nothing to give me further pleasure in this life, and that by frequent looking on these words and by computing the swiftness of life's flight I may be admonished that now, with the breaking of my strongest chain, it is time to flee out of Babylon. And this by the prevention of God's grace will be easy for me, when I consider with insight and resolution my past life's idle cares, the emptiness of its hopes, and its extraordinary issues."

The death of Laura removed an element of storm and stress from Petrarch's life ; at the cost of a great sorrow it gave him final deliverance from passion.   Years afterwards, when he sat down to write in all candour the autobiographical fragment which he called his *Letter to Posterity*, he could even speak of his bereavement as "timely for him, in spite of its bitterness."   That was the calm judgment of retrospect ; it is the note in the Virgil which expresses his feeling at the time, and helps us to realise the deep sincerity underlying the elaborate art of his poems *On the Death of Madonna Laura.*   In poetical quality the second part of the *Canzoniere* does not differ from the first ; there is the same faultless workmanship, the same delicate play of fancy, the same felicitous rendering of the subtlest shades of emotion. To take only a single illustration, the sonnet to the bird that sang in winter may rank with the sonnet to the waters of the Sorgue as a lyric born of the poet's sympathy with nature. But in sentiment the poems of the second part differ widely from their predecessors; their prevailing tone is exactly that "bitter sweetness" of which the note in the Virgil speaks, and they are permeated by a spirit of piety, which reminds us of Petrarch's saying in the *Secretum* that "through love of Laura he attained to love of God."

The composition of these poems extended over more than a decade, and we cannot assign dates to them with even an approach to exactitude. Criticism which relies entirely on appreciation of spirit and tone is always risky, for it gives undue scope to the temperament of the critic; and it is doubly dangerous in dealing with Petrarch, who was for ever correcting and polishing his works, and whose faculty of reminiscence was so acute that it could carry him back almost at will into the temper of a period that had long passed away. Neither can we trust the position of any given poem in the collection as a proof of its place in the order of composition; there can be little doubt that in the final arrangement of the *Canzoniere* Petrarch was guided chiefly by his sense of artistic fitness. Still it is reasonable to suppose that many of the lyrics were the immediate fruit of his sorrow, and that, speaking generally, the earlier in place were also the earlier in time ; it is difficult, for instance, to believe that at least the inspiration of the ode *Che debb' io far* was not due to the poignancy of recent grief.

All through the summer the plague infested Avignon, and on July 3rd Cardinal Colonna fell a victim to it. Stefano the Elder had now outlived all his seven sons. However great was the strain put upon their relations by recent events, Petrarch had till a year ago been like a son of the House, and even in the pain of parting he had not for a moment forgotten or concealed his debt of affectionate gratitude to his patron. He could not avoid writing to old Stefano, and he accomplished the task of condolence much better now than in the previous autumn. It was not an easy letter to write ; he could not pour out his soul, and he would not be guilty of an insincerity. He solved the difficulty in a way characteristic of him and of his age, by composing with extreme care an elaborate epistle graced with rich ornaments of classical learning. Nothing could be more foreign to the sentiments of our own day ; but it was what a past generation would have called "a beautiful letter," and there can be no doubt that its recipient would take as a compliment the pains bestowed on its composition. Throughout its length Petrarch keeps his emotion under restraint ; but its formality is rather grave than cold, and in one passage, which speaks of Giovanni as having attained to the cardinalate and of Giacomo as having been surely destined to rise even higher had life been granted to him, the sincerity of the emotion is almost intensified by the restraint put upon its expression.

If grief could have been assuaged by public honours, Petrarch would have found no lack of consolation. The "storm of obloquy" which he anticipated from his association with Rienzi never burst. On the contrary, hardly a month passed without his receiving some signal mark of esteem from persons high in place and power. Whatever the rulers of Italy might think of Rienzi's abortive political Renaissance, they vied with each other in doing honour to Petrarch as the leader of its intellectual counterpart. Humanism was now in the air, and the sure instinct which guides men swayed by a general impulse pointed to Petrarch as its prophet. Heedless of political differences, the rulers of Ferrara, of Carpi, of Mantua, and of Padua were at one in welcoming him to their cities, and that the Pope regarded him with undiminished favour was testified by his presentation in 1348 or 1349 to the archdeaconry of Parma, of which he took formal possession in 1350.

Of these new connections by far the most important was his friendship with Jacopo II da Carrara, the ruler of Padua. History affords no more typical example of an Italian despot than this remarkable man, who obtained his lordship by murder and forgery, and used it to promote the welfare of his city and the interests of art and learning. Better, perhaps, than any of his contemporaries he appreciated the value of Petrarch's work, and this just estimate made him, if possible, more eager

than the others to do honour to the poet and to
enjoy the luxury of his companionship.   It was in
1345 that he seized the government of Padua;
over and over again in the next few years he sent
letters and messages entreating Petrarch to come
and live with him there; at last, in March, 1349,
Petrarch paid him a visit and was received, "not
like a man, but with such a welcome as awaits the
souls who enter Paradise."   To ensure his new
friend's future residence in Padua, Jacopo procured
him a canonry there, to which he was formally
inducted on the Saturday after Easter.   Loaded
thus with honours and benefits, Petrarch may be
forgiven if he ignored Jacopo's crimes, which he
had not personally witnessed, and celebrated in
terms of unstinted eulogy his friend's virtues and
charm, of which he had daily experience in the
intimacy of private life.   Jacopo was evidently a
man as fascinating to his friends as he was dangerous to his enemies.   When he set himself to win
Petrarch's love and gratitude, he succeeded so completely that the latter could write to Luca Cristiano,
to whom he would certainly not be guilty of an
insincerity, " I have another residence equally tran-
quil, equally fit to be our joint home, at Padua, in
the valley of the Po, where no small portion of our
happiness would consist in the privilege of living
with my benefactor whose qualities I have so
extolled to you."

This letter was written to Luca on May 18th,
very soon after Petrarch's return to Parma, where
he found that, as he prettily says, "the one draw-

back to his stay in Padua had been that he had thereby missed a visit from Luca and Mainardo." Bitterly indeed did he regret his absence when some weeks later he learnt that it had lost him his last opportunity of seeing that loyal soldier and true friend alive. Finding him away from home, the two had supped in his house and slept together in his bed. The next morning they left a letter telling him that they had just come from Avignon after saying good-bye to Socrates, and were on their way, Mainardo to Florence and Luca to Rome, but that a little later on they hoped to come back and stay with him in Parma. Finding this letter on his return more than a month afterwards, Petrarch began to wonder why he heard no further tidings of them, and presently dispatched a confidential servant to Florence with a letter to Mainardo, and a request that he would send the servant on to Luca. Eight days later the messenger reappeared with the lamentable news that, as the friends were crossing the Apennines, they had been ambushed by armed banditti; that Mainardo, who was riding ahead, had been instantly slain, and Luca, who dashed to his assistance, had at length escaped, no one knew whither, so severely wounded that it was feared he must have died. Perils of this kind were common enough in the Italy of the fourteenth century; Petrarch himself, as we have seen, had had more than one narrow escape from a similar fate. But his wrathful indignation knew no bounds when he heard that these banditti were under the protection of certain great men of the neighbourhood "unworthy of the name of nobles," who prevented the peasants from coming to Luca's help and avenging Mainardo's death, and gave the robbers shelter in their fortresses. Petrarch was for some time in doubt about Luca's fate. He made fruitless inquiries at Florence, at Piacenza, and in Rome ; at length a member of his household happened to meet a Florentine of position passing through Parma, and, knowing his master's anxiety, made bold to entreat the stranger to see Petrarch and tell him all he knew. From this stranger Petrarch heard to his great comfort that Luca was still alive, but the melancholy story of Mainardo's death was confirmed in every particular.

Many other friends died in these terrible years of plague, among them one whose loss caused Petrarch the keenest grief, though their friendship was of recent origin. Paganino Bizozero was a native of the Milanese territory whom Luchino Visconti had appointed Governor of Parma. Here Petrarch found him at the end of 1347, and here apparently he died on May 23rd, 1349, though his governorship had come to an end four months before. Their intimacy, therefore, lasted less than a year and a half, but Petrarch's account of him, given in the same letter to Socrates which tells of Mainardo's death, shows how close a bond of affection united them during that short period. " There was left to me," he says, "a friend of illustrious dignity, a high-minded and very prudent man, Paganino of Milan, who by many instances of his worth had become most congenial to me, and

seemed altogether worthy not of my love only, but
of yours too. So he had begun to be as a second
Socrates to me; there was almost the same confidence, almost the same intimacy, as well as that
sweetest property of friendship, the sharing of either
kind of fortune and the opening of the soul's hiding-
places for the loyal communication of its secret
things. Oh, how he loved you; how eagerly he
desired to see you whom indeed he did see with his
spiritual eyes; how anxious he was for your life in
this general shipwreck! so that even I marvelled
that a man not personally known could be so well
beloved. If ever he saw me sadder than my wont,
he would ask in friendly trepidation, What is the
matter? What news of our friend? And when
he had been told that you were well, he would put
away his fear and overflow with exceeding joyful-
ness. Now he, as I must tell you with many tears
. . . was suddenly seized one evening with this
sickness of the plague which is now destroying the
world. He had taken supper with his friends, and
had spent the rest of that evening entirely in talking
about us and discoursing of our friendship and our
affairs. That night he spent in enduring extreme
agony with perfect fearlessness; in the morning
death quickly carried him off; and, the plague
abating no jot of its usual cruelty, before three days
were past his sons and every member of his household had followed him to the grave."

CHAPTER IX

FLORENCE AND BOCCACCIO

1350

PETRARCH'S life may be divided into three clearly defined periods, of which the boundary marks are dates in the history of his friendships. The first period ends with the great plague, and the deaths of Laura and Mainardo; the second opens with his visit to Boccaccio, and closes with the second plague and the deaths of Socrates, Lælius, Nelli, and Barbato; the third is the last period of the poet's life, when of his earlier friends only Guido Settimo and Philip de Cabassoles remained alive, but his old age was saved from desolation by the ever-strengthening tie of affection which bound him to Boccaccio, by the veneration of his pupils, and by the devoted love of his daughter.

The last years of the first period, while afflicting him with heavy sorrows, had brought him a great accession of material wealth : he now held a priory, three canonries, and an archdeaconry, to the latter of which was attached a large official house, of which he made occasional use, while retaining for ordinary purposes the more modest residence, which he had bought and beautified. His personal expenses, apart from the cost of travel, cannot have

been large, for wherever he went he found welcome
and entertainment. His income, then, was more
than sufficient to supply his personal needs, and
to allow him to make provision for his son and
daughter. Characteristically, he spent the surplus
in furthering his life's work. From this time forward, he was hardly ever without a copyist or two
in the house—sometimes he had as many as four
at once—engaged in making transcripts from the
precious manuscripts, which he had either hunted
out himself, or borrowed from friends, with a
view to their reproduction. He still did much of
this work himself, and more than once we find him
complaining, not that good copyists were dear, but
that they were scarce. We shall never know with
certainty how much we owe to this employment of
his money, but we may safely assume that if he had
remained poor, many a library would be without
some of its richest treasures. Even as things were,
his industry and Boccaccio's were taxed to the
utmost limit of human capacity.

He divided the earlier months of 1350 between
Padua, Parma, and Verona; on Valentine's Day he
was present at the solemn translation of the body
of St. Anthony of Padua from its first place of
burial to the church newly erected in the saint's
honour. A document discovered by Fracassetti
fixes June 20th as the day on which he took formal
possession of his archdeaconry; immediately afterwards he must have left Parma for a flying visit to
Mantua, for it was on his way back from that city
that some members of the Gonzaga family enter-

tained him on June 28th to a sumptuous supper in their castle of Luzzera, which Petrarch describes in a humorous letter to Lælius as "a home of flies and fleas enlivened by the croaking of an army of frogs."

Meanwhile the year of Jubilee was being celebrated in Rome, with the more solemnity as the terrors of the plague had inclined the minds of many to religion, and disposed them to obtain the indulgences promised to those who went on pilgrimage to Rome. Petrarch tried unsuccessfully to persuade Gulielmo da Pastrengo to accompany him thither. Failing in this, he set out alone, about the beginning of October. He travelled by way of Florence, a journey ever memorable as the occasion of his first meeting with Boccaccio.

History contains no more satisfactory episode than the friendship of these two men of letters. From their society their companions must have derived the same kind of pleasure that the eye finds in looking at a harmonious arrangement of complementary colours. Their natures were made to supplement each other; the life of neither could be reckoned complete till he had found his fellow. Petrarch had an anxious spirit; under every rose he looked for the thorn, and if he failed to find it, he vexed his soul with questioning whether it ought not to have pricked him. Boccaccio plucked the flower and wore it with a gay assurance that took no count of thorn-pricks. Petrarch's worst troubles were the offspring of his own soul; Boccaccio's were imposed on him by the rub of circumstance.

BOCCACCIO

FROM A PORTRAIT IN THE BRITISH MUSEUM

Petrarch was introspective, self-conscious, jealous to a fault of his reputation, but laudably anxious to deserve it. Boccaccio was too well amused by the follies of others to be deeply concerned about his own, and too instinctively an artist to care over-much what other people thought of his art. Petrarch had the deeper nature, the higher ideals, the more sensitive conscience; in Boccaccio we are captivated by a rich generosity of sympathetic humour. In intellect no less than in character each of them was his friend's complement. They were alike in their enthusiasm for learning and in their indefatigable industry, but they were alike in hardly anything else. Petrarch was incomparably the riper scholar, the sounder critic; he had a more reasoned judgment, a more cultivated taste; Boccaccio had the more fertile imagination, the brighter wit. Petrarch was lucid in argument, but apt to be prolix in narrative; Boccaccio showed little talent for disquisition, but his was the story-teller's inimitable gift.

There is therefore a quality in Petrarch's intercourse with Boccaccio which distinguishes it from all his other friendships. Close and intimate as it was, there were others which for some years to come surpassed it in intensity of feeling; Boccaccio was very dear, but Socrates, Lælius, and Francesco Nelli, of whom we shall have to speak immediately, were dearer still. All these, however, were Petrarch's followers in the battle for culture; Boccaccio stood by his side, a comrade-in-arms. True, that with unfailing reverence he styled himself his pupil, and that the title was accurate as well as modest. Petrarch possessed, in a degree rare even among great leaders, the divine gift of kindling enthusiasm, and Boccaccio's glowing tributes may express without exaggeration the magnitude of his debt; none the less, he stands out above the rest, his master's sole intellectual peer.

In Boccaccio's house Petrarch found another Florentine, with whom he fell at once into a friendship that reminds us of Lombez and the earlier days at Avignon. Francesco di Nello Rinucci, commonly called Francesco Nelli, came of an influential family; his father had held the office of Gonfalonier of Justice, the highest executive dignity in the republic. He was himself in Orders, and Prior of the Church of the Holy Apostles, but had some talent for affairs, for which he found scope later in the post of Secretary to the Grand Seneschal of Naples; at home Petrarch seems to have thought that his abilities were insufficiently appreciated, in spite of the fact that he was a most loyal patriot. He was an intimate friend of Boccaccio, and an enthusiast for learning. He took his place at once in the inmost circle of Petrarch's friends, and the latter, with his familiar habit of bestowing gracious nicknames, called him his Simonides.

Here, too, Petrarch met the eminent scholar and lawyer Jacopo or Lapo da Castiglionchio, of whose accomplishments Coluccio Salutati, himself a distinguished follower of Petrarch in humanistic studies, could write after his death : " Whom has our State ever produced more diligent in pursuit of our

studies and of those which pertain to eloquence?
Which of the poets was unknown to him, nay,
rather, which of them was not a hackneyed writer
to him? Who was better versed in the works of
Cicero? Who more abundant in gleanings from
history? Who more deeply imbued with the pre-
cepts of moral philosophy? Good heavens! How
he abounded in sweetness, and in weightiness of
discourse; how ready he was in dictation, or in
setting himself to the task of writing!"

With all these three men Petrarch had already
been in communication by letter. Lapo had sent
him Cicero's *Pro Milone* the year before, and
thenceforward the two kept up a constant commerce
of books. In addition to the *Pro Milone*, Lapo
sent him at different times the *Pro Plancio* and the
Philippics, of which Petrarch had copies made by
trustworthy scribes before sending them back; and
in return he communicated to Lapo his own precious
discovery, the *Pro Archiâ*. Lapo was a fervent
admirer of Petrarch's genius, and possessed a manuscript of the last thirteen books of his *Familiar
Letters*, which is now preserved in the Laurentian
Library at Florence. It contains some interesting
marginal notes in Lapo's own handwriting.

How long Petrarch had been in communication
with Boccaccio and Nelli is not quite certain. If
one of his letters to Socrates is rightly ascribed to
the year 1350, he was already on terms of affectionate intimacy with them both; and this is confirmed
by Boccaccio's statement that he was devoted to
Petrarch for forty years or more. This passage

has led to a conjecture that the two may have met
in Paris, while others have dated their intimacy
from Petrarch's first visit to Naples; but Boccaccio's
words do not necessarily imply more than devoted
admiration, and Petrarch's own statement that Boccaccio had not previously known him by sight is a
conclusive reason for assigning the year 1350 as the
date of their first meeting face to face.   We must
suppose, then, either that the sentence in the letter
to Socrates is a later interpolation, or that the
earlier intimacy had been one of letters which have
not come down to us.   The first extant communication is a copy of verses sent by Petrarch to
Boccaccio in 1349.

This first visit was a very short one; Petrarch
hastened on to Rome, but on October 15th he was
delayed at Bolsena by an injury to the thigh caused
by a kick from his horse.   In spite of this mishap,
he was in Rome by November 1st, but his wound
still gave him much pain.   In December he left
Rome for his birthplace, Arezzo, whose citizens
received him with extraordinary honour.   Thence
he went on to Florence for a second and probably
longer visit to Boccaccio; and it was here, not at
Arezzo as Fracassetti states, that Lapo gave him
a copy of the newly discovered *Institutions* of
Quintilian.   As was his wont, Petrarch eagerly
devoured the new treasure, and then sat down to
an appreciation of it in the form of a letter to its
dead author.

He left Florence about the new year, and three
months later he received a return visit from Boc-

caccio, of which the occasion must have been singularly gratifying to both. Technically Petrarch was still a banished man; the decree which exiled Petracco two years before his son's birth applied to his descendants, and Petrarch was theoretically in peril of his life when in his forty-seventh year he visited the city of his ancestors. Practically there was no fear of any attack on him. Florence was eager to claim her share in the distinction achieved by her illustrious son. But for very shame she could not speak of Petrarch as a Florentine while her own records proclaimed him an exile. Petrarch's visits to Florence gave an appropriate opportunity of redressing the wrong done to him through his father, and his friendship with Boccaccio enabled the reparation to be made in a singularly agreeable manner. At the beginning of April Boccaccio went to Padua as the bearer of a letter from the Priors of the Guilds and the Gonfalonier of Justice of the People and State of Florence, revoking the sentence of banishment, restoring the property confiscated nearly fifty years before, and inviting Petrarch in terms of honorific compliment to fix his abode in the city of his forefathers. Petrarch replied in cordial and dignified terms. It is noticeable that even as an exile he had always spoken of Florence as his " Patria," and he must now have felt a new pleasure in acknowledging his Tuscan descent. For a time he may even have thought seriously of accepting the invitation to go and live among those who now addressed him as " fellow-citizen."

However this may be, Padua had for the moment lost its charm, and had become a place of mourning for him. He had returned there on January 7th, to find that a fortnight earlier Jacopo da Carrara had been assassinated by a bastard nephew. Petrarch's grief was profound. His lamentations, loud and bitter as they are, have no note of exaggeration; his praises of his dead friend, though pitched in the highest key, are absolutely sincere. Jacopo's death must have made him not unwilling to leave Italy for a time, when in the summer of 1351 it became convenient for him to return to Vaucluse.

Alinari

THE TOMB OF JACOPO II. DA CARRARA, WITH INSCRIPTION BY PETRARCH

CHAPTER X

VAUCLUSE

1351-1353

ON May 3rd he left Padua, accompanied by the boy Giovanni, after dictating an impromptu epitaph for Jacopo's tomb, on which he might profitably have spent a little more time. The genuineness of its sentiment makes inadequate amends for the extreme flatness of its composition. Petrarch had the pen of a ready writer, but the fluency of his poetic style always needed the correction of his maturer judgment.

That night he stayed at Vicenza, and found there, to his amusement and delight, an old man more enthusiastic about Cicero than himself, or at least more intemperate in praise of him. The talk of the company after supper fell upon the great Latin author, the old man abounding in unqualified admiration of him. Here was Petrarch's pet subject brought ready to his hand; he put forward his favourite view that Cicero was flawless as a writer and an orator, but somewhat unstable as a politician, and he gave the audience the rare privilege of hearing him read his own two letters to Cicero, which are written upon this theme. But the old man was unconvinced; he threw out his hands

piteously, crying, "Spare, oh spare my Cicero!"
And when pressed by arguments that he could not
answer, shut his eyes and turned away his head as
if in pain, moaning, "Ah me! Ah me! So they are
finding fault with my Cicero!"

Petrarch stayed some days at Verona, and then
went on to Piacenza, whence, on June 11th, he
dispatched a letter to Socrates, written some weeks
earlier, but held back for want of a trusty messenger. To this he added a few sentences announc-
ing that he was on his way to Vaucluse, and hoped
that Socrates would soon meet him there. He
actually arrived there by way of Mont Genèvre on
June 21st.

For nearly two years Vaucluse was once more
his home, and he seems to have lived there for
weeks and even months together without interrup-
tion. Of course he went sometimes to Avignon;
during the whole period, indeed, business of various
kinds took him there much oftener and kept him
there much longer than he liked. Not a few such
visits were paid in connection with a little incident
of monastic intrigue, which gave him a good deal
of occupation and must surely have afforded him
some amusement. To the great Benedictine abbey
of Vallombrosa were attached several dependent
religious houses, among which was the abbey of
Corvara, near Bologna. In 1351 the post of Abbot
of Corvara fell vacant; the right of nomination was
vested in the Abbot of Vallombrosa. Petrarch and
his Florentine friends desired that the dignity should
be conferred on a certain Don Ubertino; Nelli was

especially eager to back Petrarch in procuring this appointment, and the Bishop of Florence also used his influence in Ubertino's favour. The Abbot was a saintly person, unused to the ways of a place-hunting world. He yielded to all this pressure and nominated Don Ubertino; then almost immediately he repented of his decision, revoked the appointment, and made a second nomination in favour of Don Guido, another brother of the Order. Ubertino refused to give way; he had got his presentation, and he meant to have the place. Guido was equally firm in his determination to be Abbot of Corvara. The dispute went for judgment to Avignon; and the Abbot of Vallombrosa found himself in a pitiable position. He was of course disposed to maintain his second nomination, and had forwarded papers in support of it to Avignon. But again the Bishop and Nelli intervened, and induced him to promise neutrality. He wrote a letter to his lawyer at Avignon full of praises of Ubertino, and ending with the cryptic statement that he could not speak more explicitly because he had once already been accused of inconstancy, and he would not incur the reproach a second time. To the ordinary man's intelligence it seems rather as if he had now incurred it from both sides. The affair dragged on for months; the law was not more expeditious at Avignon than elsewhere, and the decision was further delayed by the Pope's illness. Petrarch threw himself heart and soul into Ubertino's cause; Fracassetti even represents him as arguing it in court; his own letters give no warrant for this, but show that he left nothing undone that influence and solicitation could achieve. " I have become in another's behalf what I never have been in my own," he writes, "a busy importunate canvasser." The case was heard at last in full Consistory; Petrarch's opinion was quoted, and his wishes carried weight with Pope and Cardinals, and much to his delight Ubertino was declared lawful Abbot of Corvara.

After settling this little matter of ecclesiastical patronage, Petrarch still had occasion for frequent visits to "Babylon." But he stayed there no longer than he could help, and the period from Mid-summer, 1351, to the middle of April, 1353, may be regarded as practically spent in his "Transalpine Helicon." It was a period of profuse letter-writing; the *Familiares* are not arranged in quite trust-worthy chronological order, but, speaking roughly, more than five books of them, from the middle of the eleventh to nearly the end of the sixteenth, were written at this time. From frequent allusions in these letters, we know also that it was a time of much reading and hard literary work, though we cannot name with certainty the books on which Petrarch was engaged. There is a passage in the lamentable letter to Socrates of June, 1349, in which Petrarch says that his friends are looking for great men's histories from his pen, but that he has now no heart for anything but mourning. The allusion must surely be to his great and long-forgotten work, the *Lives of Illustrious Men*, and we may infer that this history of the Roman

Republic, written in the form of a series of biographies, from Romulus to Julius Cæsar, had been
well advanced in the earlier periods of his residence
at Vaucluse ; it is reasonable to conjecture further
that on getting back to his books, and resuming his
usual habits of work, Petrarch would devote himself
anew to its composition, but he did not quite complete it, for at the end of 1354 he told the Emperor
that "he still wanted time and leisure to give it the
final touches." Italian politics, too, as we shall have
occasion to note later, occupied much of his time
and thought during these years. But above all,
this is a period of happy country life in the beautiful valley of the Sorgue, and there are no more
delightful passages in the whole range of Petrarch's
writings than those in which he describes its
charms. A complete collection of these passages
would fill a fair-sized volume. Here we must be
content with the description of his life given in a
letter to Nelli in the summer of 1352. He writes
as follows :—

"I am spending the summer at the source of the
Sorgue. You know what comes next without my
saying it, but as you bid me speak, I will tell you in
a few words.

"I have declared war on my body. May He
without whose aid I must fail so help me, as gullet
belly, tongue, ears, and eyes often seem to me to be
not my own members, but my undutiful foes. Many
are the evils which I remember having suffered
from them, especially from the eyes, which have
led me into all my falls. Now I have shut them up

here so that they can see hardly anything but sky, hills, and streams; neither gold, nor jewels, nor ivory, nor purple cloth, nor horses, except two mere ponies, which carry me round the valleys in company with a single lad. Lastly, I never see the face of a woman, except that of my bailiff's wife, and if you saw her, you might suppose yourself to be looking on a patch of the Libyan or Ethiopian desert. 'Tis a scorched, sunburnt countenance, with not a trace of freshness or juice remaining; had Helen worn such a face, Troy would still be standing; had Lucretia and Virginia been thus dowered, Tarquinius had not lost his kingdom, nor Appius died in his prison. But let me not, after this description of her aspect, rob the goodwife of the eulogy due to her virtues; her soul is as white as her skin is swarthy. She is a bright example of female ugliness boding no harm to man. And I might say more on this head, if Seneca had not dealt with the theme at length in his letters which allude to his Claranum. My bailiff's wife has this singular property, that while beauty is in general an attribute proper rather to woman than to man, she is so little affected by the want of it that you may reckon her ugliness becoming to her. There never was a trustier, humbler, more laborious creature. In the sun's full blaze, where the very grasshopper can scarce bear the heat, she spends her whole days in the fields, and her tanned hide laughs at Leo and Cancer. At evening the old dame returns home, and busies her unwearied, invincible little body about household work, with such vigour that you might suppose her a lass fresh from the bed-chamber. Not a murmur all this time, not a grumble, no hint of trouble in her mind, only incredible care lavished on her husband and children, on me, on my household, and on the guests who come to see me, and at the same time an incredible scorn for her own comfort. This woman of stone has a heap of sacking on the bare ground for her bed. Her food is bread well-nigh as hard as iron, her drink wine which might more justly be styled vinegar drowned in water; if you offer her anything of mellower flavour, long custom has taught her to think the softer victual hard. But enough about my bailiff's wife, who would not have engaged my pen except in a country letter. Well, this is my eyes' discipline. What shall I say of my ears? Here I have no solace of song or flute or viol, which, elsewhere, are wont to carry me out of myself; all such sweetness the breeze has wafted away from me. Here the only sounds are the occasional lowing of cattle and bleating of sheep, the songs of the birds, and the ceaseless murmur of the stream. What of my tongue, by which I have often raised my own spirits, and sometimes perhaps those of others? Now it lies low, and is often silent from dawn to dusk, for it has no one except me to talk to. As to my gullet and belly, I have so disciplined them, that my herdsman's bread is often enough for me, and I even enjoy it, and I leave the white bread, brought me from a distance, to be eaten by the servants who fetched it. To such an extent does custom stand me in the stead of luxury. And so my bailiff and good friend, who humours all my whims, and has himself a constitution of stone, has no quarrel with me on any subject, except that my fare is harder than he says a man can put up with for any time. I, on the other hand, am persuaded that such fare can be tolerated longer than luxurious living, which the satirist declares to be most wearisome, and not to be endured five days together. Grapes, figs, nuts, and almonds are my delicacies. And I thoroughly enjoy the little fish which abound in this river, especially the catching of them, a pursuit in which I am most diligent, and very fond of handling both hook and net. What shall I tell you of my clothes and shoes? They are changed from top to toe. Not such was my old fashion. 'Mine,' I say, because of the surpassing vanity with which, while observing the proprieties, I trust, and holding fast by seemliness, it was my pleasure of old to shine among my equals. Now you would take me for a ploughman or a shepherd, though all the while I have finer clothes here with me, but there is no reason for changing my dress except that the clothes which I choose to wear first get dirty first. My old bonds are loosed, and the eyes which I once sought to please are closed for ever; and I think that, even if they were still open, they would not now have their wonted mastery over me. But in my own eyes I never look so well as when loose-girt and free. And what can I tell you of my dwelling? You might take it for the house of Cato or Fabricius. There I live with a single dog and

VAUCLUSE; THE SORGUE AND PETRARCH'S GARDEN

Brun

only two servants. I gave the slip to all the rest in Italy, and would that I had given them the slip on the journey so that they could never get back to me, for they are the one hurricane that wrecks my peace. My bailiff, however, lives in the adjoining house, always at hand whenever he can be of service, but with a door that can shut off his quarters at any moment, if I feel the least symptom of boredom at his being always in waiting.

"Here I have fashioned me two little gardens, the most apt in the world to my fancy and desire; should I try to picture them to you, this letter would be long drawn out. In a word, I think the world scarce holds their like, and if I must confess my womanish frivolity, I am in a huff that such beauty should exist anywhere out of Italy. The one I always call my Transalpine Helicon, for it is bowered in shade, made for study as for nothing else, and consecrated to my Apollo. It lies close to the pool in which the Sorgue rises, beyond which is only a trackless crag, quite inaccessible except to wild animals and birds. My other garden lies close to my house; it has a better-tilled appearance, and Bromê's nursling (Bacchus) has his favourite plant there. This, strange to say, lies in the middle of the beautiful swift river, and close by, separated only by a little bridge at the end of the house, hangs the arch of a grotto of natural rock, which under this blazing sky makes the summer heat imperceptible. It is a place to fire the soul to study, and I think not unlike the little court where Cicero used to declaim his speeches, except that his place had no Sorgue flowing by it. Under this grotto, then, I sit at noon; my morning is spent on the hills, my evening in the meadows, or in that wilder little garden, close to the source, where design has embellished nature, where there is a spot in mid-stream overshadowed by the lofty crag, a tiny spot indeed, but full of lively promptings by which even a sluggard soul may be goaded to high imaginings. What would you have? I might well spend my life here, if it were not at once so far from Italy and so near to Avignon. For why should I try to hide from you my twin weakness? Love of the one soothes my sorrow and plucks at my heart; hatred of the other goads and exasperates me, and seeing that the loathsome stench of her breeds plague throughout the world, is it any wonder if her too near neighbourhood pollutes the sweet air of this little country-side? It will drive me away from here; I know it will. Meanwhile you know my mood. The one thing I long for is the sight of you and my few surviving friends; the one thing I dread is a return to city life. Farewell."

Only a few months after this letter was written, the faithful farm-bailiff, Raymond Monet, who had been truly a friend as well as a servant to his master for many years, died, and Petrarch, then at Avignon, wrote to the Cardinals Talleyrand and Gui de Boulogne, asking them to sanction his immediate return to Vaucluse. Regulus, he says, asked leave to return from Africa at a critical moment to look after his farm at home on account of his bailiff's death, and Gnæus Scipio similarly asked leave of

absence from Spain to portion his daughter. "Now
I," says Petrarch, writing on January 5th, "may
support my appeal for leave of absence by the
precedent of both these great generals; for by my
bailiff's death yesterday not only does my farm run
the risk of neglect, but my library, which is my
adopted daughter, has lost her guardian. For my
bailiff," he goes on, "though a countryman, was
gifted with more than a townsman's forethought
and refinement of manners. I think earth never
bore a more loyal creature. In a word, this one
man by his surpassing fidelity compensated and
made amends for the sins and treacheries of the
whole race of servants, as to which I have not only
to make daily complaint by word of mouth, but
have sometimes put my complaints into writing.
And so I had given into his charge myself, my
property, and all the books which I have in Gaul;
and whereas my shelves contain every sort and
size of volume, mixed big and little together, and I
myself have often been absent for long periods,
never once on my return have I found a single
volume missing, or even moved from its proper
place. Though unlettered himself, he had a devotion to letters, and he took special pains with the
books which he knew I valued most. Much handling of them had by this time taught him to know
the works of the ancients by name, and to distinguish my own small treatises from them. He
would beam with delight whenever I gave him a
book to hold, and would clasp it to his bosom
with a sigh. Sometimes under his breath he

would call upon its author by name, and, strange
as it may sound, the mere touch of the books
gave him an enjoyable feeling of advancement
in learning.   And now I have lost this excellent
guardian of my property, with whom for fifteen
years I have been wont to share all my troubles,
who was to me, so to speak, as a priest of Ceres,
and whose house served me for a temple of
fidelity.   Two days since, in obedience to your
Eminences' summons, I came away, and left him as
I thought slightly indisposed.   He was an old man,
it is true, but, as Maro says, of a hale and green old
age.   Yesterday at evening he left me, called hence
to attendance on a better Master.   May He grant
uninterrupted repose to his soul after the many
labours of his body here.   His one prayer to God
was for repose.   This he seeks at Thy hands; deny
him not this, O Christ.   Grant him to dwell no
longer in my house, but in the house of the Lord,
to regard the Lord's pleasure, not mine, and to
have his conversation in His temple, instead of in
my fields, where he laboured many years with
limbs hardened to cold and heat alike.   In my
service he found toil; in Thine let him find rest.
At Thy command the bonds of his old prison-house
have been loosed and he has come to Thee.

"One of my servants, who happened to be present
at his death, brought me the sad news as quickly as
possible, and arriving here late last night, told me
that he had breathed his last, after making frequent
mention of my name, and calling with tears on the
name of Christ.   I grieved sincerely, and my grief

would have been still more bitter, had not the good man's age long since warned me that I must look for this bereavement.

"So I must go. Give me leave, I pray you, most eminent Fathers, and let me go from the city where I am of no service, to the country where I am wanted, and where I am more anxious about my library than about my farm."

Great as were the joys and sorrows of life at Vaucluse, they were far from monopolising Petrarch's attention. His spirit had regained its buoyancy, and once more he threw himself heart and soul into the great drama of Italian politics. The years 1351–3 were fruitful in episodes of that drama. The war between Venice and Genoa, the pacification of Naples, the appointment of a Commission to regulate the government of Rome, and the imprisonment and release of Rienzi at Avignon, the death of Clement VI, and the election of Innocent VI to succeed him, all belong to these eventful years.

With the struggle for the supremacy of the sea Petrarch had no very direct concern, but no one who valued the safety of Europe, least of all an Italian patriot, could see without alarm the two great maritime republics wasting their strength on internecine war, while the weakness of Constantinople and the constant growth of the Moslem power might at any moment create a situation of urgent peril to the West. Clement was probably a shrewder politician than those who saw only the pleasure-loving side of his nature suspected ; he did his best

to bring about peace, and it may have been at
his instigation that Petrarch, whose letters received a consideration that would not now be
accorded to the appeals of even the most distinguished amateur diplomatist, wrote in terms of
eloquent entreaty and fervid exhortation to the
rulers of both states.   But neither formal nor informal diplomacy availed to stay the war.   In
February, 1352, the fleets had a drawn battle.
Eighteen months later, the Venetians under Pisani
gained their overwhelming victory off Sardinia.   A
shameful flight saved the Genoese Admiral Grim-
aldi and a third of his force; the rest of the
Genoese fleet was either sunk or captured.   For
the moment Venice remained mistress of the
Mediterranean.

In the affairs of Naples Petrarch took a closer
personal interest, though apparently no active share.
Here again the Pope was chief mediator.   After
months of negotiation, in the course of which he
did a stroke of business for the Papacy in buying
the Countship of Provence from Queen Joanna,
Clement succeeded in bringing the hostile factions
to terms.   The King of Hungary recognised Lewis
of Tarentum, Joanna's cousin, paramour, and second
husband, as King of the Two Sicilies, and for a
while the land had peace.   Lewis was now first in
rank at Naples; but first in influence and power
stood the King's tutor in the art of statesmanship,
the great Florentine, Niccolò Acciaiuoli, who became Grand Seneschal of the realm.   Though not
yet personally acquainted with Petrarch, Acciaiuoli

was excellently disposed in his favour, for he knew intimately the whole circle of his Florentine friends : his own brother Angelo, in fact, the Bishop of Florence, was included in that circle, and enjoyed Petrarch's hospitality at Vaucluse in the spring of 1352. In the Grand Seneschal, Petrarch saw a not unworthy successor to King Robert, alike as a ruler and a patron of letters.

Interesting as were the politics of the maritime republics and of Naples, the magic word Rome evoked a far deeper sentiment. Since the fall of Rienzi, confusion had reigned in the city. The Jubilee had brought a kind of truce, for the Romans thoroughly understood the value of their city as a place of pilgrimage. But Clement was too sensible to take the temporary toleration of his Legate as a sign of settled order, and appointed a Commission of four Cardinals to advise him on the necessary reforms. In the autumn of 1351 this Commission asked Petrarch to lay his views before them, and he did so in two letters, which illustrate and empha-sise in a remarkable manner the sincerity and con-sistency of his views. Writing under a full sense of responsibility, and writing to Princes of the Church, whose sympathies would naturally be with the ruling class, he repeats the conviction expressed five years earlier to Rienzi, that the Baronial Houses were the eternal enemies of Rome's peace, and that if good government was to be made possible in the city, the magistracy must be recruited, not from them, but from the ranks of the people.

Only a few months after this correspondence with

the Cardinals, Rienzi himself appeared in Avignon, a prisoner in peril of his life. He had taken refuge with the Emperor : the latter cannot be severely blamed if he showed scant sympathy with the upstart who had summoned to his bar the heir of the Cæsars. The Pope wanted to have Rienzi ; the Emperor had no pleasure in keeping him : to the Pope he went. The chamber which was his prison is shown to all who visit the Papal palace, and they are told that he was released from it at the intercession of his friend Petrarch. There is no written authority for this gracious legend, but two things are certain : Petrarch was in a fury of indignation at Rienzi's imprisonment, and the reason which he assigns for his release could have no validity outside Crotchet Castle. He was in a fury because, as he thundered, Rienzi was arraigned not for his bad deeds, but for his good ; not for betraying the cause of Rome, but for having dared to assert her sovereignty. Rienzi was in the grip of wicked men ; how could he ever expect deliverance ? Hear the astonishing story. Through the modern Babylon ran a rumour that Rienzi was a poet. What ! A sacred bard lies chained in this city of culture. Off with his gyves ! And Rienzi comes out a free man. As history this is a little thin, and it is pleasant to think that he who circulated it may, after all, have had a hand in the happy deliverance.

In August, 1352, occurred a curious little episode, of which the details are somewhat obscure, though the main fact is clear. The papal secretaryship was

again vacant, and two of Petrarch's friends among
the Cardinals used secret influence to get it offered
to him. Again he wisely shrank from the uncongenial burden, and in his turn took secret
measures to defeat his friends' well-meant but unwelcome scheme. What reason can there have
been for all this mystery? Once before the office
had been openly offered and declined; the same
kind of thing was to happen, formally or informally,
three times more in the course of the next twelve
years. Why this manœuvre of sap and countersap
now? Possibly the Cardinals may have wanted to
confront him with a *fait accompli;* possibly he may
have feared to wound their susceptibilities by open
opposition. The reasons are all conjectural, but
there is ample warrant for the fact.

This was not the only preferment resigned by
Petrarch in this year. In the autumn he was
appointed to a canonry at Modena, but being
already provided with a sufficient income, he sent
the presentation to Luca Cristiano on October 19th,
and the terms of the accompanying letter in which
he explained his action are a model of that delicate
tact which makes it possible for one friend to accept
a service of this kind from another.

Rienzi had been set free in August, 1352. At
the end of the year the Pope, who had admired his
eloquence, tolerated his power, and profited by his
fall, was no more. For some time Clement had
been in failing health. In the spring of the year
Petrarch, who held all physicians for quacks, as
indeed at that time of the world's history most of

them were, wrote the Pope a letter warning him to beware of their practices. This brought on the poet the hatred of the medical profession, and a controvery ensued of which we can read only one side. Our estate would be the more gracious if we could read neither : to those who love Petrarch best as a man, he must appear most detestable as a controversialist. Whether in spite of his physicians' exertions or because of them, Clement died on December 6th, 1352, and twelve days later the Sacred College, spurred to haste by information that King John of France meditated a visit to their neighbourhood, chose Stefano Alberti, Cardinal of Ostia, to succeed him.

Clement's successor took the name of Innocent VI ; to those who regard innocence as synonymous with ignorance, the choice must have seemed admirable. It is only fair to add that the new Pope had a better title to it in the exemplary austerity of his life. He checked the licence of the Papal Court, reformed abuses, and insisted on bishops living in their dioceses ; but his ignorance was appalling. Here in the middle of the fourteenth century, at the head of the Church, which numbered in her ranks five-sixths of the educated men of Europe, was a Pope who, at the suggestion of a malevolent Cardinal, seriously proposed to excommunicate Petrarch as a necromancer, on the sole ground that he was a student of Virgil. The absurd sentence was never passed ; many of the influential Cardinals were well affected to Petrarch, and it so happened that his especial friend

Cardinal Talleyrand had been instrumental in procuring Innocent's election. But for a moment the ridiculous accusation was a serious danger, and however abominable Petrarch may have found Avignon in the past, its neighbourhood must have seemed yet more destestable when the rude bigotry of Innocent had taken the place of Clement's refined taste and kindly tolerance.

CHAPTER XI

MILAN AND THE VISCONTI

1353-1354

PETRARCH had meant to spend the winter in Italy. On November 16th, 1352, he started from Vaucluse in fine weather, which had been unbroken for many weeks, but he had hardly left the valley when a gentle drizzle set in, which presently turned to a heavy rain, and as the day wore on to a veritable deluge. He took shelter at Cavaillon, where he found the Bishop indisposed, but declaring himself cured by the sight of him. Philip besought him to give up the idea of his journey, and in the course of the night came news that the roads round Nice were closed to travellers by armed bands of the mountaineers. All through the night the rain fell in torrents, and in the morning Petrarch found his friend's entreaties, which in themselves had been nearly enough to turn him, supported by the fact that "one route was made impassable by war, and all by flood." It seemed, he thought, as if God would not have him go forward, and he returned presently to Vaucluse. In the spring of 1353 he resumed the project. In April he paid a visit to his brother Gherardo, whom he had not seen for more than five years, but of whose courageous conduct, when Montrieu was devastated by the plague, he had heard an account some two years before, which had filled him with joy and admiration. Not only had Gherardo refused to desert the post in which he believed Christ had set him, but when the plague came, and brother after brother fell a victim to it, he spent his whole time nursing the sick, giving absolution to the dying, and burying the dead. Then he found himself, with one faithful dog, the sole survivor of a house which had numbered over thirty brethren. Marauders came to pillage the defenceless shrine ; Gherardo opposed their entrance, and they slunk away abashed. Then, having saved the sacred edifice and its contents, he set himself to have it repeopled, and applied to the principal monastery of his Order, not for any reward or recognition of his services, but to have new brethren given him and a new prior set over him. To this brother, whom Dr. Koerting has aptly called "Francesco without the modern elements," the latter had a whole-hearted attachment. From an unsteady, headstrong youth, Gherardo had grown to be a man of singularly resolute character, and the elder brother, whom his conduct had formerly inspired with grave anxiety, now looked with unqualified admiration on his piety and self-devotion. His visits to Montrieu were rare, but they evidently gave him unqualified pleasure, and he warmly recommended the monastery, through his brother-poet Zanobi da Strada, another of his Florentine friends, to the favour of Acciaiuoli and the Court of Naples. From Montrieu he went

back to Vaucluse, and on April 26th paid what
proved to be his last visit to the city which had so
deeply influenced his fortunes, where so much of his
life had been spent, and which, in spite of its associa-
tions with Laura and with Socrates, he so cordially
detested. He went back to make preparations for
what he intended, as in fact it proved, to be his final
departure from Provence.

Early in May he set out, travelling as he had
come two years before, by the direct route over Mont
Genèvre. As on his descent from the top of the pass
he left the clouds behind him, and "the soft, warm air,
rising from the Italian valley, caressed his cheek,"
the sight of Piedmont spread out to the eastward
smote him with gladness, and in a poem of eighteen
hexameters he poured out a salutation to "the land
beloved of God, the land of unmatched beauty, the
land rich in wealth and in men, the mistress of the
world, on whom art and nature had lavished their
choicest favours, and to whom he was now eagerly
returning, never again to depart from her." It is
not pretended that in workmanship these lines can
equal the hexameters of Virgil, or even of Politian,
but they are veritably a great lyric, for almost alone
among Petrarch's Latin verses they utter the note
of rapturous inspiration.

This salutation to Italy was written on the spot.
It is very probable that the sight of those glorious
valleys stretching away from Mont Genèvre inspired Petrarch also with the idea of his greatest
Italian poem, the *Ode to the Lords of Italy*. Various
dates have been assigned to this supreme lyric, but

the best choice seems to lie between 1345, the time approximately assigned by De Sade and Fracassetti, when the earlier depredations of the Great Company inflicted new sufferings on Italy, and 1353 or 1354, the time suggested by Gesualdo and preferred here, when Petrarch, returning to the valley of the Po, found the princes and republics of his country bidding against each other for the service of similar bands of foreign mercenaries. Every line of this glorious ode burns with the fire of purest patriotism ; it is a cry of lamentation over his Italy's wounds, of passionate entreaty to her princes for union and for peace, and of prayer to God, wrung from the suppliant's very soul, that He, who for pity of man came down from heaven, will turn and look upon the beloved sweet country, and soften the hard hearts of those who afflict her with war.   Here is the real national hymn of Italy; for five hundred years it haunted the imagination of those who dreamed of her unity, gave inspiration to the counsels of her statesmen, and nerved the arm of her soldiers.   The unsurpassed beauty of the poem as a lyric is almost equalled by its fruitfulness in political result.

If this was, indeed, the time at which the ode *Italia Mia* was composed, there is a pathos which can without exaggeration be called tragic, in the fact that it coincides with the least excusable error of Petrarch's life, the one action in which he seemed to fall below his high standard of patriotism.   He had hardly touched Italian soil, when he accepted the shameful patronage of the Archbishop of Milan.

Of all the ruling families who afflicted Italy in the fourteenth century, the Visconti were the most odious. It is true that their fellow-tyrants could not be excelled in the magnitude of their vices, but few were so ill-provided with compensating virtues. The viper was the appropriate cognisance of the House, and its present head, the Archbishop Giovanni, habitually goes by the name of the Great Viper in the pages of Villani's chronicle. In truth he had just the qualities with which the serpent is credited—its cunning, its callousness, and its poison. If he had not the wanton ferocity of his great-nephew Bernabò, his cold, deliberate ruthlessness seemed almost more hateful. That he was a consummately able and successful statesman is indisputable, but we find no hint in his career that his lust of power was ever checked by a scruple, or lit by a ray of magnanimity.

Luchino had died in his bed in January, 1349: an event not quite so rare in the Visconti family as in some others. Giovanni succeeded him, and the power of Milan stood higher than ever. With Luchino Petrarch had had some amicable correspondence, initiated by the ruler of Milan, who asked for a copy of verses and some plants from the poet's garden. Both verses and plants were sent, accompanied by a letter couched in the courtly terms of compliment required by good manners in that age, but giving Luchino not ambiguously to understand that the encouragement of men of letters is the chief glory of princes. Now as Petrarch passed through Milan in uncertainty where

THE EQUESTRIAN STATUE OF BERNABÒ VISCONTI

to go next, Giovanni, "the· greatest of Italian princes," laid on him hands of friendly compulsion, and persuaded him to fix his abode there.   From Petrarch's first narrative, written before he realised any need for apology, we gather that the interview went somewhat as follows: The Archbishop couched his request in the most flattering terms; he whose lightest word was usually treated as a command condescended to ask for Petrarch's presence in Milan as a favour.   Petrarch was on the point of objecting that he was pledged to work, that he hated a crowd and longed for quiet, but the Archbishop anticipated all his objections and answered them before they were made.   He would place at his disposal a healthy house in a delightful part of the city, with the church of St. Ambrose on one side, and a view over the plain to the Alps on the other; could the country offer a more peaceful retreat?   His time should be his own, he should be absolutely his own master; no service should be expected of him, no obligation imposed.   Petrarch yielded, and yielding incurred a reproach from which his warmest partisans cannot wholly clear him.

The news brought utter dismay to some of his best friends.   There is indeed no hint of disapproval from Socrates; to that loyal and affectionate heart, we may suppose, whatever Petrarch did seemed right. But the Florentines could not possess their souls in even a show of patience, and no one who realises the situation can refuse them his sympathy.   A good Florentine could not help hating Milan, and no better

Florentines than Boccaccio and Nelli ever breathed the Tuscan air. It was not merely that Florence and Milan happened to be inveterate enemies; their antagonism was derived not from a mere accident of history, but from a conflict of principles. Whatever the faults of her government, the great Guelf Republic stood for civic liberty; whatever the merits of Milanese order, the name of Milan's rulers symbolised tyranny. In going to live with the "Great Viper," the master whom they revered seemed to them, not without reason, to have fallen below the most elementary standard of patriotism. From Nelli came a letter of remonstrance, the tenor of which can be pretty accurately inferred from Petrarch's reply. Boccaccio took a rod from the master's own cupboard; he employed Petrarch's favourite device of allegory and in a pastoral dialogue upbraided "Silvanus" (as Petrarch often called himself in compositions of this kind) for deserting and betraying the nymph Amaryllis (Italy) and giving himself into the hands of her oppressor, Egon (the Archbishop), the false priest of Pan, a monster of treachery and crime. Petrarch replied to his friends in letters which give the genuine explanation of his conduct, but do not touch the main issue. The real gist of the remonstrance is that he, the Italian patriot, has gone over to the enemy's camp. He replies that the Archbishop is a very powerful and very courteous prince, that great men's commands have to be obeyed, especially when they take the form of entreaties, and that he feared to incur the reproach of arrogance by refusing. All this is quite sincere: he had a delicate sensitiveness which made it very difficult for him to say "No" to those who went out of their way to be kind to him, and the Archbishop was a man to whom few people would dare to refuse anything for which he condescended to ask. He meant to have the World's Laureate as an ornament to his Court, and he got him. By sheer strength of will and suppleness of method he dominated Petrarch; but he did not win him, as Azzo and Jacopo had won him, by the heart, even though, like every one else, he showed him only the best side of his nature. The last thing a man could do with Giovanni Visconti was to love him.

One consideration, at which Petrarch just hints, may have had legitimate weight with him. The Archbishop offered him a "healthy" house; with the Great Plague fresh in remembrance that was an inducement worth thinking about, and strangely enough Milan had hitherto entirely escaped the pestilence. Petrarch was a very brave man; many a time we have seen him hazard his life for a whim, and go unarmed through a country swarming with brigands. But the bravest man may prefer Goshen to a charnel-house, and having no special duty to combat the plague, he might avoid it if he could.

So in Milan he stayed and believed himself his own master. The Visconti kept their promise, and put no constraint upon him. They knew their man; he would have wriggled free from chains, but the silken bonds of courtesy and kindness held him fast. If he attended a public ceremony, it was as an honoured guest; if he represented his patrons abroad, it was as chief spokesman of a distinguished embassy. The close scrutiny of his friends' eyes discerned that his residence in Milan was derogatory to his highest ideals, but it must be acknowledged that in the view of society at large those very ideals were exalted by the exceeding honour done to his person.

His first attendance at a state ceremonial nearly cost him his life; he rode out in the train of the Visconti brothers to meet the new papal legate, Cardinal Albornoz. Night was falling when the Cardinal arrived, and the darkness was increased by clouds of dust from the two cavalcades. Petrarch rode forward in his turn to make obeisance, and was resuming his place when something frightened his horse; the animal jibbed and backed, and dropped his hind-legs over the precipitous and unguarded edge of the road. Petrarch was saved from a fall that would probably have been fatal by the promptitude and dexterity of young Galeazzo Visconti. The horse hung on by his fore-feet only, and Petrarch fell off into some brambles, which arrested his fall for a moment, and just gave Galeazzo time to grasp him by the hand and pull him up in safety. The horse too, lightened of its burden, managed to scramble up. Petrarch might well consider that he owed his life to Galeazzo.

A few weeks later he attended a far more imposing if somewhat melancholy ceremonial. As already mentioned, the crushing defeat of the Genoese off the mouth of the Loiera took place in August.

Wounded in her honour by the flight of her admiral, and crippled in power by the loss of more than half her best ships, the city turned upon her rulers, and after driving them from power, took the desperate course of seeking help from Milan. The Archbishop's aid was to be had only on his own terms; the price of it was the lordship of the city. Men scarcely believed their ears when it was known that the Genoese were ready to pay the price. Even Petrarch, the Archbishop's honoured guest and counsellor, was shocked for a moment at the proud city's humiliation. But the shameful bargain was struck, and on October 10th the Archbishop received from the ambassadors of the city the submission of Genoa. He made them a dignified and encouraging reply; he had got what he wanted, and was not the man to grudge stately phrases. It must be allowed that he had the graces of external deportment. It must be allowed also that he did not neglect his share of the bargain. He made serious efforts to negotiate an honourable peace with Venice, and Petrarch was among the envoys entrusted with the delicate task. The victorious republic rejected his overtures with contempt, and a year later suffered in her turn the retribution that waits on arrogance. In November, 1354, the Genoese admiral, Paganino Doria, with a new fleet, sailed up the Adriatic, and surprised and utterly destroyed the naval force of the Venetians at Porto Lungo. The war was over, and it was Venice who in the following year had to sue for peace. The strategy and tactics of this great achievement were

Doria's, but men noted that the turning point in the struggle had been the intervention of Milan. It seemed as though Giovanni Visconti had only to put his hand to an enterprise, and its success was assured. But by a strange coincidence, neither he nor the great Venetian Doge, Andrea Dandolo, lived to see the issue of the struggle ; Dandolo died in September, and Giovanni Visconti on October 3rd.

He was succeeded in his sovereignties by his great-nephews Matteo, Bernabò, and Galeazzo, who kept the territories of Milan and Genoa as a common possession, and divided the rest of the inheritance. Their accession was made the occasion of a magnificent ceremony, at which Petrarch delivered the inevitable harangue, and was much disgusted at having it interrupted in the middle by an astrologer, who declared that this was the one propitious moment for executing the deed of partition. The brothers continued to him the full measure of their great-uncle's favour, and Bernabò shortly afterwards asked him to stand godfather to his infant son Marco. The enduring result is a birthday poem in Latin hexameters, of which the first few lines are not without elegance, but which presently degenerates into a catalogue of the incredible number of persons who, unfortunately for the conscientious student of Petrarch, have borne the name of Marcus.

A rather painful incident of a private character has to be noticed as belonging to this period. In 1352 the boy Giovanni, though only fifteen years old, had been appointed to a canonry at Verona,

THE TOMB OF ANDREA DANDOLO, WITH INSCRIPTION BY PETRARCH

and his father had sent him from Vaucluse to take possession of it, commending him to the care of his old schoolmaster Rinaldo and of Gulielmo da Pastrengo. Now, probably owing to his connection with the Visconti, Petrarch lost the favour of Can della Scala, Mastino's heir ; and Giovanni, who may have given a handle to his enemies by some youthful irregularity of conduct, was deprived of his benefice, and returned to live with his father.

The year which brought this domestic anxiety brought also a notable addition to Petrarch's library. In January, 1354, he received from the Greek general, Nicholas Sygerus, who was equally distinguished as a soldier and a scholar, a manuscript of the Homeric Poems in Greek, probably the first copy of Homer sent from East to West since the severance of the Churches. His delight in the possession of this treasure furnishes a touching illustration of his enthusiasm for the classics. " From the extremity of Europe," he writes, "you have sent me a present, the worthiest of yourself, the most acceptable to me, the noblest in intrinsic value that it was possible for you to send. . . . . What gift could come more appropriately from a man of your talent and eloquence than the very fountain-head of all talent and eloquence ? So you have given me Homer, whom Ambrose and Macrobius have well named the fount and origin of all divine imagination. . . . Your gift would be complete indeed, if only you could give me your own presence together with Homer's, so that under your guidance I might enter on the strait path of a foreign language, and enjoy your

gift in the happy fulfilment of my own wish. . . .
Your voice, if only I could hear it, would both
excite and assuage the thirst of learning that possesses me; but it reaches not my ears, and without
it your Homer is dumb to me, or rather I am deaf
to him.   Nevertheless, I rejoice in the mere sight
of him; often I clasp him to my bosom and exclaim
with a sigh, 'Oh, great man! How do I long to
understand thy speech!' . . . Take then my thanks
for your exceeding bounty.   Strange to say, Plato,
the prince of the philosophers, was already in my
house, sent to me from the West. . . . Now
through your generosity the Greek prince of poets
joins the prince of philosophers. . . . If there is
any book that you wish to have from me, I beg
you to let me make a return for your great kindness; use your right to command me.   For I, as
you see, use my right over you; and since success
in begging breeds boldness in the beggar, send me
Hesiod, if your leisure allows, send me, I pray you,
Euripides."

CHAPTER XII

CHARLES IV AND PRAGUE

1354-1357

CHARLES of Luxemburg, Prince of Bohemia, son of the blind King John, was elected King of the Romans in 1346, a few weeks before his father's death at Crécy. Strictly speaking, he should have borne no higher title previous to his coronation, but the stringency of the old rule had become relaxed by courtesy, and we find him constantly addressed as Emperor from the first. His election was the result of a papal intrigue, carried out during the lifetime of his predecessor Lewis "the Bavarian," who had been deposed and excommunicated by three successive Popes. Naturally it was displeasing to those who considered that an Emperor's main function should be to annoy the Pope. Lewis had lived up to this simple view of his duties; he had even, as we have seen, revived the good old imperial practice of setting up an Anti-Pope. Charles IV was the Papacy's effective rejoinder, nearly twenty years delayed, but the Papacy could afford to wait. Militant German imperialists nicknamed him "the Priests' Kaiser," but after the death of Lewis in 1347 his title was generally accepted.

Now, if ever, the White Guelf ideal of Pope and Emperor ruling the world jointly seemed to have its chance. Yet it was not even seriously tried. It is easy for us, who have been enlightened by the genius of Macchiavelli, to comprehend the failure ; for since the days of the great Florentine it has been an accepted axiom that human nature is the most important factor in politics. The White Guelf theory never had a chance precisely because of its logical perfection. Admirable as an embodiment of ordered thought and philosophic synthesis, it lacked just the one thing needful, in that it made no allowance for the friction of human passions. There was just a chance that Petrarch might see this. He had broken loose from the methods of the schoolmen, and had taken the classical writers for his models. If you had said to him that systems were useless unless you could get suitable men to work them, he would have accepted the statement without demur, and would have quoted you a dozen instances of the fact from Livy, and as many illustrations of the principle from Cicero ; in the last year of his life he might even have cited his own admirable treatise *Concerning the Best Methods of Administering a State.* But he did not realise this truth in practical politics, or see how fatal it must be to his hopes, precisely because he stood too near to the Middle Ages, and his own life too closely resembled the lives of the men who had evolved the theory.

Not that he was its bigoted adherent. As we have seen in considering his relations with Rienzi,

the sovereignty of Rome was to him the supreme
end of politics, and he would have welcomed any
means by which that end could be attained. Personally his warmest sympathies were with a revival
of the Roman Republic; but this had been tried and
had failed; and with mingled feelings of disillusionment and hope he took up again the White Guelf
idea, and wrote letter after letter to Charles IV,
urging him by every incentive which could stimu-
late his ambition or rouse his conscience to come to
Italy and cherish his rightful bride. The first of
these letters is assigned by Fracassetti to February,
1350, but contains a passage which makes 1351
seem the more probable date. At the latest, it
was written only about three years after Rienzi's
fall. Frequently during the intervening years there
were rumours that the Emperor was coming to
Italy, but as frequently the Emperor put off the
visit with what seemed to Petrarch frivolous excuses.
The poet spared neither rebuke nor reproach, but
the Emperor bore him no grudge for his plain
speaking. When at last he arrived in Italy, he
invited him to spend a week at his Court, and even
sent Sagramor de Pommières, an officer of his body-
guard, to escort him thither.

Charles had come to Italy with the full assent of
the Pope, to whom he had promised not to spend
more than the actual day of his coronation in Rome,
and to respect the papal sovereignty over the States
of the Church. Early in November, 1354, he
arrived in Padua, where Jacopo's sons and successors received him with every honour, and were

rewarded with the title of Vicars Imperial. Then
came his first disillusionment : Can della Scala shut
the gates of Verona against him. The Visconti
were of course hostile, for, being but a novice in
diplomacy, he had made no secret of his wish to
form a league against them. He went to Mantua,
where the Gonzaga received him well, and where
he expected to find ambassadors from the cities of
Tuscany. Here was his second disappointment; as
the Pope's ally, he had found himself unwelcome to
many of the old Ghibellin families ; now he was
to learn that his imperial title deprived him of all
countenance from the Guelf republics ; of the
Tuscan states only Pisa, pathetically faithful to
her traditions, sent envoys to welcome once more
an Emperor to Italy. The " Priests' Kaiser " had
fallen between two stools. But Charles was no
fool ; he could listen to unpalatable advice and
profit by experience ; and in Italy the lessons of
statecraft, if learnt at all, were learnt quickly.
Charles agreed with his adversaries while he was
in the way with them. He no longer talked of
taming the Visconti's insolence ; on the contrary, he
proposed to receive the Iron Crown of Lombardy
at their hands.

Petrarch's visit must have been useful to Charles
in this change of front. If he wanted an occasion
for opening communications with Milan, here was
one which could be either kept free from the taint
of politics, or made to serve as an introduction to
them. The visit was also a great success from the
point of view of the visitor. He travelled through

the coldest weather in living memory, but the warmth of his welcome made ample amends. Charles received him with frank courtesy, and to his vast delight kept him talking night after night into the small hours. Charles asked him about the *Lives of Illustrious Men*. Petrarch seized his opportunity, and while telling him that it was not yet ready for publication, promised to dedicate it to him if his actions were such as to deserve it, and if he himself were spared to finish it. And to keep him in mind of the great men whom he was to imitate, Petrarch made him a present of some very beautiful gold and silver medals of the Cæsars, among which the portrait of Augustus especially almost seemed to have the breath of life. We must credit Charles with rare magnanimity, or perhaps it were juster to say we must credit Petrarch with rare charm, when we find that at the end of the discourse which accompanied the gift the Emperor urged his lecturer to go with him to Rome. Petrarch's account of the visit, written in a letter to Lælius, leaves us with the impression that both he and Charles must have had an insatiable appetite for talk.

Presently the Emperor moved on to Milan and became the Visconti's guest. This was not a happy visit; Galeazzo excelled in the art of polite discourtesy, and while nothing was done that must necessarily provoke a rupture, nothing was omitted that could bring home to the Emperor the sense of his own weakness and the power of his hosts. On the Feast of the Epiphany, 1355, Charles received

the Iron Crown of Lombardy, not at Monza, but in
the church of St. Ambrose at Milan.   When he left
the city, Petrarch, though unable to accept his invitation to go to Rome, accompanied him as far as
the fifth milestone beyond Piacenza.   He went on
to Pisa, where Lælius waited on him with a letter
of introduction from Petrarch, and so to Rome,
where he received the imperial crown on April 4th.
He returned by way of Pisa, where he was pleased,
on May 14th, to bestow the Laurel Crown of Poetry
on Zanobi da Strada, Niccolò Acciaiuoli's secretary,
who has been already mentioned as a friend and
frequent correspondent of Petrarch.   The meaning
of this strange freak has never been quite clear.
The obvious suggestion is that it must have been
meant as a snub to Petrarch, perhaps a hint that
there were other poets, who might be less exigent
in the matter of an Emperor's deeds before they
praised him; but the history of the three men's
personal relations makes against this easy explanation.   There is no hint of anything but extreme
cordiality between Charles and Petrarch, and only
the merest conjecture that the latter's amicable
relations with Zanobi were ever interrupted.   Besides, Charles was not a fool in literature any more
than in politics; he had taste and judgment; and
he would have been fully alive to the absurdity of
setting up this painstaking grammarian, capable
private secretary, and respectable writer of verse as
a rival to Petrarch.   Such folly could only have
emphasised the latter's superiority to all living
poets.   Perhaps the explanation may be simply that

the Emperor wanted a laureate of his own making, and took what he could get. From Pisa Charles made his way northwards, and, to Petrarch's indignation, returned to Germany in June. His Italian tour had given him two crowns, and rid him of a few illusions.

During the whole month of September Petrarch suffered from an unusually violent and prolonged attack of the tertian fever, to which he was always liable at that season. He rose from his bed at the beginning of October so weak in body that he could hardly hold a pen, but with his temper exasperated afresh against the physicians. He took up the old feud with renewed acrimony, and the violent *Invective against a Physician* is the unhappy result. It is not to be doubted that much of the medicine of that day was mere quackery, and a calmly reasoned exposure of the knavery of many practitioners and the folly of their dupes, put forth by a man of Petrarch's influence, might have served as a useful aid in the promotion of serious research; but the intemperate vehemence of Petrarch's invective, though it seems to have commanded Boccaccio's admiration, could only defeat its own object. Not only the quacks whom he was justified in attacking, but the earnest students who were labouring to better the rudimentary science of their time, must have been set against the man who thus vilified the whole profession. Yet in spite of this furious diatribe Petrarch had pleasant relations with more than one physician to whom he was personally known; and in later years the eminent Dondi dell'

Orologio enjoyed his intimate friendship, and possessed the precious Virgil after his death.

Meanwhile a tragedy had happened in the Visconti family. On September 26th Matteo, the eldest brother, was found dead in his bed. That his brothers should be accused of poisoning him was only natural; but even in that age men heard with horror that the bereaved mother was the loudest accuser of her surviving sons. The brothers denied the charge, and their partisans plausibly attributed Matteo's death to debauchery. Their guilt is doubtful, but they certainly divided the inheritance.

About this time the whirligig of Italian politics brought Petrarch a new friend. For two years the warrior-priest, Cardinal Albornoz, had been fighting and negotiating as the Pope's Legate in Italy, and so successful had he been alike in arms and in diplomacy, that he had brought the greater part of Romagna and the March, as well as the ancient States of the Church, either into direct obedience to the Holy See, or to an admission of its overlordship. Among the great houses reduced to obedience were the Malatesta of Rimini, whom the Legate deprived of the great bulk of their usurped possessions, while allowing them to retain Rimini itself and three other cities, as vassals of the Church. Their diminished possessions hardly gave scope enough to the more ambitious younger members of the House, and Pandolfo Malatesta, who was at once the best soldier and the best scholar of the family, took service with Galeazzo Visconti as

general of his cavalry.   Before knowing Petrarch
personally, he had conceived so great an admiration
for him, that he commissioned an artist, whose
name is unknown to us, to paint him a portrait of
the poet.   The picture is declared by Petrarch to
have been at once expensive and bad, but he was
undoubtedly flattered by the compliment and predisposed to like Pandolfo.   They met in Milan, and
a warm and lasting friendship resulted.

But clients of the Visconti could not hope for
the continuous enjoyment of each other's society.
The general of cavalry in particular was not left
long in idleness.   To narrate the intrigues of these
years in detail would require a good-sized volume ;
briefly, it may be said that leagues against the
Visconti were perpetually being formed, dissolved,
and formed again.   In the winter of 1355-6,
Giovanni Paleologo, Marquis of Montferrat, and
Milano Beccaria, tyrant of Pavia, both of them once
the allies and now the opponents of the Milanese
Princes, joined in organising such a league.   The
Marquis's share in its operations was to excite a
rebellion against Galeazzo in Piedmont, and Pandolfo Malatesta found plenty of occupation for his
sword in fighting the revolted cities.   A still more
serious incident connected with the same affair soon
afterwards took Petrarch on a distant errand of
diplomacy.   It was more than suspected that the
Emperor, who had not forgotten the humiliation
inflicted on him the year before, was secretly sup-
porting the Visconti's enemies, and still more alarm-
ing rumours were current of a proposed invasion of

Italy by the allied forces of Bohemia, Hungary, and Austria. The Visconti had no mind to apologise for the past, but their hands were full enough for the moment, and partly to put the Emperor in good humour, partly to spy out his intentions, they dispatched an embassy to him, with Petrarch as its orator. It is not to be supposed that the practical business of the embassy was entrusted to him; he was to be its ornamental figure-head, and we can see from the letter in which he tells Nelli of his appointment that he quite grasped the situation. He had showered reproaches on Charles at the time of his departure from Italy; now he would catch him in his own kingdom, and have at him again for his ignoble and most unimperial flight. "So," says he, "whether my journey be for any profit or no, at any rate I shall be my own ambassador." To tell the king to whom you are accredited that he is but a poor creature would not strike a conventional diplomatist as the best way of propitiating him; but once again we may take it that the Visconti knew their men.

Petrarch set out on May 20th, and again enjoyed the pleasure of having Sagramor de Pommières for a travelling companion. They went first to Bâle, where they expected to find the Emperor, but Charles was not there, and, after waiting some weeks, they started for Prague. They had left just in time. Only a few days later the whole basin of the Rhine was shaken by a tremendous earthquake. Over eighty castles are said to have been destroyed by the successive shocks, which continued at in-

tervals for many months; and in every town from
Bâle to Trèves houses fell and the citizens had to
camp in the fields. The first shock, which Petrarch
and his companions just escaped, was especially
severe at Bâle, and laid almost the entire city in
ruins.

The ambassadors found the Emperor in Prague,
and Petrarch's colleagues must have noted with
satisfaction that his hands were much too full of
German business to permit of his present intervention in Italy. He, whose own election had been
secured by every device of trickery, was busy with
his famous Golden Bull—the Reform Bill of Imperial
Elections. Also, however unworthy a successor he
may have been to Augustus in politics, he was
diligently following his example in the embellishment of his capital.

We have no details of this visit to Prague. We
know only that Petrarch was received with undiminished cordiality by the Emperor, and that he
spent much time in the congenial society of two
great ecclesiastics of the Court, Johann Oczko,
Bishop of Olmutz, and Ernest von Pardowitz,
Archbishop of Prague. Petrarch's acquaintance
with these two distinguished men, begun in Italy,
now ripened to friendship, and many of his later
letters are addressed to them. But perhaps the best
fruit of his embassy was the intimacy with Sagramor
de Pommières, which resulted from their companionship in travel, and grew so close that a year or two
afterwards he could speak of Sagramor as "privy
to his every thought and act." The visit brought

him also the dignity of Count Palatine, conferred
on him by the Emperor some months after his
departure, and later still the honour of an auto-
graph letter from the Empress Anna, informing him
that she had been safely delivered of a son.

He returned to Milan at the beginning of September, and declared to Lælius that the more he
travelled abroad the more he loved Italy.

In the following year (1357) occurred an incident,
the memory of which Petrarch's admirers would
willingly let die. During the winter events had
happened at Pavia which curiously anticipated by a
century and a half Savonarola's celebrated revolution in Florence. An eloquent and earnest monk,
named Jacopo Bussolari, set himself to combat from
the pulpit the vices and bad government of the
Visconti. So far, his sermons were heard without
distaste by the Beccaria, but their attitude changed
when, from denunciation of the Milanese tyrants,
Bussolari proceeded to crusade against tyranny
and vice in general, with pointed allusions to the
occupants of the adjoining palace. The Beccaria
tried the usual tyrant's answer to criticism ; but all
their plots to assassinate Bussolari were discovered,
and the successive discoveries raised him from the
position of a popular preacher to that of a national
prophet, saint, and hero. At last he ended a sermon
of surpassing eloquence by bidding the people
organise a free government under leaders whom he
designated by name. The people rose as one man
at his call, and a republican government was installed under the eyes of the Beccaria, who were

expelled one by one from the liberated city. In
desperation they turned to their old allies and
recent foes, the Visconti, surrendered to them their
fortified country houses, and organised a plot to
put them in possession of the city. This plot also
failed, and for a time Pavia enjoyed the blessings
of freedom. Surely this was a movement with
which he who applauded Rienzi should have sym-
pathised. Alas! Pavia was not Rome, and the
iron-willed Visconti held Petrarch in a grip far
stronger than that of the House of Colonna. At
Galeazzo's instigation, he managed to persuade
himself that Bussolari was a mere adventurer, a
charlatan, who had deluded the people with empty
phrases, that he might use them as his instruments
to work out the selfish aims of unbridled ambition.
He wrote Bussolari a letter of insolent reproof and
impertinent exhortation, which we can hardly read
for shame and would gladly delete from the manuscripts which it deforms. Affection for Galeazzo,
to whom he considered himself indebted for his life,
is the one admissible palliation, and it is pitiably
inadequate. True, that liberty in the fourteenth
century did not imply democracy, and that Petrarch
would conscientiously have pronounced mob-rule
the worst of tyrannies. Still Bussolari's cause was
that of civil liberty, self-government, and moral
purity; Galeazzo stood prominent, the champion
of a tyranny which encouraged every vice. Surely
the man who could bid Charles live up to the
standard of Augustus might have used his influence
with Galeazzo to soften, if he could not turn aside,

his wrath against Bussolari. But communication with the Visconti had corrupted Petrarch's manners; Nelli and Boccaccio were justified of all their fears. Let it be added, however, that this is the single instance of Petrarch's degradation ; in no other case did he accept a commission from the Visconti which he could not honourably fulfil.

CHAPTER XIII

DOMESTICA

1357-1360

SO far as regards Petrarch's connection with
public affairs, the years to be dealt with in this
chapter are the least eventful of his life. But they
are notable for some interesting personal experi-
ences, and, above all, as the period at which the
poet himself took a review of his past life and work.
They offer, therefore, an admirable occasion for
a similar review by his biographer, and an attempt
will be made in the following chapter to take advantage of the opportunity.

First, however, we must notice the few domestic
events which belong to the period.

One of these shows Petrarch at his very best.
A most distressing thing had happened in the circle
of his friends. After all these years of unbroken
affection, Socrates and Lælius had quarrelled; worst
of all, they had quarrelled about Petrarch. Some
slanderous liar had told Lælius that Socrates had
represented him as opposing Petrarch's interests at
Avignon. Lælius was furious, Socrates heart-
broken, Petrarch in a state of mind which without
hyperbole he describes as agony. The moment he
heard of the miserable business, he sat down and

wrote Lælius a long, impetuous letter of loving remonstrance with him for having believed the lie, and of most loving entreaty that he would believe the truth now and make it up with Socrates. He was your friend, says Petrarch, even before he was mine. We have lived eight-and-twenty years together, the three of us, in the closest union of souls. You know him incapable of such baseness; how could you believe it of him for a moment? You should have thrust the calumny from you, as Alexander did when his friend and physician was accused of being bribed to poison him, and he drank off the draught before showing the accusation to his friend. "Friendship is a great, a divine thing," he goes on, "and quite simple. It requires much deliberation, but once only and once for all. You must choose your friend before you begin to love him; once you have chosen him, to love him is your only course. When once you have had pleasure in your friend, the time to measure him is past. 'Tis an old proverb that bids us not to be doing what is done already. Thenceforward there is no room for suspicion or quarrel; there remains to us but this one thing—to love." Compare with this admirable passage the equally beautiful sentence in a letter to Nelli, written a few years earlier: "In my friendships I practise no art, except to love utterly, to trust utterly, to feign nothing, to hide nothing, and, in a word, to pour out everything into my friends' ears, just as it comes from my heart." Petrarch's pleading was irresistible, and to his delight he heard before long that Lælius had no sooner read his letter, than he had gone straight with it to Socrates, and with tears and embraces they had knit afresh the ancient bonds of affection. The friend who had brought them together was as happy in their reconciliation as he had been miserable at their estrangement. "All your life you have done me pleasure on pleasure," he wrote to Lælius, "but never a keener pleasure than this."

This was by no means the only time in his life that Petrarch played the part of peacemaker among his friends. We find him, for instance, doing the same office for Nicolò Acciaiuoli and Barili, and with equal success; but the matter never went so near his heart as in this quarrel between Lælius and Socrates. "Till this day," he wrote in this letter to Lælius, "we had lived together not merely in harmony, but, as one might say, with only one mind in the three of us." And nothing can be more charming or more touching than the grace with which in the letter of congratulation he gives Lælius all the credit for his prompt act of reconciliation, and is satisfied for his own part with the pure delight of his friends' reunion. Whatever may have been his qualities or his defects as an Ambassador of State, the world has not seen his superior in the delicate diplomacies of friendship.

In the congratulatory letter to Lælius, there is a passage which makes it clear that once again Petrarch's friends at the Papal Court had proposed to get him the offer of the papal secretaryship, and once more he had been able to defeat their well-meant intentions, this time without mystery or

secret machination.   He was less than ever inclined
for the office.   He had fewer friends among the
Cardinals than of old, and Pope Innocent, as we
have seen, had been violently prepossessed against
him at the beginning of his reign.   That temper,
indeed, must have changed already, or Lælius and
the rest could not have dreamt of getting the
appointment for Petrarch.   Still, Innocent was not
his friend as Clement had been, and he says himself
that his position at the Curia was very different
now from what it had been a dozen years before.
The post was given to Zanobi da Strada, at whose
promotion Petrarch sincerely rejoiced, reckoning that
he had now a new friend in Avignon, and regretting
only that Zanobi would have no more time for
poetry.   The language of this passage sufficiently
refutes the absurd calumny, for which there is not
a scrap of first-hand evidence, that Petrarch was
jealous of Zanobi.

To avoid the tediousness of perpetually recurring
to the subject of the papal secretaryship, it may be
mentioned here that Pope Innocent's old hostility
to Petrarch presently changed into so cordial a feeling towards him, that in the last year of his pontifi-
cate he made him a direct and formal offer of the
post, and that a year later his successor, Urban V,
repeated the offer.   Petrarch was still resolute in
declining, but none the less the incident of 1361
shows both men in an agreeable light.   The Pope
who could thus revise his own judgments must
have possessed a sense of justice rare among bigots,
and there must have been something singularly

INNOCENT VI

attractive about the man in whose favour such judgments could be reversed.

In the early autumn of 1358 he suffered an accident which may be narrated in his own words. "You shall hear," he writes to a friend, "what a trick Cicero, the man whom I have loved and worshipped from my boyhood, has just played me. I possess a huge volume of his Letters, which I wrote out some time ago with my own hand because there was no original manuscript accessible to the copyists. Ill-health hindered me, but my great love of Cicero, and delight in the Letters, and eagerness to possess them, prevailed against my bodily weakness and the laboriousness of the work. This is the book which you have seen leaning against the door-post at the entry to my library. One day, while going into the room thinking about something else, as I often do, I happened inadvertently to catch the book in the fringe of my gown. In its fall it struck me lightly on the left leg a little above the heel. 'What! my Cicero,' quoth I, bantering him, 'pray what are you hitting me for?' He said nothing. But next day, as I came again the same way, he hit me again, and again I laughed at him and set him up in his place. Why make a long story? Over and over again I went on suffering the same hurt; and thinking he might be cross at having to stand on the ground, I put him up a shelf higher, but not till after the repeated blows on the same spot had broken the skin, and a far from despicable sore had resulted. I despised it though, reckoning the cause of my accident of much more weight than the accident itself. So I neither gave up my bath, nor put any restraint on myself in the matter of riding and walking, but just waited for the thing to heal. Little by little, as if hurt at my neglect of it, the wound swelled up, and presently a patch of flesh came up, discoloured and angry. At last, when the pain was too much not only for my wit, but for sleep and rest, so that to neglect the thing any longer seemed not courage but madness, I was forced to call in the doctors, who have now for some days been fussing over this really ridiculous wound, not without great pain and some danger to the wounded limb, as they insist, though I think you know just what reliance I place on their prognostications either of good or evil. At the same time I am bothered with constant fomentations, and am cut off my usual food, and obliged to keep still, to which I am quite un-accustomed. I hate the whole business, and especi-ally I hate being obliged to eat sumptuous fare. But health is now in sight, and you may hear of me, as I have of you, that I am well again, before knowing anything of my having been ill. . . . So this is how my beloved Cicero has treated me ; he long ago struck my heart, and now he has struck my leg."

Before the wound was fully healed, two days in fact before the above letter was written, he paid a visit which is notable as showing how enthusiasm for the revival of learning was spreading through different classes of Italian society ; it also illustrates the lines of social cleavage in fourteenth-century Italy.

There lived at Bergamo a goldsmith named
Enrico Capra, an old man who had grown rich by
skill in his handicraft, for he was a working smith,
and not to be confounded with the banker gold-
smiths of Florence or Genoa. As a young man
he was little versed in letters, but had always a
natural inclination to them. Late in life he heard
of Petrarch's reputation as a scholar; his imagination was kindled, and he resolved to give up everything for study. Petrarch was his hero. His
highest ambition was now to be a humble scholar
in the studies of which Petrarch was the master.
He consulted his idol, and Petrarch, with that
practical good sense which is so disconcerting to
people who would like to put poets and sensible
men into separate pigeon-holes, advised him strongly
to stick to his trade. "For," said he, "it is late for
you to strike out an entirely new line, and your
private affairs may suffer." In this one thing, Capra
was deaf to his hero's advice. He gave up his
business and set himself to school. One supreme
desire now possessed him, to have the honour of
entertaining Petrarch as his guest, if it were but for
a single night. Petrarch's fashionable friends would
have dissuaded him from the visit, representing
that it was beneath his dignity to be a tradesman's
guest. He knew better, and was too much a
gentleman to be ruled by them. He has often been
accused of courting great men, and it is perfectly
true that he did like to sit on the right hand of
princes. But what he liked in it was the feeling
that he had power to influence the powerful. He

was no vulgar devotee of mere riches or mere rank. He would have been worse than a barbarian, worse than a wild beast, he declares, if he had refused Capra's request. The man carried the fervency of his desire writ plain in eyes and brow. So to Bergamo he went, and with him rode some of his fine friends, curious to see how the goldsmith would deport himself. The goldsmith was above everything anxious that Petrarch should not be bored; he abounded in conversation, and the fine gentlemen had to acknowledge that the excellence of their entertainment made the way seem short. When they reached Bergamo it seemed as if the whole town had turned out to receive Petrarch. There were the governor, the captain of the militia, and all the city dignitaries, pressing on him a public reception at the palace and entertainment at the house of one of the chief men. Again Capra trembled with apprehension, but Petrarch knew what good manners and good feeling required of him. He was the goldsmith's guest, and with civil excuses to the great folks he went to the goldsmith's house. There he found such entertainment as Prague itself had not provided for him. He dined off gold plate, and slept in a bed hung with imperial purple, in which, vowed his host, no other man had ever slept, or ever should. There were plenty of books too, "not a mechanician's books, but those of a student and a most zealous lover of letters." Petrarch might have stayed more than one night if he could have been left alone with his delighted host, but he ran away from the otherwise

inevitable civic festivities. The governor and the
town councillors, unable to keep him as a guest, accompanied him a great part of the way home, but
it is pleasant to know that they were outridden by
Enrico Capra, who saw his hero safe to the very
threshold of his home.

Petrarch spent a good part of the winter at
Padua, where he had business to transact, and at
Venice, where he stayed for pleasure; and in the
spring of 1359 he enjoyed the exquisite pleasure
of a visit from Boccaccio. We feel a kind of pride
in human nature when we see how completely their
difference of opinion about Petrarch's residence in
Milan had failed to impair their friendship. Silvanus cannot have enjoyed being told that his
new friend Egon was a blood-thirsty renegade;
but Nelli and Boccaccio might say to him what
they liked. To them he had given his heart, and
he lived up to his own fine sentiment, that when
once you have given your heart, there is nothing
left for you but to love. Moreover, he held that
there should be no concealments between friends;
it was Boccaccio's duty, then, to show him all that
was in his heart. Boccaccio's attitude seems to
have been equally pleasing. He did not retract
his opinion, but he had had his say, and the decision
did not lie with him. His relations with Petrarch
illustrate the modesty of which genius may be
capable : he constantly insisted on taking the place
of a disciple ; and he would not be fatuous enough
to suppose that the master must always see eye to
eye with him. So this loyal Florentine made his

pilgrimage to the city which he hated and the friend
whom he loved. There had been a constant inter-
change of letters and poems between them since
their last meeting. Boccaccio had sent on one
occasion St. Augustine's Commentary on the Psalms,
on another some works of Cicero and Varro copied
with his own hand for his friend's library. Then
we find Petrarch acknowledging the receipt of
several letters, and alluding to one of his own which
had been lost in transmission. And Boccaccio
having protested against being called a poet, Petrarch rallies him on his petulance. "A strange
thing," he says, "that you should have aimed at
being a poet only to shrink from the name." And
from what follows, we may gather that Boccaccio
felt legitimately aggrieved that his poetical work
had not won him the recognition of the laurel. We
gather too that the Milanese visit was a project
of long standing. At last in the early spring of
1359 it was realised, and Petrarch writes to Nelli :
"I should send you a longer letter, but that I am
prevented by a want of time which is of my own
making, to wit, through the most delightful companionship of our common friend, to whose visit
there are only two drawbacks—the shortness of it
and your absence. The pleasant days have slipped
away silently and unperceived. But our friend's
own voice will tell you what my pen has no time
for ; you can trust implicitly in his report, for he
knows perfectly my every thought, my every action,
my manner of life, in a word my whole self, and all
my little haps and hopes."

Boccaccio left about the end of March in wild weather, but reached Florence without accident. Soon afterwards he sent Petrarch a copy of the *Divina Commedia*, together with a poetical Latin letter, in which he begged "Italy's glory and his own dear friend and single hope" to accept, read, and admire the great work of the poet-exile, who first showed the world of what achievements in verse his mother-tongue was capable; his brow deserved the laurel which it failed to obtain; Florence, the great mother of poets, bore him and takes her place of pride among cities under the championship of his glorious name; in honouring him, his brother-poets do honour to themselves and their craft. In this last sentiment, or in the exhortation to read Dante, Petrarch may have seen ever so delicate a hint of the common belief that he was jealous of the latter's fame, though Boccaccio had spared no possible words of compliment to himself. His answer is quite candid, and gives a faithful picture of his sentiments. The supposition that he was jealous of the elder poet's fame rests on a far different basis from the silly gossip that he envied Zanobi. "Jealousy" of Dante is not, indeed, the right word, but want of appreciation must be admitted. He is quite sincere in saying to Boccaccio that "Dante easily carries off the palm among writers in Italian," and this is not the language of jealousy; nor is his protestation that he "admires and venerates" Dante less sincere. But the pith of the whole matter lies in that passage of unconscious self-revelation, where he protests that his admiration of the great Florentine, as of every one else, is critical, and really implies a much higher compliment to its object than the indiscriminate gush with which his ignorant worshippers bedaub their idol. Exactly; Petrarch admired Dante "critically," but he read him very little, and radical difference of temperament made it impossible that he should be in sympathy with him.

The autumn of 1359 brought a very sad incident in Petrarch's domestic life. For years Giovanni's character and conduct had been a source of painful anxiety to his father. At last the young man's faults of temper, aggravated by the elder's faults of management, resulted in an open breach. We have only Petrarch's side of the story, and not very much of that, but it is enough to show us quite clearly the cause and the nature of his unhappy relations with his son. He was a man predisposed to affection, predisposed also to count his geese swans. He was the last man in the world to belittle the virtues or exaggerate the sins of those who belonged to him. There can be no doubt that the lad was slothful, sullen, and prone to a disorderly life. Only by very judicious handling could his better qualities, of which Petrarch's friends discerned the rudiments, have a chance to win the day. Judicious handling was exactly what Petrarch could not give him. Sarcasm and sermonising are the very worst tools for fashioning the character of such a boy, and Petrarch, honestly anxious to shame Giovanni into industry and instil into him a virtuous ambition, was at once sarcastic and didactic. The

circumstances of their relationship probably aggravated the evil. Petrarch, as we have seen, had
procured letters of legitimacy for Giovanni, which
of course involved an admission of paternity, and
his friends knew the whole story. But the word
"son" was seldom if ever used in the intercourse
of daily life, and though Nelli, to whom the lad
paid an apparently happy visit at Avignon in 1358,
spoke of him as Giovanni Petrarca, his position
was one which only devoted love and tactful sympathy could have rendered tolerable. Now, in these
years, Petrarch, sick of town life, had found himself
a retreat entirely to his mind, which he called
Liternum after Scipio's famous Campanian villa,
a few miles outside the city walls. While he was
living there a robbery occurred in his house at
Milan, which was traced to members of his own
household. Coincidently, Giovanni was guilty of
misconduct so grave that Petrarch expelled him
from his house. This is all that can be said with
certainty, but we may surely infer that Giovanni
was found to be a participator in the robbery, if not
its instigator.

It may have been this unhappy occurrence which
finally determined Petrarch to give up his house in
Milan, and transfer himself and his possessions to
the Benedictine monastery of San Simpliciano,
where, though only just outside the city, he could
enjoy all the pleasures of life in the country, and
where his precious books would, in his absence, be
under the guardianship of the brothers. He chose
his rooms with judgment. They contained a con-

venience which had been wanting in his town house
—a little secret door which he could use as a bolt-
hole to escape from unwelcome visitors.   Here he
settled on November 3rd, and here in the following
August he received a visit from Niccolò Acciaiuoli,
with whom, as we have seen, he had long been in
friendly communication, but whom he appears never
to have met till now.   The Grand Seneschal was
an expert in ceremonial; Matteo Villani even hints
that he carried ostentation to a fault; and nothing
was omitted that stately pomp and gracious dignity
could contribute to mark the homage which he paid
to Petrarch's genius.   But the pleasantest touch in
the visit was the eagerness with which he pounced
on the poet's books, and his unwillingness to tear
himself away from them.

THE TOMB OF NICCOLÒ ACCIAIUOLI

CHAPTER XIV

THE FOUNDER OF HUMANISM—
PETRARCH'S WORK AND ITS RESULT

IT was in 1359 that Petrarch faced that worst ordeal of a writer's life, the revision of his papers. The letter to Socrates, which serves as preface to the collection of *Familiar Letters*, shows him in a retrospective mood of rather melancholy sentiment. "We have tried wellnigh all things, my brother, and nowhere is rest. When are we to look for it? Where to seek it? Time, as the saying goes, has slipped through our fingers. Our old hopes lie buried in the graves of our friends. It was the year 1348 that made us lonely men and poor; for it took away from us treasures which not the Indian or the Caspian or the Carparthian Sea can restore. . . . Now what thought you are taking for yourself, my brother, I know not; for my part, I am just making up my bundles, and, as men do on the eve of a journey, am looking out what to take with me, what to share among my friends, and what to throw into the fire; for I have nothing to sell." So he dived into the rusty chests, and presently found himself "ringed round with heaped piles of letters, blockaded by a shapeless mass of paper." His first impulse was to save bother by throwing the lot into the fire; and after a little indulgence in the pathos of retrospect, he began the work of destruction. "A thousand or more compositions, some of them stray poems of every kind, the rest familiar letters, were thus given over to Vulcan's revision, not without a sigh indeed, for why should I be ashamed to own my weakness?" While these were burning, he bethought him of another bundle lying in a corner, and containing letters many of which had already been transcribed by friends. These he thought would give little or no trouble, so he spared them, and in fulfilment of an old promise resolved to dedicate the prose to Socrates, the verse to Barbato. Here one might well suppose the story of the *Epistolæ de Rebus Familiaribus* and of the *Epistolæ Poeticæ* to be complete; but he who expects finality little knows his Petrarch. What follows may serve as a characteristic instance of his method of work; he was for ever polishing, correcting, interpolating. Two years after writing the preface he nominally closed the *Familiar* series with a second dedicatory letter to Socrates. "With you I began," he writes, "with you I finish; here, my Socrates, you have what you asked for. . . . I began this work in youth, I finish it in old age, or rather I am still continuing what I then began. For this is the one pursuit of mine to which death alone will put the finishing touch. How can I expect to cease from chatting with my friends till my life ceases? . . . Whatever I may write in this kind henceforward will be classed in another volume under a title derived from my time of life, since my friends are so fond as to forbid my withholding any of my writings from them." Even this was not the final arrangement. Socrates died, probably before receiving the letter just quoted, and the collection, made as a token of devoted friendship, became its pathetic record. As such Petrarch once more revised it, and while doing so actually inserted a few letters belonging to the four intervening years. At last, in 1365, with the help of one of his pupils, he arranged the series practically as we have it to-day. He meant it to contain 350 letters; in Fracassetti's edition, which is the most complete, it contains 347; but possibly some of those which Fracassetti published as an appendix were intended by Petrarch to have a place in the body of the volume. The collection is divided into twenty-four books, of which the last contains the *Letters to Illustrious Men of Antiquity;* the rest, Petrarch tells us, are "for the most part" in chronological order, but the qualifying words require a pretty liberal interpretation. Besides these, he preserved some other letters which, to avoid repetition and tediousness, he kept by themselves; these formed the nucleus of the single book of *Various Letters*, intended to contain seventy and actually containing sixty-five epistles. The earliest letter of all was written in 1326, the latest in 1365; but substantially the series extends from 1331 to 1361, with which year the series of *Letters written in Old Age* begins. Of the authorised prose letters, we have thus three classes—the *Familiar*, the *Various*, and the *Senile*. In addition to these, a ᴏᴏᴋ is extant of *Letters without Title* (*Sine Titulo*), diatribes against the corruptions of Church and clergy, which Petrarch kept carefully secret during his life. But as he preserved the manuscript of them, we may suppose that he intended them to be published after his death.

Of all Petrarch's writings the prose letters are the most important; of all his Latin writings they are, by a happy coincidence, the most delightful reading. As evidence of the events of their author's life, they outweigh all the other biographical materials put together, and this is perhaps the least of their many merits. The extracts given in these pages must have been ill-chosen and ill-translated if the reader has not realised from them that the letters reveal a personality of singularly human interest and poignant charm. So far as regards mere facts, Petrarch's habit of revision and interpolation occasionally—though very seldom and only in matters of secondary importance—tends to weaken or confuse the testimony. But there is not a page, not a line, not a word, which does not bear the true stamp of its author's individuality. "If we must needs keep ourselves before the eye of the public," he once wrote, "by all means let us show ourselves off in books and chat in letters." Exactly; the man stands revealed in the "chat" of the letters written to his intimate friends.

Not that he was ever indifferent to style. He might say with truth that he wrote to his friends whatever came uppermost in his own mind; and he might believe himself to be equally truthful in

saying that he was not careful about the adornment of these familiar talks. But he simply could
not be careless about workmanship; nature had
given him the instinct for style, and whatever he
wrote must be written with the inborn grace of the
artist.

He knew too that a letter from him was regarded
as a literary star of the first magnitude; eager
friends copied the precious manuscript and circulated
it through Europe. Boccaccio speaks of these
letters with a kind of rapture as equal to Cicero's;
and though the pronouncement shows that criticism,
which Petrarch had brought anew to the birth, was
still in its infancy, it shows also the extreme importance of the letters in furthering the main work of
their author's life—the revival of learning.

In attributing to Petrarch the initiation of this
mighty movement, a word of caution may be found
in season. People sometimes talk as if history
could be likened to a row of pigeon-holes, and as if
events once classified and docketed as belonging to
pigeon-hole B could thenceforward be regarded as
quite dissociated from the contents of pigeon-hole
A. Of course nobody maintains such an absurdity
in theory, but classification is so useful an aid to
memory, that in practice we are continually tempted
to draw hard-and-fast lines of division. No error
is more fatal to the right understanding of history;
it robs even definite events of half their meaning;
much more does it distort and obscure the significance of intellectual developments. The life of the
world's mind is like the life of a forest; birth,

growth, death, go on side by side; while the forest is older than its oldest tree, its youngest sapling may claim an immemorial lineage. When therefore we say that Petrarch founded Humanism and inaugurated the New Learning, we do not mean that he created something out of nothing; we mean that he inspired ideas and modes of thought, which preceding scholars had possessed in their own brains, but could not communicate to society at large. It is true that few successive periods are as sharply contrasted as the Middle Ages and the Renaissance; but even so it is false history to represent the Middle Ages as a night of pitchy blackness, the Renaissance as a blaze of unheralded light. Scholarship had never died; our own England furnishes proof of that. John of Salisbury in the twelfth century was as good a Latinist as Petrarch, and Robert Grosseteste in the thirteenth had a competent knowledge of Greek. None the less it is to Petrarch, not to his predecessors, that we rightly attribute the inauguration of the Renaissance; they were its forerunners, not its founders; they handed down the torch of learning unextinguished; some quality in him enabled him to fire the world with it.

His method was not merely to study the classics as ancient literature, but to bring the world back to the mental standpoint of the classical writers. To do this it was essential to spread the knowledge of those writers as widely as possible, and we have seen how diligent he and his friends were in the discovery and reproduction of texts. Then men had to be convinced that the affairs of old Rome were of vital interest to fourteenth-century Italy, and so Petrarch gave to the world the stimulating conception of the continuity of history. Lastly, it was necessary to set up again the fallen standard of criticism. Criticism does not mean fault-finding; the correction of error is only one of its functions. Its main business is to look below the surface of things, to apprehend their true significance, to appraise their just value. This intellectual faculty was conspicuously lacking in the men of the Middle Ages, but the classical men possess it in rich abundance. Now of all the classical writers known to Petrarch he esteemed Cicero "far and away the chief captain," the wisest thinker, the most discerning critic, the supreme master of style. Saturated himself with the Ciceronian spirit, he set himself to diffuse it through Europe. He was no slavish worshipper even of Cicero; he paid his great master the higher compliment of discriminating enthusiasm. Like all true apostles, he was less concerned to imitate the manner of his models than to preach their gospel. This was probably the secret of his success; the revival of classical learning became in his hands a resurrection of the classical spirit.

Judged as mere compositions, his own Latin writings fell far short of the masterpieces which inspired them, and he himself was fully conscious of their inferiority. Once, he tells Boccaccio, he had thought of writing solely in Italian, moved thereto by the consideration that the ancients had written so perfectly in Latin as to be inimitable.

This must have been a mere passing thought; from earliest youth onward he felt instinctively that to write the best Latin he could was the way to propagate the Roman culture.

This sound instinct explains the depreciatory tone in which he sometimes spoke of his Italian poems. It is not to be supposed that the man who could write the *Canzoniere* was blind to its beauty; and the pains which he undoubtedly took to polish and perfect it show that he appreciated the exquisite art of its workmanship. He knew, too, how greatly it was instrumental in winning him the fame that he loved. But, almost as if he had foreseen the degradation of the Petrarchist school, he seems to have felt that not here would lie his real claim to the world's gratitude. It is easy to go too far, as Petrarch himself went, in minimising the importance of the *Canzoniere*. The poems are quick with the genius of Humanism, and their revelation of the subtlest workings of a human soul must have done much to imbue mankind with a thirst for the study of man. Still it remains a curious fact that Petrarch's most beautiful poetry was precisely the least influential of his writings in furthering his life's work.

It has already been said that the most influential were the prose letters, which contain samples of everything that can possibly be put into epistolary form. Far inferior to them in charm, but almost equally important in the history of literature, are the three books of poetical letters. These too contain an infinite variety of subjects, from impassioned appeals to successive Popes for the re-

storation of the Papacy to a graceful description of
his "battle with the Nymphs of the Sorgue" for
the reclamation of a garden for the Muses. It is
hardly possible for us to appreciate these poems at
their full value. Petrarch indeed handles Latin as
a living language, his idiom is seldom seriously at
fault, his diction is choice and his versification
fluent; his hexameters might quite well be mistaken, as actually happened in the case of a passage
from the *Africa*, for those of some poet of the
Silver Age. But our ears have been attuned to
finer harmonies, and Petrarch's verses cannot stand
comparison with those of Virgil and Horace, or even
with the graceful compositions of Politian, the most
accomplished Humanist of the following century.
Moreover, defects of form are much more noticeable, not to say more irritating, in verse than in
prose; and rich as are these poetical letters in
biographical and literary interest, we cannot read
them with quite the enjoyment that the prose collection affords.

Yet more tedious to our modern taste, but of
superlative historical value, is the Book of Eclogues,
containing twelve so-called "pastoral" poems. Here
we have the completest fusion ever achieved between the mediæval and the classical methods.
The mediæval doctrine that poetry is allegory is
taken up by Petrarch, approved, and acted on. But
the allegory takes a classical shape. Arcady, that
migratory realm of poetic fancy, is transported to
Provence; in the guise of the shepherds and
nymphs who inhabit it we are introduced to Petrarch

himself — usually designated Silvius or Silvanus, the lover of forest and hill — to his brother, to Socrates and Laura, to Popes and Cardinals, to personifications of the city of Avignon and of the Spirit of Religious Consolation, and to no less a personage than St. Peter himself. These all take part in "pastoral" dialogues, which thinly veil the expression of the poet's feelings or the discussion of contemporary events. It is all tiresomely artificial and unreal; but Petrarch was persuaded that Virgil had done just the same in the eclogues on which his own were modelled. Whatever we may think of them now, these "pastoral" poems hit the taste of the day and enjoyed an extraordinary vogue.

Petrarch's most considerable work in Latin verse, the *Africa*, remains to be noticed. The story of its composition has been told already, how it was conceived and partly written during the first residence at Vaucluse; then put aside for a year or two; then, under the stimulus of the recent coronation, resumed during the walks in the Selva Piana, and finished with a rush at Parma. So far as any work of Petrarch's could be called complete during his lifetime, we have it on his own authority that the *Africa* was completed in 1341. But he did not hurry its publication; he kept it by him for the usual revision, and some years passed before even his closest friends were allowed a glimpse of it. Presently he so far yielded to Barbato's importunity as to send him the passage which narrates the death of Sophonisba. This is the passage which a French critic in the eighteenth century declared had been stolen from the *Punica* of Silius Italicus ; and it is noticeable, as evidence of the quality of Petrarch's Latin, that the refutation of the calumny, complete as it is, rests on external evidence and on the obvious appropriateness of the lines to their position in the *Africa*, not on any marked inferiority of Petrarch's hexameters to those of Silius. With the exception of this detached extract, the poem was still kept for many years secluded in its author's library; and as time went on he came to regard it with mingled feelings of hope and disappointment. It was to have been the supreme effort of his imagination, the choice fruit of poetic genius which should justify in the sight of all posterity his reception of the laurel crown, the proof that an Italian of the fourteenth century could write a Roman epic, not perhaps quite a rival to the *Æneid*, but not altogether unworthy of a place beside it. He never quite resigned the hope that in the *Africa* this high ambition was achieved ; but he suffered grievous pangs of doubt, and more than once declared his intention of throwing the poem into the fire, "being far too severe a critic of his own performances," says Boccaccio.

How far the *Africa* can be called a success must depend on our estimate of the effect produced by it. Judged by a purely literary standard, it must be pronounced a meritorious failure, though in justice to its author stress should be laid on the merit. The conception is a fine one, and the whole poem is inspired by enthusiasm for Rome. In Scipio Petrarch was celebrating his ideal hero, and it would be hard to find an historical subject more congenial to epic treatment than the end of the Second Punic War. Petrarch was fully alive to these advantages and spared no pains to give effect to them. Unfortunately the art is a little too obvious; the epic stage-properties are unmistakably second-hand, the machinery creaks, the magic spell of illusion is wanting. The whole poem is reminiscent of the *Æneid* and of what Petrarch knew about the *Iliad;* we have a palace decorated with numberless pictures from the mythology, a banquet followed by a sketch of Roman history, the death of an unhappy queen, a prophetic apparition of Homer. Only a journey to Hades and a conclave of the gods are wanting; instead of them we have an astonishing scene in heaven, in which the Almighty expounds Christian dogma to allegorical impersonations of Rome and Carthage. Here we touch the root of the whole failure. Petrarch is too earnest in his plea for Rome to lose himself in his subject; for once he is too much a missionary to be quite successfully a poet.

Artistically, then, the *Africa* is a failure, but historically it holds a notable place in the revival of learning. Though it was never definitely "published," we must infer from Boccaccio's allusions that some scholars at least had access to it; and the mere fact of its existence inclined men's minds to consider the possibilities of poetry. They heard with admiration that a contemporary of their own had dared to follow in Virgil's footsteps, and to compose a great epic in the tongue which made it the common property of scholars in all lands. Boccaccio, in the passage already quoted, mentions the *Africa* among Petrarch's most important works, "which," he says, "we will read, and on which we will comment even during the lifetime of their author."

In the same category Boccaccio places several of those treatises and disquisitions which also played an important part in fostering the humanistic spirit. The books *On the Solitary Life* and *On the Remedies of Good and Bad Fortune* in particular had in their day an extraordinary reputation and a potent influence. Nobody reads them now; and that is a pity, for they are much better reading than a good deal of the literature that has superseded them. Petrarch would have based on them his claim to be ranked as a "philosopher," and the men of his day would have allowed the claim. Nothing could more clearly mark the difference between the new learning and the old. Mediæval philosophy was the science of exact thought, and had as little as possible to do with literature; its burning question, the Nominalist and Realist controversy, was concerned with metaphysical definitions in just that region of metaphysics that lies nearest to theology. Similarly we find that even Dante, incomparably the greatest man of letters of his day, in composing his treatise *De Monarchiâ*, handled theoretical politics by the deductive method. Petrarch breaks loose from the austere discipline of logical process and formula. In his treatises, as in his letters, he takes his readers back to the Ciceronian standpoint and invites them to investigate

truth by literary methods.   Not for a moment does
he exalt style above matter; what we call "style
for style's sake" is an abomination to him.   But he
requires that a man of letters shall employ a good
style for the adornment of good matter; and if a
man will only take example by Cicero, he shall
know how to achieve the combination.

Exactly the same is true of his work as an historian; he discards the methods of the chroniclers
and reverts to those of Plutarch.   His greatest
work, the *Lives of Illustrious Men*, is a history of
classical Rome set forth in thirty-one biographies
of great men from Romulus to Cæsar.   Considering the materials at Petrarch's disposal, this is a
stupendous achievement; and the scale on which it
is planned no less than the method of its execution
marks it as the first of modern histories.   In the
1874 edition it occupies over 750 octavo pages, of
which over 350 are given to the life of Cæsar.
The knowledge that Petrarch was engaged on it
created no small stir in the world; we have seen
that Charles IV eagerly questioned him about its
progress.   Its very excellence, indeed, probably
hastened the day of its supersession; it must have
kindled an interest in historical research fatal to its
continued use as a textbook.   Before the invention
of printing it had been forgotten, and only the
jejune *Epitome*, on which Petrarch was engaged at
the time of his death, appears in the earlier editions
of his works.   Domenico Rossetti, the editor of
Petrarch's lesser Latin poems, unearthed the original
and corrected the erroneous attribution of part of it

to Giulio Celso; Luigi Razzolini published the complete text with an Italian translation in 1874; thanks to these two scholars, we now have easy access to the work which most completely illustrates Petrarch's sense of the continuity of history, his zeal for Rome, and the methods by which he enabled the world to possess once again the splendid heritage of her literature.

Yet when all is said and done, it is not by the letter but by the spirit of his Latin writings that Petrarch holds his rank among the great masters whose work endures through the ages. He was not the only man of his day who had the right instinct for culture or the power to discern the beauties of classical literature. But he was the one whom nature had gifted with the magnetic power to kindle men's zeal and make their enthusiasm fruitful. His personality impressed itself on the whole movement; his very foibles are the characteristic foibles of his successors. Like him, they were self-conscious men whose eagerness about their personal reputation was not free from the taint of vanity. Many of them carried to excess the faults which in their master had been the trivial blemishes of a most lovable character. But if the world inherited from Petrarch a little restlessness, a little vanity, a little self-consciousness, he bequeathed to it also a faculty of right judgment, a tradition of unwearied diligence, a noble ardour of research. Therefore, and not because he wrote the *Africa*, the *Lives of Illustrious Men*, or even the *Letters*, we hail him in Boccaccio's phrase as "our illustrious teacher, father, and lord."

CHAPTER XV

THE SORROWFUL YEARS OF THE SECOND PLAGUE—DEATHS OF FRIENDS

1360-1363

IN 1360 the French had at last succeeded in raising their King's ransom, and the Peace of Bretigny was signed on May 8th. A considerable contribution to the ransom had come out of the coffers of Galeazzo Visconti, who furnished six hundred thousand florins on condition that his son Gian-Galeazzo should marry the Princess Isabelle of France. The bargain was duly carried out, and in October the two children, whose united ages amounted to twenty-three years, the bride being a year the elder, were solemnly joined together in holy matrimony at Milan.

The connection with the House of Valois was a good stroke of business for Galeazzo, but his first embassy to Paris was sent on an errand of courtesy rather than of negotiation. It went in December, to offer Galeazzo's congratulations to King John on his return to his capital, and who so fit as Petrarch to be its spokesman? At the state reception Petrarch delivered a harangue, in which the leading theme was the vicissitudes of fortune. To our modern sensitive ears the subject seems rather a

ticklish one under the circumstances, but people in
the fourteenth century underwent too many of these
vicissitudes to be squeamish in talking about them.
And the orator had evidently gauged the taste of
his principal auditors, for the King and his heir
apparent not only pricked up their ears at the mention of fortune, but proposed to recur to the subject
on a less formal occasion, when they even promised
themselves the sport of confuting their learned
guest. So after dinner up came the Prince with
Peter of Poitiers, the translator of Livy, and a
bevy of other scholars at his heels, and demanded
a discourse upon the nature and attributes of
Fortune. A friendly colleague, zealous for the
honour of his fellow-Italian, had given Petrarch
a hint of what was coming, so that he was not
quite unprepared, though he would dearly have
liked time for a peep at some books of reference.
Still he came off with credit, and the company was
not inclined to contest his dictum that Fortune was
a mere name, a popular superstition, but of service
now and then to the learned in the embellishment
of their phrases. The credit of Italy was saved,
and her champion went victorious to bed. The
Prince, who must have been a very glutton of talk,
was for renewing the discussion in the morning,
when the ambassadors had audience of the King.
But the talk went off on other matters, and in spite
of prompting nods and becks from the disappointed
Prince, the topic had not been reached when the
time came to terminate the audience.

Petrarch spent altogether about three months

over this embassy. After making full allowance
for the probable delays of Alpine travel in mid-
winter, we may suppose that two-thirds of the time
would be spent in Paris, for we do not hear of the
ambassador's staying at intermediate places, but
only of his passing through a country which thirty
years ago had seemed to him a picture of wealth and
prosperity, but which he now found desolate and
barren, with farms deserted and houses tumbling to
decay. A feature of his visit which gave him
especial pleasure was the renewal of his acquaintance with Peter of Poitiers, who had testified his
admiration for him years before by going to seek
him out at Vaucluse.

In March he was back at Milan, and a few
months later received there a fresh token of the
Emperor's esteem and regard. Charles sent him
his own golden drinking-cup, and accompanied the
gift with a letter of profuse compliment in which he
invited him to return to Prague. Petrarch thanked
him for both bowl and letter in the warmest terms,
and very gracefully accepted the invitation of which
he hoped he might avail himself when the unhealthy
season of late summer and early autumn was past.
But he did not forget to say roundly, though with
perfect courtesy, that the better course would have
been for the Emperor to accept *his* invitation to
come to Italy. "Yours is the upper hand in virtue
of your position, Cæsar," he writes, "but mine by
the goodness of my cause. You summon me to
honourable—I grant you that—and delightful enjoyment ; I call you to high emprise, to your

enforced and bounden duty, which is indeed so plainly your duty that you may be thought to have been brought to birth for no other purpose." And this is only one of many similar appeals addressed to Charles in the years now under review.

From the middle of 1361 to the end of 1363, the story is little else than a record of deaths. The plague, never entirely subdued, broke out again with a virulence that in some places even exceeded that of the first terrible visitation. One after another Petrarch's dearest friends died, till of those who had made the season of his manhood so fruitful in affection only three or four remained to share with him the joys and sorrows of age. Younger men, indeed, were gathering round him, who would cherish his later years with filial piety, but only Guido Settimo, Philip de Cabassoles, and Boccaccio were left of those who had cheered him in youth's struggles, or rejoiced, with a joy that no achievement of their own could have inspired, in the triumphs of his maturer manhood.

The first bereavement of which he had knowledge, though not the first in order of occurrence, was the death of his son. All Giovanni's misdeeds had not quenched the flame of natural affection in Petrarch's heart. "I talked of hating him while he lived," he wrote to Nelli; "now that he is dead, I love him with my mind, hold him in my heart, and embrace him in memory. My eyes look for him, alas! in vain." The Virgil fly-leaf has this entry: "Our Giovanni, a man born to bring toil and grief to me, afflicted me with heavy and constant anxieties during his life, and wounded me with pangs of sorrow by his death. For having known but few happy days in his life, he died in the year of our Lord 1361, the twenty-fourth of his age, at midnight between Friday the ninth and Saturday the tenth day of July. The news reached me on the fourteenth of the month, at evening. And he died at Milan, in that unexampled general slaughter by the plague from which that city had previously been exempt, but which then found its way thither and invaded it."

Three weeks later he heard first a vague report and then only too certain news of a still greater sorrow, the greatest, indeed, that could possibly befall him : Socrates had died exactly three months ago in Avignon, and all this time Petrarch had been ignorant of his loss. It sounds incredible, but the note in the Virgil is positive and precise ; Petrarch, often so careless of chronology, noted these days of bereavement with the closest exactitude. "In the same year," the note proceeds, "on the 8th of August, first a doubtful report from one of my servants on his return from Milan, and presently on Wednesday the 18th of the same month sure intelligence brought by a retainer of the Cardinal Theatine coming from Rome, reached me of the death of Socrates, my friend and best brother, who is said to have been dead since last May in Babylon, otherwise called Avignon. I have lost my life's companion and comfort ; Christ Jesus, receive these two and the other five into Thine everlasting habitations, that as they cannot be longer with me here below, they may enjoy the blessed exchange of life with Thee." And to Nelli he writes: " Socrates was born in a different part of the world from ours, but from the very moment of our meeting, his look, his disposition, and his worth made us of one mind, so that never from that day have I known his zeal for my interests falter or his devotion slacken for a single instant."

The latter part of the year was brightened by an event of happy omen destined to be happily fulfilled: Petrarch's daughter Francesca, now eighteen years old, was married to Francesco da Brossano, a Milanese of good family, whom Boccaccio describes as a very tall young man of placid countenance, sober speech, and refined manners. Francesca and her husband made their home with Petrarch; she was a devoted daughter, Francesco a model son-in-law; with them, and by and bye with his little grandchildren, Petrarch found the chief happiness of his later years. The eldest of these was the little Eletta, born in the following year; a boy whom they named Francesco was born in 1366, but died only two years later, in the summer of 1368.

Azzo da Correggio died in 1362. For him Petrarch had written his *Remedies of Good and Bad Fortune;* the subject was singularly appropriate to the vicissitudes of that stormy career, but only a friend's partiality could lay the blame on Fortune. Azzo had been his own architect, and had himself to thank when his house lay in ruins. Fortune, indeed, had done all that she could for him; he had brilliant talents, aptitude for statesmanship, extra-

ordinary charm of manner, and early opportunities
of employing his gifts with advantage.   He threw
everything away from sheer over-indulgence in
treacheries.   It was not fickleness, but a kind of
natural obliquity which set him scheming, as soon
as he had concluded a bargain, how to get more
gain by breaking than by keeping it.   Mere lack of
scruple would not have hindered him; on the
contrary, morality was nothing accounted of among
the princes of Italy, and a man might very easily
be too nice in his sense of honour to serve them ;
but there comes a point at which a reputation for
treachery makes the traitor still more unserviceable
as a tool than the honest man.   Azzo reached that
point, and passed it ; and so he, who might have
ruled Parma and founded a great library, died, a
discredited exile, after losing most of his property
by confiscation, and having to spend nearly all that
remained in ransoming his wife and two children
from the prison in which the third child had miser-
ably perished.

In the early spring of 1362 Petrarch thought of
returning to Vaucluse, and actually started on his
journey, but the disturbed state of Lombardy made
travel impossible, and he was forced to return.
Then came a pressing invitation from the Emperor
to fulfil his promise of visiting Prague ; again he
started, and again the presence of hostile armies
forced him to go back first to Padua, and thence, to
escape a virulent outbreak of the plague, to Venice.
It was just at this time, when he might well have
been excused if the miseries of the past year had

broken his nerve, that he gave a signal instance of
his self-possession and freedom from those super-
stitions to which his contemporaries were so prone.
A fanatical Carthusian monk, to whom all secular
learning seemed a snare of the devil, visited
Boccaccio and told him that a certain holy man,
named Peter of Siena, a worker of miracles, had had
on his death-bed a vision telling him that Boccaccio,
Petrarch, and some others would very soon die,
and that if they would escape damnation, they must
amend their lives and give up profane literature.
For once, Boccaccio was thrown off his mental
balance ; in times of pestilence very sane men may
lose their heads, and in Boccaccio's versatile nature
there was a strain of melancholy, which in a man
of narrower sympathies might have degenerated
into moroseness. For the moment he was thoroughly
frightened, and wrote to Petrarch that he must obey
the divinely sent command, get rid of his books,
and devote himself to an ascetic life. Petrarch
replied in a letter which ranks among the noblest of
his prose writings.

You tell me, he writes in effect, that this holy
man had a vision of the Saviour, and so discerned
all truth: a great sight for mortal eyes to see.
Great indeed, I agree with you, if genuine ; but
how often have we not known this tale of a vision
made a cloak for imposture ? And having visited
you, his messenger proposed, I understand, to go to
Naples, thence to Gaul and Britain, and then lastly
to me. Well, when he comes, I will examine him
closely ; his looks, his demeanour, his behaviour

under questioning, and so forth, shall help me to judge of his truthfulness.   And the holy man on his death-bed saw us two and a few others to whom he had a secret message, which he charged this visitor of yours to give us; so, if I understand you rightly, runs the story.   Well, the message to you is twofold : you have not long to live, and you must give up poetry.   Hence your trouble, which I made my own while reading your letter, but which I put away from me on thinking it over, as you will do also; for if you will only give heed to me, or rather to your own natural good sense, you will see that you have been distressing yourself about a thing that should have pleased you.   Now, if this message is really from the Lord, it must be pure truth. But is it from the Lord?   Or has its real author used the Lord's name to give weight to his own saying?   I grant you the frequency of death-bed prophecies; the histories of Greece and Rome are full of instances; but even if we allow that these old stories and your monitor's present tale are all true, still what is there to distress you so terribly? What is there new in all this?   You knew without his telling you that you could not have a very long span of life before you.   And is not our life here labour and sorrow, and is it not its chief merit that it is the road to a better?   Do not philosophers, writers of Holy Scripture, and fathers of the Church all agree in telling us that death is more to be desired than life?   All this you know, and I am teaching you nothing new, but only bringing back to your mind the knowledge which it held before this shock paralysed your memory. This at least all must grant, that we ought not greatly to love life, but that we are bound to endure it to the end, and seek to make its hard way the path to our desired home. Yes, it is not death that is to be feared, but life that is to be lived by the Christian rule. Ah! but you have come to old age, says your monitor. Death cannot be far off. Look to your soul. Well, I grant you that scholarship may be an unreasonable and even bitter pursuit for the old, if they take it up for the first time, but if you and your scholarship have grown old together, 'tis the pleasantest of comforts. Forsake the Muses, says he; many things that may grace a lad are a disgrace to an old man: wit and the senses fail you. Nay, I answer, when he bids you pluck sin from your heart, he speaks well and prudently; but why forsake learning, in which you are no novice, but an expert able to discern what to choose and what to refuse; which has become not a toil, but a delight to you, and which you have skill to use for the furtherance of knowledge, eloquence, and religion? What! Shall we Christians who know exactly what to think of the gods of the mythology renounce the classics and yet read the really dangerous books of the heretics? 'Tis the sure mark of ignorance to despise what it cannot understand and to try to bar against others the way in which it has no skill to walk. Learning rightly used does not hinder, but helps the conduct of life. It is like a meat which may disagree with the sick, but gives strength to the healthy. All history is full of examples of good men who have loved learning, and though many unlettered men have attained to holiness, no man was ever debarred from holiness by letters. Good men all have one and the same goal, but the roads to it are many. Each man travels his own way, but the lofty ways are better than the low ; piety with learning is better than piety without it, and for every unlettered saint you can name me, I will name you a greater saint proficient in letters.

But if, in spite of all this, you persist in your intention, and if you must needs throw away not only your learning, but the poor instruments of it, then I thank you for giving me the refusal of your books. I will buy your library, if it must be sold, for I would not that the books of so great a man should be dispersed abroad and hawked about by unworthy hands. I will buy it and unite it with my own ; then some day this mood of yours will pass, some day you will come back to your old devotion. Then you will make your home with me : you will find your own books side by side with mine, which are equally yours. Thenceforth we shall share a common life and a common library, and when the survivor of us is dead, the books shall go to some place where they will be kept together and dutifully tended, in perpetual memory of us who owned them.

There is no need to enlarge upon the excellence of this remarkable letter. It tells its own comforting tale of sane piety, loyalty to a high calling, and considerate devotion to a friend. Only a true lover

PETRARCH'S HOUSE IN VENICE

of books and men could have written the concluding sentences.

The libraries, however, were never united; Boccaccio was soon healed of his mental sickness, and went back to his books with a convalescent's appetite. But Petrarch made the intended provision for his own books. He reserved the whole property in them to himself for his lifetime, but assigned them not by a mere will, but by a memorandum intended to be embodied in an irrevocable deed, to the Republic of Venice after his death. There is no evidence that this deed was ever duly signed, sealed, and delivered; but the validity of the bargain is indisputable, for Petrarch accepted and enjoyed the consideration. The Palazzo Molina, or Palace of the Two Towers, was assigned to him, and became his chief residence till war between Venice and Padua made sojourn in the former city unpleasant to him. His books therefore should have gone to Venice, and to this day visitors are told that they formed the nucleus of the Marcian Library; it has also been constantly asserted that the State which accepted the precious legacy left it to rot in the packing-cases that contained it. There is no truth in either of these statements, though there is some justification for the second in the condition of some books discovered two hundred and fifty years later, and erroneously believed to be Petrarch's. After his death, the Republic was either unable to claim her inheritance or indifferent to it, and the real nucleus of the Marcian Library is the collection bequeathed by Cardinal Bessarion in the following century. Petrarch's books were probably dispersed soon after his death ; somehow or other a good many of them found their way to Gian-Galeazzo's library at Pavia, and most of these are probably now in Paris ; others are to be found in various Continental libraries.

In September, Innocent VI died. For his successor, the Cardinals went outside their own body, and chose the Abbot Guillaume Grimoard, of Marseilles. Frenchmen now formed the majority of the Sacred College. The new Pope was a Frenchman, supposed to have a special attachment to his country. Everything seemed to point to the definite establishment of the Papal See at Avignon, but a story related by Villani credits Grimoard before his election with the wish to return to Rome and to deliver Italy from her tyrants. Whether there is any foundation for this story or not, the new Pope certainly took the earliest opportunity to give a hint of possible change ; he was proclaimed by the name of Urban V. Joyfully Petrarch hailed the omen ; that the immediate offer of the secretaryship proved the new Pope personally favourable to him was least among the causes of his gratification. With enthusiasm he spoke of "this most holy, liberal, and truly *urbane* Father, raised to the highest place of human dignity by the express will of God, for the comfort of all good men, and the rescue of the world."

The story of 1363 is again an almost unbroken record of deaths. Its one happy episode is Boccaccio's three months' visit to Venice in the summer.

He brought Leonzio Pilato with him, and we can imagine the zest with which the friends must have discussed the teaching of Greek. Hardly had Boccaccio left when the hand of death fell again heavily on the diminished circle of Petrarch's friends. In this sad year the plague took from him Lælius, the last survivor of the Lombez-Avignon group, Barbato, whose friendship with him dated from the triumphant year of his coronation, and—last-known, but perhaps best-beloved of all, save only Socrates—Francesco Nelli, his dear *Simonides*, for twelve years the sympathetic recipient of all his confidences. " You alone are left to me of all my friends," he cries, in his agony, to Boccaccio, and the words were almost literally true. Guido Settimo and Philip de Cabassoles were the only exceptions, and it does not appear that either of them was personally known as yet to Boccaccio.

CHAPTER XVI

THE MASTER AND HIS PUPILS—
VENICE, PADUA, AND PAVIA

1364-1367

PETRARCH had not yet completed his sixtieth
year, but already he must be counted an old
man. In some respects the second plague made an
even greater change in his life than the first: after
1363 he made no new friendships of the old intimate kind with men of his own age. The nearest
approach to such a new tie was the ripening of his
acquaintance with Francesco Bruno, the new Papal
Secretary, into a feeling of warm attachment and
regard. It is evident that the longer Petrarch knew
Bruno, the better he liked and trusted him. But the
word friendship covers many degrees in the scale of
human sentiment, and though Petrarch and Bruno
were friends in no mere conventional sense, they
never met in the flesh; however intimate might
be their knowledge of each other's minds—and
Petrarch testifies that it was very intimate indeed—
they could never be on those terms of more than
brotherly affection which we have learnt to associate
with the names of Socrates, Lælius, and Simonides.
For the rest, the names which crop up for the first
time in the *Letters written in Old Age* are chiefly

those of scholars with whom Petrarch exchanged the courtesies of their common calling, or men of a younger generation, some of them his pupils in literature, others the sons of old friends.

The later letters accurately reflect the changed condition of their writer's life. They contain a much larger proportion of treatises and disquisitions than the earlier collection; of really "familiar" letters there are comparatively few. One long and delightful letter of reminiscences addressed to Guido Settimo is our principal authority for the events of Petrarch's early years. There are half a dozen addressed to Philip de Cabassoles, which show that neither long absence, nor Philip's promotion, first to the Patriarchate of Jerusalem and then to the Cardinalate, could weaken the ties contracted in the intimacy of Vaucluse. Best of all, there is a whole series of letters to Boccaccio, which prove that Petrarch had at least one friend left with whom there need be no shadow of concealment.

If he did not contract new friendships, still less was he likely to take up new themes or attack the solution of new problems. The interests of his earlier years were enough to fill the lives of half a dozen ordinary men; they could still satisfy even his appetite for work, and there is not a sign of slackening in the ardour with which he pursued them. Still we may note that the last decade of his life is a time of strenuous diligence on the old lines, not of any effort to strike out new ones.

One change observable in his habits was entirely for the better: Venice now counted for much more, and Milan for much less in his life. His attachment to the republic was of recent growth. Only ten years before he had been a strong partisan of Genoa, and had written to Guido Settimo, then Archdeacon and on the point of being made Archbishop of that city, a letter in which he identified himself with the Genoese, and spoke of the Venetians as a "haughty and implacable foe." Next he did his best both by letter and as the Visconti's ambassador to bring about peace between the two great maritime states. From the first Venice treated him with such distinguished honour as must have inclined him favourably towards her. Presently came the revolution, by which, after three years' subjection, Genoa shook off the yoke of Milan : Petrarch's personal friendship with Guido was now the only tie that connected him with Genoa, and there could be no shadow of reason why he should not cultivate closer relations with Venice. These were facilitated by his friendship with Benintendi de' Ravegnani, Chancellor of the Republic. He accepted her invitation to write Andrea Dandolo's epitaph, paid her frequent visits, and at last, as we have seen, gave her the reversion of his library, and accepted the usufruct of a house as a mark of her gratitude. It was not surprising that Venice in these days of her early greatness should cast over him the spell which for six hundred years has charmed the imagination of men. There was a good old Roman ring about the word Republic which always appealed to him ; and here was a republic which embodied his ideas in the stability of her institutions, and gratified his taste by the dignified splendour of her civic life. He speaks of her as "that most august city of Venice, the one remaining home of liberty, peace, and justice, the one refuge left to good men, the one harbour where the ships of those who desire to live worthily may still find shelter when battered by the storms of tyranny and war. 'Tis a city rich in gold, but richer in repute; powerful in her resources, more powerful in her worth; built on a solid foundation of marble, and established on the yet more solid base of civic concord; girt with the salt of the waves, and safeguarded by the still better salt of good counsel." To modern ears, indeed, it may sound a little strange to speak of the Venetian oligarchy as the one defender of liberty; and when we read of the "civic concord" that prevailed in Venice, we cannot help remembering that she had very recently beheaded a doge. But once again it must be remembered that by liberty Petrarch means the people's assent to the form of their government, not their participation in its working; and the suppression of Marino Faliero's puerile conspiracy might well be regarded as a testimony to the strength of the Venetian Constitution, not as evidence of any weakness inherent in it.

Not that he broke with the Visconti; far from it. Only from this time he appears in the character of Galeazzo's personal friend, rather than as a client of the family. He was as deeply interested as ever in the politics of Milan as part of the general politics of Italy; and when a new papal envoy,

Cardinal Androuin de la Roche, came to treat for peace between Bernabò Visconti and the Church, Petrarch waited on him at Bologna. His visit was probably paid just before the conclusion of the Peace of Lombardy, by which Bernabò Visconti waived his claim to the possession of Bologna on condition that Androuin, not Albornoz, should be deputed by the Holy See to govern it.

The sight of Bologna distressed Petrarch sadly; he had known it as a peaceful and opulent university town; now it had been for some years the bone of contention between rival armies, and the result to both university and city was deplorable; "it looked just like a hungry desert."

He seems to have spent Lent and Easter, as was now his habit, at Padua; in May we find him once more in Venice. The Venetians were now busy with their expedition to Crete, which was in full rebellion against their authority. The Peace of Lombardy enabled them to offer the command of their forces to Luchino del Verme, one of the most celebrated *condottieri* of the day. For some years Luchino had been Galeazzo's Captain-General, and the Milanese successes against the Marquis of Montferrat must be credited to his skill in leadership. The peace threw him out of work, and Petrarch, apparently at the instance of the Doge Lorenzo Celso, wrote him a letter congratulating him on the offer of the Cretan command, and urging him to accept it; to this practical exhortation he added some five folio pages of disquisition on the qualities of a great general, as illustrated by instances from

history.   Luchino accepted the command, was
solemnly sworn in, and sailed from Venice on
April 10th; less than two months afterwards arrived
the news of a decisive victory.   On June 4th
Petrarch was standing with his friend and guest,
the Archbishop of Patras, at the window of his
house on the Riva degli Schiavoni, when he saw a
galley making at full speed for the harbour; her
oars were wreathed with garlands, and on the prow
stood a band of youths crowned with laurel and
waving flags; evidently she brought news of victory.
The sentinel in the watch-tower gave the signal
that a ship from abroad was entering the port.   The
people flocked down to the quays, and soon all
Venice had heard the joyful news that, almost without loss to her own army, the enemy had been
routed, the Venetian captives liberated, the rebel
fortresses surrendered, and the whole island reduced
to submission.   Then Venice showed the world
how a great nation rejoices in a great triumph.   A
huge procession followed the Doge and chief officers
of state to a solemn thanksgiving in St. Mark's,
and then paraded the Great Square.   Games and
sports followed; the square was packed so close
that it seemed as if the whole people must be met
together, but in all this throng "there was not a
sign of tumult or disorder or quarrelling; the city
was full of joy and thankfulness, of harmony and
love; and while magnificence ruled supreme, modesty
and sobriety were not banished from her kingdom."
Two months later, when the victorious general had
returned with his troops, the celebrations were

renewed on a still more elaborate scale ; four whole days were devoted to a magnificent spectacle, of which the chief features were an equestrian display by twenty-four young Venetian nobles, and a tournament in which Venetians and foreign guests of the republic took part together.   Among the jousters were included some Englishmen of high rank, members of King Edward's Court and family, who had come by sea to Venice a few days before. The Doge witnessed the spectacle from the marble platform behind the bronze horses of St. Mark, and for two days out of the four Petrarch sat in a place of honour at his right hand.   He was invited, indeed, to attend the whole performance, but excused himself for the other two days on the ground of his well-known occupations.

In the following year, as we learn from the Florentine historian, Scipione Ammirato, the Republic of Florence asked the Pope to confer on Petrarch a canonry either in her own Church, or in that of Fiesole.   The object of the request was, of course, to induce Petrarch to take up his residence in Florence, but nothing came of the proposal.   The Pope, however, had his own plan for attracting Petrarch back to Provence, and nominated him to a canonry at Carpentras.   But before the presentation was actually made, a false report of the poet's death was circulated in Avignon, and universally believed.   Petrarch hints that this report, and many others of the same kind, were set about by the malice of a personal enemy.   If this was the case, the lie for once succeeded in doing its victim a mischief, for before the error could be rectified, Urban had conferred all Petrarch's benefices on others. Those which he had actually held were of course restored to him as soon as he was found to be alive; but as he had never been formally presented to the canonry of Carpentras, it remained with its new possessor. It is doubtful whether Petrarch very much regretted the loss of it. He had been gratified by the spontaneous mark of Urban's goodwill, and especially by the considerate thoughtfulness of a gift which would have brought him back to the neighbourhood of Vaucluse and Philip de Cabassoles; all this he warmly acknowledged in a subsequent letter to Bruno. But as years went on he became steadily less inclined to leave Italy; and when at last, to his exceeding joy, Urban brought the papacy back to Rome, he could declare with evident sincerity that the good Pope's blessing was the only favour that he desired of him.

The chronology of these years is not quite clear; the letters belonging to them are certainly not placed in exact order of composition, and Fracassetti assigns to 1364–5 some events which in this narrative are placed a year later. But the matter is one of curiosity rather than of importance. The general tenor of Petrarch's life throughout the period is clear enough.

It was probably in the summer of this year that he first took up his residence in Pavia. That town had now been for six years in the power of Galeazzo Visconti. For a short time, indeed, it had seemed as though Bussolari might succeed in his heroic attempt to found a state on the principles of morality and freedom, but the powers of evil were too strong. The Beccaria, acting as Galeazzo's jackals, made themselves masters of the surrounding country. Pavia was closely besieged, and though Montferrat made many attempts to relieve it, only a single convoy got through. In October, 1359, hunger produced the usual pestilence, and Bussolari saw that he must yield. With his own hand he drew up the terms of capitulation, by which Galeazzo agreed to respect the new Constitution, and maintain the people in full enjoyment of their liberties. For himself, Bussolari asked not so much as a safe-conduct ; his concern was for the people, and he had absolutely no thought for his own safety. Galeazzo signed the treaty, and it is superfluous to add that he broke it. By inducing Bussolari's superiors to keep the friar in strict monastic confinement, which soon ended in his death, Galeazzo did not indeed commit any breach of faith ; he only gave the expected measure of Visconti generosity. To the citizens of Pavia he was both mean and treacherous. The liberties which he had sworn to maintain were at once destroyed, and his breach of faith was made worse by his subornation of servile lawyers to furnish him with a pretext for its justification. One thing he did for Pavia : he brought money into the place. The Milanese historian Corio says that his wife and family persuaded him to leave Milan, lest Bernabò, in one of his frenzies, should offer him violence ; whether this were his

THE CASTLE OF PAVIA

motive or not—and Bernabò in a frenzy was certainly a person to be avoided—Galeazzo left Milan in 1360, and built himself a magnificent palace-castle in Pavia. Petrarch was always welcome at his Court, and from 1365 onwards we find him making a practice of spending the late summer and autumn there, and sometimes prolonging his visit to the end of the year.

This period is rich in letters to Boccaccio. One of these gives us a glimpse of the Italian minstrels who went about singing and reciting the compositions of well-known poets. These, if Petrarch's description is to be trusted, ranked far below the jongleurs of Provence. The latter, though not to be confounded with the courtly poets known as troubadours, were as often as not the authors of the compositions which they sang or recited. But the Italian minstrels are characterised by Petrarch as " men of no great parts, but with great powers of memory, great industry, and still greater impudence, who frequent the halls of kings and great men, with not a rag of their own to cover their nakedness, but tricked out in the trappings of other men's songs, and who earn noblemen's favour by their declamatory recitations of this or that man's best compositions, especially of such as are written in the vulgar tongue." Naturally these reciters were for ever pestering Petrarch for a copy of his latest poem. In his early days he was in the habit of gratifying them, but presently took a disgust at their importunity, and not only refused all their applications, but would not so much as see the applicants.

Occasionally, however, he received visits of thanks from men whom he had formerly sent away starving and in rags with a poem to recite, and who now came back well fed and clad in silk to assure him that his kindness had saved them from utter poverty. This made him consider the granting of their requests to be a kind of alms-giving, and he would often relax his rule of refusal, especially in favour of those whom he knew to be poor and honest. When he had speech of these men, he would ask them why they plagued him with all their importunities, and especially why they did not go and give Boccaccio a turn. One day he got an answer which throws a charming light on the foibles which almost equally with his great qualities make Boccaccio dear to us, and on the complete frankness with which he and Petrarch spoke and wrote to each other. It was no use going to Boccaccio, it seems, for Boccaccio was in a huff; he was no poet, he said; Dante and Petrarch were your only poets, and no one else need apply for the title. It is not to be supposed that for a single moment Boccaccio allowed himself to be jealous of the reputation of those whom he thus exalted above himself. He did not claim to be put on a level with his two great masters; it was Petrarch who rightly told him that his place was by their side. But Boccaccio, like all impulsive men, had his fits of depression. Poverty pressed hard on him, and he was amply justified in feeling now and then that the fruits of his genius and industry deserved more than they received in the way of material reward, and perhaps of reputation too. In such a mood, which we may be sure was only transitory, he was for throwing his Italian poems into the fire. What was the use of keeping this stuff, when Italy had the *Divina Commedia* and the *Canzoniere*? Petrarch's reproof is at once sensible and affectionate. He tells Boccaccio about an old man of Ravenna, who was no mean judge of poetry, and who always put Dante first, Petrarch himself second, and Boccaccio third among the poets of Italy. For his own part Petrarch accepts the verdict; but if Boccaccio thinks he ought to have second place, it is entirely at his service; there can be no quarrels for precedence between them. If such a thing were possible, it would mean that their friendship was incomplete; for his own part Petrarch would rather rank Boccaccio above himself than below, and he remembers old sayings by his friend which show a reciprocal affection. The thing that really matters is not relative position, but excellence of work, and if any one still remains ahead of him in the race, let Boccaccio take it as an incentive to go on working his hardest and producing his best. That is the kind of goad which stimulates a noble mind to win astonishing success. Boccaccio indeed has a legitimate grievance against this ignorant and conceited generation, which is incapable of appreciating such work as his. He may well have a mind to withdraw it from so incompetent a tribunal; but let him hold his hand, and remember that in the realm of high learning he may always take refuge from the vulgarities and ineptitudes of the day.

In the autumn of 1365 Boccaccio went to Avignon as the spokesman of an important Florentine embassy to the Pope. He returned early in December by sea to Genoa, and Petrarch hoped that he might come thence to pay him a visit at Pavia, but Boccaccio was obliged to go straight home to Florence. He wrote Petrarch an account of his stay at Avignon and an expression of his regret at not being able to visit him ; in reply Petrarch sent a long letter dated from Pavia on December 14th, in which he alludes with special pleasure to Boccaccio's account of his first meeting with Philip de Cabassoles. "Greatly do I rejoice," he writes, "that in Babylon itself you saw those few friends whom death has spared me, and above all that veritable father of mine, Philip, Patriarch of Jerusalem, a man, to describe him in a brief phrase, altogether worthy of the dignity to which he has attained, and not unworthy to attain to that of Rome, if ever the turn of events should bring him the office for which his merits fit him. Though he had never seen you before, he welcomed you as my second self, you tell me, embracing you long and tenderly with sincere affection in the presence of the Pope himself, and under the eyes of the Cardinals, and after loving kisses and pleasant conversation, with anxious inquiries about my welfare, he begged that I would send him presently my book *On the Solitary Life*, which I wrote years ago in his own country district, when he was Bishop of the diocese of Cavaillon, and dedicated to him. In truth he asks what is only fair, since I have really finished that little treatise; but I call God, who knows

everything, to witness that ten times at least I have
tried and tried again to send him the writing in
such a state that, however much its composition
might fail to satisfy the reader's ears and intelligence, at least its penmanship should be pleasing
to his eye. But every attempt to carry out my
wish has been frustrated by the obstacle of which I
am always complaining. You know just what value
to set on a copyist's trustworthiness and diligence;
they are not the least of the plagues which afflict
your talented writer. And so, incredible as it
sounds, this book which was written in a few months
has never got copied in all these years." The
treatise was actually copied soon after, and sent to
Philip in 1366.

The same letter, like many others which precede
and follow it, contains a reference to the Greek
Leonzio Pilato and the Latin translation of Homer
which Petrarch had commissioned him to make.
The story of Leonzio is a veritable tragi-comedy.
He was born in Calabria, but when in Italy passed
himself off as a native of Thessalonica; in Greece
it pleased him to boast of his Italian origin. Boccaccio had picked him up on the journey from
Venice to Avignon, and persuaded him to come
back with him and teach Greek in Florence.
Leonzio claimed to be a disciple of Barlaam, but
not much reliance could be placed on any account
that he gave of himself. Doubt has even been
thrown on his qualifications as a teacher of Greek,
but Boccaccio certainly regarded him as thoroughly
proficient in the language and conversant with its

literature. By his influence in Florence, he managed to get a chair of Greek founded specially that Leonzio might fill it, and, poor as he was, took private lessons from him, and so supplemented his professional income. Petrarch too took a share in contributing to Leonzio's maintenance; he had heard with enthusiasm of Boccaccio's scheme for establishing a chair of Greek, and eagerly seized the opportunity of commissioning the new professor to make a Latin translation of Homer. Hitherto there had been nothing of the kind; to persons ignorant of Greek, Homer could be known only through a sort of compendium, so badly compiled that its faultiness was apparent on the face of it, even to students wholly ignorant of the original. Now, thought Petrarch and Boccaccio, was the opportunity for getting a really good translation, and Petrarch gladly undertook to bear the whole expense, if he might have the pleasure of putting the book on the shelves of his library. After many delays and repeated anxious inquiries, the precious volumes at length arrived, and were installed in their place of honour in February, 1366; but before the translation reached its purchaser, the translator had come by a strange end; it seemed as if the fates had ordained him a death to match the extravagant oddities of his life. Whatever his merits as a professor, Leonzio could not be pronounced a social success. In appearance he was a grotesque little man with preternaturally hideous features, coarse rusty-black hair, and a beard of enormous length. His habits were not nice; and

Petrarch says that he wrote letters longer and dirtier than his beard. In character he could only be compared to the troll in the fairy story, whose caprice showed itself in perpetual discontent with the conditions of his existence, and grumblings at the people who were kind to him. While he was in Italy, Greece was the only land for decent folk to live in. No sooner had he disregarded Petrarch's and Boccaccio's advice, and betaken himself to Greece, than he was begging them to have him back in Italy. Petrarch at least had had enough of him, and left the letters unanswered; but Leonzio, who must have been a pretty shrewd judge of character, felt sure that he would not be turned away if he presented himself as a suppliant in the house which for three months had endured him as a guest. He set sail from Constantinople with a manuscript of Sophocles, or so he said, as a peace-offering, and got safely as far as the Adriatic, when a terrific storm arose, and Leonzio was killed by a flash of lightning, which struck the mast to which he was clinging for safety. So died the first professor of Greek in a Western University.

From the same series of letters we find that Boccaccio was once more anxious about his friend's independence. He did not quite like Petrarch's long rhapsody on the beauties and amenities of Pavia; Galeazzo's new palace might be as fine as Petrarch painted it, but Boccaccio could not be persuaded that a Visconti castle was the home of liberty. Petrarch wrote at some length to reassure him, and this time with better reason than thirteen

years earlier. In 1353 he had been nominally the
free guest of the Visconti, but it cannot be denied
that effectively he was their client; now, in 1366,
though the court phraseology might still designate
them his patrons, he was really the independent
friend of Galeazzo.

In these years we find him increasingly intimate
with men of a younger generation, who were at
once his pupils in literature and the friends of his
old age. Nearest of them all in affection, and
most devoted in service to the master, was Lombardo della Sete, or da Serico, a native of Padua,
and a frequent inmate of the household. He was
a bachelor, and lived a very simple, frugal life in the
country. Petrarch mentions in his will that Lombardo had often neglected his own affairs to attend
to those of his friend; he named him among his
principal legatees, and even made him his general
heir, in the event of Francesco da Brossano dying
before him. The tie between the two was all the
closer as Lombardo was himself a man of letters
and a diligent student; he continued and finished
the *Epitome of the Lives of Illustrious Men*, on
which Petrarch was engaged at the time of his
death, and there are extant two or three treatises of
his own, one of them evidently suggested by his
studies with Petrarch, *On the Praises of certain
Ladies who have won renown in Letters or in Arms.*
Another friend and disciple, nearer perhaps to
Petrarch in age, but still a good many years his
junior, was the grammarian Donato degli Albanzani,
a native of Pratovecchio, in the Casentino or upper

valley of the Arno, and therefore called by Petrarch Apenninigena. Boccaccio speaks of Donato as a poor man, but highly respected, and a great friend of his own. For many years he taught grammar at Venice, where he probably made Petrarch's acquaintance in or about the year 1361. A firm friendship resulted ; Donato was an enthusiastic admirer of Petrarch's works, and after the latter's death published a commentary on his Eclogues and a translation of his *Lives of Illustrious Men*. He also translated Boccaccio's *Lives of Illustrious Women*.

A very eminent pupil and follower of Petrarch in literature, though perhaps not personally known to him, was Coluccio Salutati, a Florentine by birth, who while still a boy accompanied his father into exile at Bologna, and was educated there. A lawyer by profession, he was in 1368 associated with Bruno as joint papal secretary, and some years later he was recalled to Florence and appointed Chancellor of the Republic. Distinguished as was his official career, he won far higher fame as a scholar and a Humanist. Diligently following the lines laid down by Petrarch and Boccaccio, he did his utmost for the emendation of corrupt classical texts, and made the fruitful suggestion that public libraries should be instituted and trustworthy copyists placed on their staff. He was himself the best Latinist of his day, and his voluminous original works in prose and verse were accounted masterpieces. He was also well versed in Greek, and successful in promoting the study of it.

Of almost equal celebrity with Coluccio was the grammarian Giovanni da Ravenna, whom the former recommended to the lord of that city, Carlo Malatesta, in 1404, as "having been at one time the housemate and pupil of Francesco Petrarca, of famous memory, with whom he lived for the space of nearly fifteen years." There is an intricate controversy as to Giovanni's family and the exact details of his life, but it seems reasonable to conclude with Baldelli that he was the staunch friend of the Carrara family, who was successively a teacher of grammar at Belluno, at Udine, and perhaps in Venice, Chancellor of the city of Padua, and lecturer on Dante as well as on classical literature at Florence. On the other hand, Fracassetti is probably correct in discrediting the usual identification of him with the unnamed "young man of Ravenna" who was Petrarch's pupil and private secretary at this time. There is no sufficient reason for supposing that this young man's name was Giovanni, and even if it were, the possession of so common a Christian name would not establish his identity with the famous grammarian. On the other hand, it is practically certain that, whereas the grammarian spent nearly fifteen years of his youth in Petrarch's house, the private secretary was not its inmate for more than three or four.

He came to him on Donato's recommendation in 1364, a mere lad, but so apt for his work, that some two years later Petrarch wrote to Boccaccio that he had found a treasure. The boy had a prodigious memory. In eleven days he had all Petrarch's twelve eclogues perfectly by heart, and he never forgot what he had learnt. He was temperate in his habits, not greedy of money, and as keen to work as his master himself; in a word, though not above eighteen or nineteen years old, he was already the ideal pupil and private secretary. He was treated as a son of the house, and for some three years he repaid Petrarch's affectionate kindness with faultless diligence. His seems to have been the hand which made the final arrangement of the *Familiar Letters*, and to him was entrusted such work as required scrupulous care and nice judgment in scholarship.

Petrarch had found what he had been looking for all these years, a careful and trustworthy copyist. But the pleasant relation was too good to last. One fine day in 1367 the lad took it into his head that he would like to see the world. Petrarch was much more hurt in his affection than solicitous about the loss to his convenience. He loved the boy, delighted in his companionship, anticipated a distinguished career for him in literature, and had believed him to be singularly stable in character; now he thought him a little wanting in gratitude and sadly deficient in steadfastness. Doubtless he did not make enough allowance for a young man's natural wish to try his fortune in the great world; on the other hand, the lad evidently urged his point somewhat unkindly and without regard for the susceptibilities of the employer who had also been his friend and benefactor. He had his way, of course. He was for going to Naples to see Virgil's tomb, to Calabria, or perhaps to Constantinople, to learn Greek. At another time he proposed to visit Avignon. Whatever his ultimate intention, he actually crossed the Apennines and got to Pisa. Finding no ship there, and having nearly exhausted his money, he recrossed the Apennines and made for Parma, where he was nearly drowned in trying to ford the river. A passer-by caught him by the heel and fished him out, and somehow or other he made his way, penniless, ragged, and half starved, to Petrarch's house in Pavia. Here he found Francesco da Brossano at home, who persuaded him, in spite of shame and fear, to wait and see the master. To him he confessed his fault, and, of course, Petrarch took him back. " I am sure he will not stay with me," he wrote to Donato; "he will be off again when the impression of his suffering has worn off, but meanwhile I am putting by a little journey-money for him." His prognostication came true. A year later the young man left him again, this time with Petrarch's full consent. He carried with him a letter of introduction to Bruno, who seems to have employed him as a scribe in the secretary's office.

Happy as Petrarch was in seeing his work taken up by capable and eager pupils, and in the general recognition of its value throughout Europe, it is not to be supposed that the New Learning was accepted at once and without question by all the minds trained in other schools of thought. We have seen that Petrarch had involved himself in a rather un-dignified quarrel with the physicians; he was now to have thrust on him a similar conflict with that sect of philosophers who claimed to base their system on the works of Aristotle, but who knew their supposed master only through the commentaries of the Arab Averroes, which Michael Scott had translated into Latin. Nothing could be more repugnant to Petrarch's mind and conscience than the method of this school, which was at once narrow in its formalism and materialistic in its tendency. Certainly Petrarch professed himself a devotee of philosophy, but the word philosopher has many shades of meaning. Petrarch took it in its literal and general sense of a man who loves wisdom ; he did not conceive that in order to claim the title you must have thought out a coherent scheme of the universe. He was content to take such philosophical doctrines as pleased him from any writer in whose pages he found them, and never dreamed of co-ordinating them into a dogmatic system. In a word, his philosophy was that of a man of letters, not of a metaphysician ; and as a man of letters, anxious that fine thought should be expressed in fine style, he hated the uncouth formalism of the Averroists, while as a devout Christian he held the tendency of the school towards materialism to be a still viler abomination. It was of the Averroists that he was probably thinking when he so frequently deplored the ignorance, and worse than ignorance, prevalent at the universities. On the other hand, the Averroists were not the people to take their correction mildly. They were the dominant school, and who was this writer of

verses that he should set himself up as a judge
of thinkers? Of literature and of history they were
perfectly ignorant and scornfully contemptuous.
The jargon of their scheme was the only language
they regarded, and what could not be expressed in
its formulæ, simply was not knowledge. Matters
came to a head in 1366, when four graceless young
men published in Venice a mock-solemn judgment
to the effect that Franciscus Petrarca was a good
man, but uneducated. It is a sad pity that Petrarch
took up so silly a challenge. Surely he, whom every
scholar in Europe acknowledged for his chief and
master, might have ignored the offensiveness of the
young men's action and laughed at its folly; but he
was wounded to the quick both in his self-esteem
and in his zeal for the honour of his calling. He
answered the attack in the treatise, the writing
of which occupied him for the next two years, *On
his own and many other people's ignorance:* a work
which contains some fine passages, and some
thoughts entirely worthy of its title, but is deformed
by that intemperate vehemence and that note of
personal rancour which disfigure all Petrarch's con-
troversial writings.

To help him in the controversy, he tried, apparently without result, to enlist the pen of a distinguished young friend. The Augustinian friar
Luigi Marsili was a native of Florence, and either
there or at Padua, where he received part of his
education, he was presented while still a mere boy
to Petrarch. The poet, struck by the lad's manner
and address, conceived great hopes of his future;

he welcomed his visits, and became more and more firmly convinced that a distinguished career was in store for him. Keen must have been the stimulus afforded by such encouragement to a boy of brilliant talents and eager desire for knowledge. Marsili's subsequent career justified the high hopes which Petrarch entertained of him; alike in Paris and in Italy he was reputed one of the foremost scholars of his day, and Coluccio Salutati more than once paid him the compliment of consulting his judgment. Some years passed between Petrarch's first intimacy with him and its renewal about this period; Marsili was now a young man of whom Petrarch could say that he had come back to him, in Ovid's words, "a youth to manhood grown, more comely than himself." He conceived so strong an affection for him that in 1373 he gave him the copy of St. Augustine's *Confessions* which he himself had received from Fra Dionigi forty years earlier, and accompanied it with a short letter, which, though written in the last year of his life, may be quoted here :—

"By your leave, my friend, I should say that my services to you, which you cite as many, are nothing at all; it is merely that I have loved you from your boyhood, for even then I had some presage of what was coming, and that now I love you better and better every day, now that I have a present hope of finding in you such a man as I wish. Gladly do I give you the book for which you ask; and I would give it yet more gladly if it were still in the condition in which I had it as a gift in my youth from the celebrated Dionysius, an eminent brother of your Order, a man distinguished in learning and every kind of merit, who was a most kind father to me. But I was in those days, by disposition perhaps as well as by my age, inclined to travel; and because this book was very pleasant to me both for its matter and its author's sake, and was also little enough to be easily handled and lightly carried about, I took it with me continually wellnigh all through Italy and Germany, so that the book and my hand seemed to be almost of a piece, so inseparable had they become by constant companionship. And, to say nothing of other falls by river and land, I will tell you of a wonderful adventure when it went down to the bottom of the sea with me off the coast of Nice, and undoubtedly it had been all over with us both had not Christ plucked us out of this imminent danger. So in going hither and thither with me it has grown old, till its old pages have become hard reading for old eyes; and now at last it takes its way back to the house of Augustine, whence it came forth, and will soon be starting afresh on its travels with you, I suppose. Be it your good pleasure then to take it such as it is, and henceforth treat anything that I have as at your disposal; save yourself the trouble of unnecessary explanations, and take without asking whatever pleases you. Farewell, and may good fortune be with you; and pray to Christ for me whenever you approach His table."

A pleasant incident occurred near the end of the year 1366. In November Stefano Colonna, a great-grandson of old Stefano, visited Petrarch at Venice and spent an afternoon with him. The old wound was healed then, the old dissensions forgotten, and Petrarch could now write to Bruno of young Stefano and young Agapito in terms that recall the warmth of his old affection for their fathers and uncles.

CHAPTER XVII

THE POPE IN ROME

1367-1370

GREAT news came in the spring of 1367, news that filled Petrarch with joyful hope of yet seeing the dawn of that better era for which he had all his life been looking in vain—the Pope was really leaving Avignon and going back to Rome. It was not the full realisation of Petrarch's ideal, but at least it put an end to what he regarded as the very worst political evil of the day, the exile of the Papacy. Rienzi had failed and Charles IV had never tried to restore the sovereignty of Rome; but at least her "second husband" was now awake to the solemn duties and glorious privileges of his office; at least the Eternal City was once more to be the centre of the world's spiritual life. If so much could be achieved at a blow, might not all the rest follow in due course? Might not the recognition of Rome's right to be the seat of Papacy lead men to acknowledge her equally valid right to be the seat of Empire? It was even rumoured that the spiritual and temporal sovereigns of the world had arranged to meet within her walls; might not this meeting be the prelude to their permanent joint residence there?

The virulence of Petrarch's attacks on the vices of the Church and her clergy, and on her establishment at Avignon, which he regarded as the root of the whole mischief, has led some historians to regard him as a foe to the Papacy itself.   Exultant Protestants have even claimed him as a forerunner of the Reformation.   This is to turn history upside down, and to interpret the fourteenth century by the experience of the sixteenth.   The idea of spiritual freedom to be attained and spiritual truth to be upheld outside the Roman organisation never occurred to him ; if by an intellectual miracle he could have conceived Luther's great deliverance, he would have shrunk from it with abhorrence ; it would have seemed to him to be vitiated at its very origin by the double taint of ecclesiastical schism and disloyalty to Rome.   But if he was a loyal son of the Roman Church, how, it may be asked, could he possibly attack her clergy and her organisation as he did ?   There is no minimising the force and bitterness of these attacks ; he himself regarded the letters containing some of them as so dangerous that he never acknowledged their authorship, inscribed them with no recipient's name, and kept them strictly secret from all but a few carefully chosen friends.   Nor is this all ; outside the pages of the letters *Sine Titulo*, in his acknowledged works and even in his Italian poems, there are denunciations of " Babylon " so fierce that they were struck out from all editions printed under the jurisdiction of the Curia.   Yet the writer of them was really a papal idealist, intent on serving the Church

by purifying her, and quite incapable of the idea
of quitting her.   In penning these furious diatribes, he undoubtedly regarded himself as a
surgeon using the sharpest possible instrument to
cut out a cancerous growth which threatened the
patient's very life.   Nor did he stand alone ;
Catholics of unimpeachable loyalty shared his
views ; very eminent Churchmen protected and
encouraged him ; bishops and even cardinals were
among the chosen few to whom the letters *Sine
Titulo* were shown.

At last, it seemed, the Pope himself was convinced, and Petrarch might not unreasonably claim
to have had a share in the work of convincing him.
Urban was the third Pope to whom he had addressed his impassioned appeal for justice to Rome.
To Benedict XII he had written a couple of
poetical Latin letters ; to Clement VI he had addressed a rhetorical poem which Rossetti believes
to have been spoken as a harangue on the occasion
of Rienzi's embassy : now in 1366, while Urban
still seemed established at Avignon, he sent him a
long prose letter—rather, perhaps, we may call it
a treatise and an exhortation—which is one of the
most interesting of his political writings.   The form
of these appeals to successive Popes varies, but
their tenor is always the same : the sorrowful
"widowhood" of Rome, the pity of it, the shame
of it, and the glory awaiting the servant of God
who shall right her wrong—such is the theme of
them all ; and not of them only, for the letters to
Rienzi and to Charles IV bewail the same misery,

199

URBANVS V,
saco Gallus, creat.
1362. Sedit ann. 8.
ijt die 19 Decemb.

Guillelmus de Gri-
die 28. Octobr. an.
mens. i. dies 23. Ob-
an. 1370. V. S. d. ii.

URBAN V
FROM A PORTRAIT IN THE BRITISH MUSEUM

urge the same duty, glow with the same fervour,
extol the same ideal.

To the Pope, as to the Emperor, Petrarch writes
with an uncompromising freedom of speech which
shows that his high-flown compliments are the
language of conventional courtesy, not of adula-
tion. A long preface explains why the writer had
allowed more than three years to elapse since
Urban's election before addressing him; he had
delayed not from distrust of his powers, for the
zeal of his heart might well compensate for their
deficiency, nor yet from fear of the Pope's displeasure, against which his own age and Urban's
goodness gave him double protection; but partly
from unwillingness to incur suspicion of flattery by
praising one so highly placed, and partly from fear
that if he praised the good work that Urban had
already done, he might repeat with the Pope his
lamentable experience with the Emperor; the later
event might belie the early promise, and he might
have vehemently to blame one whom he had pre-
maturely praised. For often those who show brilliant promise in lesser things fail in the supreme
business of their life; and of all life's businesses
those of Pope and Emperor are the supreme ones.

Now he breaks silence, for three years and more
have passed without sign of the accomplishment of
the great work. All this while he had never lost
hope, knowing and saying to others more im-
patient than himself that great enterprises cannot
be done in a hurry. But now time enough for
reasonable preparation has gone by; he must ask

a patient hearing for exhortation, perhaps even for blame.

Let Urban consider, while he does lesser things consummately well at Avignon, in what state lies his natural home, his spiritual bride. True, the whole Church is his, and the city in which he chooses to dwell may be called his bride ; none the less Rome has a peculiar claim on him ; all other cities have their special bridegrooms ; she alone has no bishop but the Pope. He bids all other bishops reside in their sees ; how then can he leave the queen of cities in ruins, spoiled by robbers, and desolate of her bridegroom ? Surely his very name, voluntarily assumed and hailed as an omen of hope, is a call that Urban cannot ignore. His noble mind may despise world-given glory ; but let him think what merit Christ will impute to him who brings His Church back to the place where He established her. Of all six Popes who have sat at Avignon, Urban has received the clearest call to the great work ; for in his election the finger of God was almost miraculously made manifest. If the return to Rome is God's will, He will perform it through some one ; why should Urban leave to a successor the glory of being His instrument ?

Four qualities are requisite in the man who shall do the great work ; Urban possesses them all. He has intellectual ability, for lack of which some have been unable to discern the good cause from the bad. He has goodness of heart and will ; many have let their passions overpower the conviction of their minds. He has experience ; for lack of it many have maintained the superiority of Provence over Italy. Lastly, he is disinterested; many oppose the return to Rome out of regard for their worldly interests in Avignon. In a word, Pope Urban is marked out as the man to return to the Urbs.

Lately he had a magnificent reception at Marseilles; that was but a feeble earnest of what would await him in Rome. And who can say that Avignon is a safe residence and Rome a dangerous one? Safe! Why the Great Company lately held city and Pope to ransom; Urban suffered worse indignities than Boniface; and if Rome is turbulent, the Pope's absence is the main cause of her turbulence. Never can he be as happy at Avignon as in Rome, for only in Rome can he feel that he is taking his proper place and doing his duty to God and man.

Lastly, nowhere west of Rome can Pope and Emperor honourably and fittingly meet the peril from the Turks. How, if he stays at Avignon, will he answer Christ and Peter in the fast-approaching day of death and judgment?

A summary can give at best but a poor reflection of Petrarch's argument; the actual letter occupies eighteen folio pages, and from every page breathes the persuasiveness of earnest conviction. But could its author hope to succeed at this third attempt? The obstacles might well seem as formidable as ever. Once again the Pope was a Frenchman, and the French party had a stronger hold than ever on the Sacred College. Only the Pope's personality was changed, but this was a change indeed. Benedict, it is true, was not exactly the "ass" that he styled himself in the first surprise of his election, but his intellect was of the narrowest theological type, he was dull of imagination, impermeable by ideas. Clement had the wit to understand and the taste to value a fine conception, but lacked the driving power of moral purpose. Of Urban, on the contrary, Petrarch could say without flattery that he seemed to combine in himself all the requisite qualities : a great policy was congenial to his mind, unselfish devotion to duty was perhaps the keynote of his character, and he had already given proof of no little sagacity in carrying out reforms. At last, then, Petrarch might hope for success, and the course of events soon justified his hopefulness. How far his appeal actually influenced the Pope cannot be determined, but considering his great reputation and the high esteem in which his letters were held, it is reasonable to suppose that his advocacy had weight with Urban, if not in forming his decision, at least in confirming it and in hastening its execution. His letter is dated June 29th ; the year is demonstrably 1366 ; and before the end of that year the Papal Legate was busy getting ready a summer residence for the Pope at Viterbo, restoring the ruined palaces of Rome, and even arranging with Venice, Genoa, and Naples for a supply of galleys to bring the Papal Court by sea from the Rhone to the Tiber.

On April 30th, 1367, the Pope left Avignon, on June 9th he reached Viterbo, and about the end of the month went on to Rome. The Babylonish captivity was apparently at an end, and Petrarch

poured out his soul in a long congratulatory letter
to the Pope.   But even in this pæan of praise and
thanksgiving there is a characteristic note of warning and of exhortation to persevere.   Petrarch was
an enthusiast with a keen eye for actualities ; he
knew that the French party would spare no effort
to bring about a return to Avignon, and almost in
the same breath with his exultant cry that Israel
was come out of Egypt and the House of Jacob
from among a strange people, he exhorts the Pope
to endurance in well-doing, to patience in overcoming difficulties, and to vigilance against the arts
of the malcontents.   Two dangers cause him special
uneasiness.   One is the self-indulgent epicurism of
the Court.   This base motive he combats in a vein
of scornful persiflage, which overlies but does not
conceal his deep anxiety.   These people judge a
country by the quality not of its sons but of its tuns ;
they prefer the wine they get in Provence to the
vintages of Italy.   But was ever a man so desperate
a drunkard as to want to sleep in his vineyard ?
Wine is grown in the vineyard, kept in the cellar,
drunk in the hall ; the two first are the steward's
business, only the third is the master's.   Wherever
you live, your wine must be brought to the house,
and if these people must needs drink French wine
in Italy, well, a little extra toil of sailors who will
enjoy the job will bring it them, and it will have
improved on the voyage.   And so forth.   The
other chief danger is the argument from Italian
turbulence.   Already a street riot at Viterbo had
served the French party only too well as an instance

of mob-violence, and Petrarch foresaw that they would magnify such petty incidents, and possibly even provoke them, in the hope of frightening Urban back to their own country.

It is curious that, except for a brief acknowledgment of the importance of the Gallican Church, he hardly notices the one serious argument by which a statesman might have defended a preference for Avignon. The centre of European gravity had shifted northwards. France, Germany, and, above all, England were daily growing more important; and it was at least arguable that Southern France could now provide a more convenient ecclesiastical capital than central Italy. Petrarch's silence on this point was certainly not due to lack of counter-arguments; it is fairly safe to infer from it that motives of self-interest, not those of public policy, were the really formidable influences at work.

Urban took all this exhortation in the spirit in which it was given, and sent his monitor more than one cordial invitation to pay him a visit. Nothing could have been more gratifying to Petrarch, but for the moment he seems to have been unable to accept; probably the state of his health made it difficult for him to undertake so long a journey.

During the years 1367–8 he divided his time as usual between Venice, Padua, and Pavia. In the latter year his visit to Galeazzo was paid earlier in the season than usual; the interminable quarrel between the Visconti and the Church had entered a new phase, and Galeazzo, for the moment anxious for peace, sent for Petrarch to help him in treating for it. Petrarch accordingly left Padua on May 25th, and arrived at Pavia on the 29th. The Pope was represented by his brother, Cardinal Grimoard, whom he had lately placed as Legate in Bologna, and Petrarch was evidently welcomed as the friend of both parties to the dispute. But the negotiations came to nothing, and the war went on. From Pavia, according to the received story, of which however there is no confirmation in Petrarch's own writings, he went on to Milan to be present at a ceremony of no little interest to Englishmen. Galeazzo, eager for royal alliances, was not content with having married his son to a princess of France; he was now about to marry his daughter to a prince of England. Lionel "of Antwerp," Duke of Clarence, third son of Edward III, had been four years a widower; and for half that time negotiations had been going on for his marriage with Galeazzo's daughter Violante. At last the treaty had been signed at Windsor. The bridegroom contributed royal blood, a handsome person, and the theoretical ownership, derived from his first wife, of large estates in Ireland. The bride brought two hundred thousand golden florins and the effective lordship of several townships in Piedmont. After brilliant festivities in France and Savoy, the Duke of Clarence reached Milan, and one day early in June—there is the usual conflict of evidence as to the exact date—the marriage was solemnised with the utmost splendour in the church of Santa Maria Maggiore. The received tradition says that at the banquet which followed, Petrarch sat at the high table among the most illustrious guests. The Duke lived but a short time to enjoy his bride and her wealth ; less than five months after his marriage he died of fever in Piedmont. There was the usual talk of poison, but Galeazzo had much to lose and nothing to gain by his son-in-law's death, and an Englishman's imprudence in a strange climate furnishes a sufficient and probable explanation.

In July Petrarch resolved to return to Padua. But Lombardy had once again become a vast camp, divided between the rival armies of the Visconti and the league organised against them by the Pope. Travel might well seem impossible, but Petrarch would not be deterred from the attempt. He chartered a boat, coaxed a half-frightened company of boatmen to work her, took not a weapon to defend himself with, and sailed quietly down the Po. The adventure had an astonishing success. Through the river-fleets and between the massed squadrons of both armies sailed this invalid old man of a perfect courage, and the officers of both hosts vied with each other in doing him honour. His voyage was a triumphal progress, delayed not by the hostility but by the assiduous kindness of all whom he met. Hardly ever in the world's history has the soldier rendered such homage to the poet.

Even this peaceful triumph scarcely gave adequate compensation for the loss of a visit from Boccaccio. The latter had left Florence towards the end of March, meaning to go straight through to Venice and enjoy with Petrarch the mutual delight of a surprise visit. Bad weather and perils by the wayside delayed his journey, and he was still detained at Bologna when he heard that Petrarch had left Venice on his unseasonable journey to Pavia. How keen was the disappointment may be read in Boccaccio's charming letter of regret. " I almost gave up the project," he writes ; "indeed there was excellent reason for stopping short. For however many things worth seeing there may be in Venice, none of all these would have induced me to start ; and it was only the wish to keep faith with certain friends, and to see those two whom you love best, your Tullia and her Francesco (whom till then I had not known, though I think I know all your other intimates), that persuaded me to resume the journey and accomplish it at the cost of immense fatigue." And, after warmest praises of Francesca and her husband, he delightfully adds : " But what that belongs to you, or is of your making, can I refrain from praising ? "

Sorrow once more dealt heavily with Petrarch in this year, which took from him both the youngest and the oldest of those whom he loved, his baby grandson and Guido Settimo, Archbishop of Genoa. Guido had been his playmate in childhood, his constant companion in youth, his welcome guest at Vaucluse, where he found occasional relaxation from the strain of a busy life, his friend always.

The end of the year was marked by a happier event. Philip de Cabassoles, who for the last seven years had borne the honorific but empty title of

Patriarch of Jerusalem, was raised to the Cardinalate, and to this dignity was added in the following
year the Bishopric of Sabina. The immediate
cause of Philip's elevation was his conduct of a
special mission to administer the ecclesiastical affairs
of Marseilles ; but apart from his success in this
particular work, his appointment was an instance
of Urban's determination to regard character and
ability as the qualifications for high office in the
Church.

The year 1369 is notable in Petrarch's life, chiefly
as the date of his first stay at Arquà, a village
in the Euganean hills, which thereafter became his
regular summer residence, and will be more fully
described in the next chapter. In the same year he
availed himself of his favour with the Pope to
espouse the cause of Thomas of Frignano, General
of the Franciscans. The Chapter of the Order
had elected Thomas against the wish of their
patron, the Cardinal of Limoges ; other members of
the Order shared the Cardinal's dislike of the new
General, and accused him of heresy. The scandal
was so grave that Urban suspended Thomas from
his functions, and summoned him to defend himself
in Rome. Petrarch, who was convinced of the
General's innocence and held his character in high
esteem, wrote an eloquent defence of him to the
Pope, which may well have influenced Urban in
forming his decision. This was, at all events, in
Thomas's favour ; he was completely acquitted and
reinstated in his office, and his subsequent career
amply justified Petrarch's opinion of him. He was

made Patriarch of Grado by Gregory XI, and
Cardinal by Urban VI.

Towards the end of the year came another pressing invitation from Urban to visit Rome.   In reply
Petrarch wrote, on Christmas Eve, deploring his
inability to travel at that season, but promising
to obey the Pope's summons without fail in the following spring.   In April, accordingly, he made his
will and set out from Padua; but on reaching
Ferrara, barely fifty miles away, he was seized with
a fainting fit which was reported to be fatal, and
very nearly proved so.   After all, it was perhaps as
well that he was stopped on the journey : his disappointment, had he arrived in Rome, might have
been even keener than his disappointment at being
baulked of his visit.   He would have found the
Pope distraught with manifold anxieties, hampered
by the incessant intrigues of his courtiers, doubting
if he had done right in coming to Rome, and more
than half inclined to go back to Avignon.   Highly
as he esteemed Petrarch's zeal for great principles,
and much as he admired his eloquence in defending
them, it is not to be supposed that the poet's exhortations could have outweighed the pressure of untoward circumstances.   Since Urban had been in
Rome, troubles had multiplied round him.   True,
he had escaped the humiliating state of dependence
which had threatened to make the Papacy a department of the Government of France.   The verdict
of history holds, with Petrarch and with Saint
Catherine, that this great deliverance was worth all
the sacrifices necessary to achieve it.   But Urban

might be pardoned if he thought that it been bought too dear. Vexation and disappointment had been his portion in Rome. The Emperor had visited him in 1368; but the courtesies in which Charles abounded were poor compensation for the deadly mischief that he caused to the peace of Tuscany. Lombardy was ablaze with war. The Pope's enemies defied him, his friends fought more for their own hands than for Holy Church. All the time the pressure of the French party never slackened. Five of the Cardinals had flatly refused to leave Avignon ; their compatriots, wiser in their generation, accompanied Urban to Italy and gave him no peace while he stayed there. The Pope was a disillusioned man, and in the bitterness of disillusionment he yielded. He took the Curia back to Avignon in September, and died there in December.

Petrarch's last political hope was shattered: Tribunate, Empire, Papacy, each had failed ; Rome was once more a " widow." But his disappointment, bitter as it was, did not poison his mind against Urban ; he heard of his death with sincere sorrow, and in spite of ill-health, which might well have been accounted a valid excuse, he testified his veneration for the Pope's saintly character by attending his funeral at Bologna.

CHAPTER XVIII

THE LAST YEARS

1370-1374

THE record of an invalid's last years must have a certain sadness, but it would be a great mistake to represent the end of Petrarch's life as a period of gloom. On the contrary, we have to chronicle a triumph of character over circumstance. Events were untoward; but events, after all, are only the raw material of life; it is a man's way of dealing with them that makes or mars the finished article. Petrarch comes out of this test with a new hold on our sympathies, a new claim to our admiration. Continual ill-health, the pain of a patriot's disappointment, disturbance of his chosen home by turmoil of war, the defeat and humiliation of a dear friend, here surely were troubles enough to breed despondency, almost to excuse moroseness. Petrarch met them all with a serenity that illumines the dark places and sheds a halo over the whole retrospect of his life. He had a scholar's tenacity, a scholar's courage, a scholar's inexhaustible consolations.

Once, indeed, in the midst of all this calm confronting of adversity, the old Adam flashed out into vehemence of invective. But this time it was no

mere private quarrel that stirred his wrath; Rome
was attacked in the person of her champion, and it
was in defence of Rome, far more than of himself,
that he once more steeped his pen in gall. A
French Cistercian, angered by his letters of exhortation and congratulation to Pope Urban, had
published a clumsy and silly pamphlet by way of
counterblast. The quality of its wit may be judged
from the opening sentences, which compare Pope
Urban's journey from Avignon to Rome with that
of the man who went down from Jerusalem to
Jericho and fell among thieves. A little later Rome
is elegantly likened to the waning moon. There is
much ill-natured vilification of Petrarch and of
Italy, and much laudation of the superior excellences
of France and Frenchmen. Petrarch could not
leave this poor stuff alone. We have already had
occasion to note that he did not shine in controversy; the *Apology in Answer to a Frenchman's
Calumnies* bears a depressing likeness to the rubbish
which it undertakes to confute. It is not such
sheer nonsense; it is written in decent Latin, and
it has the merit of patriotic motive; but it is marred
by a note of rancour, and those who love its author
do not willingly read it twice.

Urban's successor was Pierre Roger de Beaufort,
nephew and namesake of Clement · VI, who is
famous in history under his papal name of
Gregory XI, as the friend of St. Catherine of
Siena, and the Pope who finally brought back the
Curia to Rome. He was a man of great ability
and high character, sincere in his efforts to reform

the monastic orders, and equally sincere in combating the doctrines of Wickliffe. Towards Petrarch he showed the kindliest goodwill, and soon after his accession instructed Bruno to write him a letter expressing friendship, and hinting an intention of doing something for him. Petrarch's reply is interesting, as showing that his considerable income was barely sufficient to meet the many claims upon it. He cannot say with truth, he tells Bruno, that his means are insufficient for the maintenance of a simple canon, but he can say quite truly that he has a wider circle of acquaintance than all the rest of the Chapter put together, and these friends put him to charges. Besides an old priest who lives with him, a whole troop will often turn up at meal-times; they swarm like Penelope's suitors, only they are friends, not enemies, and he has not the heart to turn them away or grudge them the victuals. Then, alas! he cannot do without servants; and he keeps a couple of horses, and usually five or six scribes. Just now he has only three, because scribes worthy of the name are not to be found: one only gets mere mechanical copyists—and bad ones at that. Then he is undertaking to build a little oratory to the Virgin. This work he will accomplish if he has to pawn or sell his books to pay for it. So if Gregory is minded to do for him what Urban had promised, and he himself hints, the gift will be welcome. Petrarch can, indeed, manage at a pinch as he has managed hitherto, but age makes the pinch harder. Only do not let the Pope expect him to ask for

anything.   Let him do anything or nothing, just as
he sees fit ; in any case, though, let him not confer
a cure of souls or any office entailing fresh labour.
Petrarch had refused secretaryships and bishoprics
from Clement.   He cannot, as an old man, take
from the nephew burdens which, as a young man, he
had refused to receive from the uncle.   Finally, he
commends the whole matter to the goodness of the
Pope and the kind offices of Bruno and Philip de
Cabassoles.   It does not appear that any additional
benefice was conferred, or that Petrarch was very
seriously straitened for want of one; in his personal
habits he was the most frugal of men, and any
accession of income would probably have been
spent on the further multiplication of manuscripts.

The letter, of which the above is a brief summary,
was written at Whitsuntide, 1371, from Arquà, where
Petrarch had now established his summer residence.
His first recorded stay in the place was, as we have
already seen, in the summer of 1369, when he took
refuge from the turmoil of the city in the hospitable
house of the Augustinian Friars there.   He was so
charmed with the beauty of the place, that he got
Lombardo da Serico to negotiate for the purchase
of a plot of ground, comprising a vineyard and an
orchard of olives and other fruit trees.   Here he
built a house, which still stands structurally un-
altered, and bears witness to the simplicity of his
domestic habits and his appreciation of beautiful
scenery.   Englishmen need no assurance of the
loveliness of the hills which inspired the Muse of
Shelley.   Arquà lies in a long narrow valley

Alinari

PETRARCH'S HOUSE AT ARQUA

hemmed in by conical peaks and their connecting ridges ; in the whole neighbourhood there is not a spot which looks out on a more enchanting landscape than the site chosen by Petrarch for his house. He built it on a little spur jutting out from a hill-side, which shelters it from the north-east ; to the west and south are glorious views up and across the valley; to the south-east the village scrambles, Italian fashion, up the lower slopes : in Petrarch's day it was crowned by a castle, of which only some ruined arches and a fine thirteenth-century tower now remain. Beyond the village is the only apparent outlet from the valley, a narrow gap in the hills leading to the flat water-meadows and isolated crag of Monselice.

All through this period, Petrarch's life hung by a thread. Four times in one year, he tells Pandolfo Malatesta, he was threatened with imminent death ; the first of these occasions must have been the fainting-fit of Ferrara already mentioned, the last, as we learn from his own letter, occurred in the spring of 1371. He had lately come back from Arquà to spend a few days in Padua, and was just going to answer Pandolfo's anxious inquiries about his health by telling him that he was getting the better of a long sickness. "But all of a sudden," he writes, "on May 8th, a most violent fit of my familiar fever seized me. The physicians flocked in, some sent by order of the lord of the city, others drawn to the house by friendly concern for me. Up and down they wrangled and disputed, till at last they settled that I was to die at midnight : already it was

the first watch of the night; see what a tiny span
of life remained to me, if these humbugging fellows'
tales had been true. But every day confirms me
more and more in my old opinion of them. They
said there was one possible expedient for prolonging
my life a little, by tying me up in some arrangement
of strings and so preventing me from going to sleep:
in this way there was just a chance that I might
last till morning—a mighty tiresome price to pay for
this little extra time! As a matter of fact, to rob
me of my sleep was just the way to kill me. Well,
we disobeyed them, for I have always begged my
friends and ordered my servants never to let any of
these doctors' tricks be tried on my body, but always
to do the exact contrary of what they advise. So
I passed that night in a sweet, deep sleep, such as
Virgil calls the very image of calm death. Why
make a long story? I was to die at midnight. In
the morning, flocking, I suppose, to my funeral,
they found me writing, and, utterly astounded, they
could say nothing but that I was a wonderful man.
Over and over again they have been baffled and
tricked about me, and yet they never stop impu-
dently asserting what they know nothing about, nor
can they find any other shield than this to cover
their ignorance. Yet if I am a wonderful man, how
much more wonderful are they! And as for those
who believe in them, they are not merely wonderful,
but astounding.''

It must be owned that Petrarch's experience lent
some colour to his quarrel with the doctors. But in
truth his condition was beyond hope of relief from

the science of that day. A year later he had another painful reminder of his physical weakness. Philip de Cabassoles had come as Legate into Umbria, and with affectionate urgency insisted that Petrarch must come to visit him in Perugia. No possible summons could have been more agreeable to the latter, and in May, 1372, he tried to obey it, but found himself unable to sit on horseback. The friends never saw each other again, for Philip died in the following August.

Meanwhile, war had broken out between Padua and Venice, and Petrarch could no longer enjoy the use of his house in the latter city. " I should be suspected there," he writes, in January, 1372 ; "here (at Padua) I am beloved." During the spring and summer he seems to have been much at Arquà, but in the autumn the progress of the war drove him thence. Things had gone badly for the Paduans, and the Venetian general camped his army within a short distance of Arquà. Residence in the country was no longer safe, and, sorely against the grain, Petrarch transferred himself and his family about the middle of November within the walls of Padua.

The Venetians pursued their success in the following year, and Francesco da Carrara, after vainly soliciting help from the King of Hungary, found himself obliged to sue for peace and accept what terms the republic would grant him. Venice was never slow to set her foot on the neck of an enemy. She stipulated that the Lord of Padua should acknowledge himself to be entirely in the wrong, and that either in his own person, or in that of his

son, he should go to Venice to entreat pardon for
the past, and swear allegiance for the future. Francesco despatched his son on this painful errand, and
begged Petrarch to accompany him as chief spokesman. The Venetian Senate gave them audience on
September 28th, but Petrarch, seized probably with
illness, found himself unable to deliver the speech
which he had prepared ; the audience was postponed
till the following day, when the speech was duly
delivered, and the humiliating ceremony accomplished.

There were probably not many men still living
for whom Petrarch would have undertaken such a
task, but he was bound to Francesco by ties of close
and peculiar affection. That prince had inherited
the leading characteristics of his father Jacopo, his
unscrupulousness in politics, his cultured intellect,
and his personal charm ; he inherited also his warm
and sincere regard for Petrarch. Francesco could
not have treated his own father with more solicitous
respect than he paid to his father's friend. Nothing
that could make Petrarch's stay in Padua agreeable
was omitted, and when he fled from the bustle of the
city to the quietude of Arquà, Francesco delighted
to visit him there and engage him in discussions on
the subjects that interested them both. It was to
him that, just about this time, Petrarch wrote the
long letter on the principles of government, which,
in the Bâle edition of his works, is printed as a
separate treatise under the title *On the best methods
of administering a State*. The pamphlet is especially notable for the stress that it lays on the ethical

basis of government, and on the moral qualities requisite to make a good ruler. Here we have a marked contrast between Petrarch and the great political thinker of the following century. Macchiavelli takes it for granted that adminstration is a prince's business, and proceeds to show how he can get through it most efficiently. Petrarch "is content to fill a single letter with a subject which might well form the matter of many books, the question what sort of man he ought to be to whom the charge of the State has been committed." The ruler, in a word, must justify his existence by ruling well.

It is to this period, too, that we must refer the writing of his autobiography, which took the form of a *Letter to Posterity*. The desire to live in the thoughts of mankind is not peculiar to any age, but it was felt perhaps with unwonted intensity by the men of the Renaissance. The world was in reaction against what is commonly called the mediæval spirit. The monastic system embodied, as it were, the principle of self-effacement ; and theology, which was the chief intellectual business of the Middle Ages, contemplates themes in face of which a mere man shrinks to nothingness. Against this withering of the individual, the new learning raised its protest, and it is characteristic of Petrarch that he could be at once the fervent devotee and the scholar athirst for fame. It was not enough for him that his influence should work as a silent leaven in the minds of men ; he wanted to be remembered as a man, as a personality. "You may perhaps have heard some report of me," he writes to the imaginary recipient of the *Letter to Posterity*, "and you may like to know what sort of a man I was, and what was the outcome of my works." The letter is only a fragment, and carries us no further down than Jacopo da Carrara's death, when Petrarch was still under fifty. Nor does it help us as much as we might have expected in solving the chronological difficulties which beset the student of its author's career. But the really significant thing about it is that the idea of writing it should have entered his head.

The letters of this period are rich in instances of the serene calm with which Petrarch awaited death. "I read, I write, I think," he says of himself at the beginning of 1372 ; "this is my life, this is my delight, just as it has been ever since the days of my youth. I envy no man, I hate no man, and whereas I wrote long ago that I looked down on no man, now I must say that I look down on many, but most of all on myself." A little more or a little less of life does not seem to him a thing to make a fuss about ; he waits God's will, and in the meantime keeps flying the flag of his allegiance to Learning. In a letter to Benvenuto da Imola, he lauds poetry as the most glorious of the arts, and in a most noble letter to Boccaccio, written in 1373, a letter which they who value learning should cherish as a priceless heritage, he declares that nothing but death shall tear him from his beloved studies.

Boccaccio had written in serious anxiety about his beloved master's health, and had advised that, having done more than enough for reputation, he should now allow himself a rest from hard work. "No counsel could be more repugnant to my mood," says Petrarch with the frank expression of contrary opinion possible between such friends. . . . "You write that my ill-health makes you ill at ease; I know that, and am not surprised at it. Neither of us can be really well while the other is ailing. You add that you suppose the Comic poet's saying is becoming applicable to me, that old age is a disease in itself. Here again is nothing to wonder at, nor do I reject this utterance; only I should modify it by saying that old age is not a state of bodily disease but of mental health. Well, would you have me prefer that these conditions should be reversed, so that I should carry a sick mind in a sound body? Far be such a wish from my mind! My desire and my delight is that, as in the body, so in the whole man, that part which is the nobler should be healthy above the rest. You instance me my years, and this you could not have done if I myself had not told you the tale of them . . . but believe me, I remember them, and every day I say to myself, 'Here is one more step towards the end.' . . . I remember them, and do not blush to acknowledge my age; why should I be more ashamed of having grown old than of having lived, when the one process cannot go on long without the other? What I should really like is not to be younger than I am, but to feel that I had reached old age by a course of more honourable deeds and pursuits; and nothing distresses me more than that in all this long while I have not reached the goal that I ought to have reached. Therefore I am still striving, if haply now at eventide it may be granted me to retrieve the daytime's sloth, and often do I call to mind the maxim of that most wise Prince, Augustus Cæsar, that 'whatever is done well enough is done soon enough;' as also the saying of Plato, the most learned of the philosophers, that 'Happy is he to whom it is granted even in old age to attain to wisdom and right opinion;' or again, that Catholic doctrine of the most holy Father Ambrose, that 'Blessed is the man who even in old age has risen from error; yea, blessed is he who even under the very stroke of death turns away his mind from unrighteousness.' With these and similar thoughts I am brought to the resolution of amending by God's favour not only the defects of my life, but those of my writings too; for neglect of these faults might in old days have been attributed to set purpose, but can now be ascribed only to an old man's torpor and slothfulness.

"And here comes in that advice of yours which, as I have said and say again, causes me utter astonishment; for who can fail to be astonished at hearing counsels of sleep and laziness from the mouth of the wakefullest of men? Read again, I pray you, and examine what you wrote; sit in judgment on your own advice, and acquit it if you dare; the passage, I mean, where by way of a medicine for old age you exhort me to sloth, a far worse evil than ever age can be; and the more

readily to persuade me, you try to make me out a
great man in one respect or another, as though I
might now come to a stand on the plea that I have
gone far enough in life and achievement and learning. But I am of quite another mind, as the saying
is, and have come to a very different resolution,
namely, to double my pace, and now at this season
of sunset, as having lost part of the daylight, to
make more haste than ever towards the goal.

"Now why do you give your friend advice which
you do not take yourself? Such is not the wont of
trusty counsellors. But herein you have recourse
to a wonderful piece of wit and craft; you say that
by my writings I have won reputation far and wide
. . . that I am known to the uttermost ends of
the earth. . . . In this your love for me deceives
you; it is a really absurd exaggeration. . . . But
granted that it were true; imagine my reputation
spread as widely as you please . . . do you think
this would be a rein to my diligence? Nay, it
would be a spur to it; the more flourishing appeared the results of my labours, the keener would
be my exertions in them; such is my mood, that
success would make me not slothful but eager and
ardent. Further, as though the bounds of earth
were too narrow, you say that I am known also
above the firmament, a form of praise bestowed
on Aeneas and Julius; and there, without any
doubt, I really am known; and I pray that I may
be beloved there too. Next you say in praise of
me that, throughout Italy, and very likely beyond
Italy; too, I have stirred up the wits of many to

engage in these studies of ours, which were neglected for so many centuries; and this credit I do not disclaim, for I am older than nearly all those who are now working at these subjects in our country. But your inference I do not admit, that I should make way for the talents of younger men, break the swing of the effort in which I have engaged, allow others to have something to write about if they wish, and not seem to want to do all the writing myself. Oh, what a difference of view between us, who have but one will! To you my writings seem exhaustive, or at any rate immense; to me they seem a mere nothing. But granted I have written a great deal, and shall write a great deal more; what better means can I possibly find of inciting the minds of those who come after us to perseverance? Example is always more stimulating than precept; Camillus, a much applauded general in his old age, did much more to kindle the young men's valour by marching to battle like one of themselves, than if he had left them in the fighting line, issued his orders, and gone to bed. As for your fear of my exhausting all the subjects, so that nothing will be left for any one else, it is like Alexander of Macedon's absurd apprehension that his father Philip would conquer the world and leave him no chance of winning a soldier's reputation. . . . But Seneca has rid us of that fear in a letter to Lucilius. . . .

" Our ancestors worked hard in old age; . . . they had no longer span of life than ours, but they had greater industry; and life without industry is not really life, but a sluggish and unprofitable loitering. . . . Now your crowning resource in persuasion is an entreaty that I will try to live as long as I can for the joy of my friends, and above all for the comfort of your own old age ; for, as you say, you hope that I shall outlive you. Ah me! this was what our dear Simonides always hoped ; and again ah me! his prayer was only too fatally efficacious, whereas if there were any regularity in human affairs, he ought to have outlived me. And now you, my brother, utter this affectionate wish more fervently than any one, and some others among my friends utter it too ; but it is the exact opposite of my wish, for I desire to die while you are still alive, and so to leave behind me some in whose memory and speech I may live on, and by whose prayers I may be profited, by whom I may still be loved and missed. . . .

" Lastly, you ask me to pardon you for proffering advice, and venturing to prescribe a mode of life to me under which I should give up mental strain and vigils and my usual tasks, and should nurse my age, worn out with years and study, in the lap of ease and sleep. Nay, it is not pardon but thanks that I give you, recognising your love for me, which makes you in my behalf what you never are in your own, a physician. But bear with me, I entreat you, in that I obey not your orders, and believe that even if I were most greedy of life, which I am not, still if I were to rule me by your advice, I should but die the sooner. Constant toil and strain are food to my spirit ; when once I begin to rest and slacken, I shall soon cease to live. I know my own strength; I am not fit for other labours; but this of reading and writing, in which you bid me slacken, is light toil, nay rather 'tis a pleasant rest, and breeds forgetfulness of heavy labours. There is no nimbler or more delightful burden than the pen; other pleasures flee away, and do you a mischief even while they soothe you; your pen soothes you in the taking up, and delights you in the laying down of it; and it works profit not only to its master but to many besides, often even to the absent, and sometimes to posterity after thousands of years. I think I speak absolute truth when I say that of all earthly delights, as there is none more honourable than literature, so there is none more lasting or sweeter or more constant; none which plays the comrade to its possessor with so easily gotten an equipment or with so total a lack of irksomeness. . . . This do I desire for myself, that when death overtakes me, he may find me either reading or writing or, if Christ so will it, praying and in tears."

Just before this letter was written—so strangely ignorant could he be of the vernacular works of his friends—he had read the *Decameron* for the first time, and had pleased himself by composing in Latin a free rendering of the tale of Griselda. An Englishman may note with keen pleasure that the story selected by Petrarch for this tribute of admiration was one of those which kindled the imagination of our own great master in the art of narrative poetry. This association of the names of Petrarch,

Boccaccio, and Chaucer is no mere accidental stroke of good luck; the connection between them illustrates, better perhaps than any other single event, the literary history of the early Renaissance. Petrarch's work, as we have seen, was to spread the knowledge of the classical authors, and revive their spirit as the dominant intellectual force of the world ; he accomplished this almost entirely through the medium of Latin. The choice was a wise one, because it gave him all the scholars of Europe for audience ; but the unlettered could feel his influence only at second hand. Boccaccio carried the diffusion of the humanistic spirit a long step further by breathing it into the vernacular literature of Italy. Chaucer in his turn did for England what Boccaccio had done for Italy ; with him the spirit of the new learning speaks in our national song and begins to mould our national life. Chaucer himself was well aware of the source from which his inspiration flowed. It is very possible that the Clerk of Oxenforde's Prologue alludes to an actual meeting with Petrarch at Padua in the summer or early autumn of 1373. However this may be, the words of that prologue make it clear that Chaucer knew Petrarch's Latin version of the story, and recognised in its author a master and chief among poets. The clerk tells a tale—

> Lerned at Padowe of a worthy clerk,
> As provyd by his wordes and his werk.
> He is now deed, and nayled in his chest,
> Now God yive his soule wel good rest !
> Fraunces Petrark, the laureat poete,
> Highte this clerk, whos rethorique swete
> Enlumynd al Ytail of poetrie.

These letters to Boccaccio are not quite the last product of Petrarch's unwearied pen, for de Sade is undoubtedly mistaken in ascribing his version of the Griselda to the last month of his life ; but, by a happy neglect of exact chronological sequence, they have been made to form the last book of the *Letters written in Old Age.*   There is a beautiful fitness in the arrangement which makes his correspondence close with these admirable letters to the friend who was his peer.

He kept the promise which he had so lately made in them.   Death found him at work.   The contradictions of evidence which beset so many incidents of his life throw some uncertainty over the exact details of his death.   One account states that he died in Lombardo's arms on July 18th ; another, at least as well supported by evidence and preferable in sentiment, represents that he was found dead in his library, with the unfinished epitome of the *Lives of Illustrious Men* on the desk before him, on the morning of July 20th, his seventieth birthday.

Alinari

PETRARCH'S TOMB

CHAPTER XIX

CONCLUSION AND SUMMARY

PETRARCH'S funeral was celebrated at Arquà with great pomp; Francesco da Carrara might be trusted to see to that. He himself attended with a train of courtiers; four bishops took part in the ceremony, and the bier was carried by sixteen doctors of law. Petrarch's body was dressed in a red gown, according to some the royal robe which Robert of Naples had given him for his crowning; according to others the dress of a Canon of Padua. The little chapel which he had hoped to dedicate to the Virgin had never been built. He was therefore buried temporarily in the parish church, and six years later in the sarcophagus of the rather clumsy Paduan type constructed for the purpose by his son-in-law. It is disgusting to have to add that his bones were not allowed to rest undisturbed. At a time when the tomb stood in need of repair, an arm was stolen which is said to be now preserved at Madrid; and among the relics kept in Petrarch's house the caretaker shows, with misplaced satisfaction, a box which contains one of the poet's fingers.

His epitaph may best be read, not in the jingling Latin triolet composed by himself, and still legible on his tomb, but in the testimony borne to his genius by the man who could most adequately appreciate it. "Your lamentable letter, my dearest brother," wrote Boccaccio to Francesco da Brossano, "reached me on October 20th; I did not recognise the writing, but, after undoing the knot and looking at the signature, I knew at once what I was to read in the letter, namely, the happy passing of our illustrious father and teacher, Francesco Petrarca, from this earthly Babylon to Jerusalem above. In truth, although none of our friends save you had written me the news, I had long since, to my exceeding sorrow, heard it bruited about by universal report, and for some days together I had wept almost without intermission, not for his ascent, but because I found myself left in bereavement and misery. And no wonder: for no mortal man ever stood closer to me than he. . . . And when I saw and read your letter, I fell to weeping again for almost a whole night." Then, after much praise of Petrarch's piety and some tender, thoughtful messages to "my sister Tullia," Boccaccio goes on to say that, as a Florentine, he must grudge to Arquà the guardianship of the illustrious dead "whose noble breast was the choicest dwelling-place of the Muses and all the company of Helicon, a shrine devoted to Philosophy and most rich in store of liberal arts; yea, a mirror and glory of such arts, and especially of that one which concerns itself with Ciceronian eloquence, as his writings clearly testify." The sailor, who brings his cargo from far lands to the head of the Adriatic and sees the tops of the Euganean hills against the sky, will say to himself and his companions that "in the bosom of those hills lies he who was the world's glory, the temple of all learning, Petrarch, the poet of sweet speech, whom kindly Rome decked with the triumphal laurel, whose many noble books live to herald forth his most sacred fame." Similarly, in his book on the *Genealogies of the Gods*, written some years earlier, Boccaccio had spoken of "Francesco Petrarca, the Florentine, my most revered teacher, father, and lord, . . . a man who should be counted among the company of the illustrious ancients rather than among modern men: who is acknowledged for a chief poet, I will not say merely by the Italians, whose singular and everlasting glory he is, but also in France, in Germany, and in that most distant corner of the earth, England, and by many of the Greeks. . . . Now there lie open to us many works of his, both in verse and prose, most worthy to be commemorated, which bear to and fro the sure testimony of his heavenly talent."

Similar testimonies might be multiplied from the writings of Benvenuto da Imola, from Coluccio Salutati, and others. But enough has been said to show that those contemporaries of Petrarch who were best qualified to judge, unanimously esteemed him their master and leader in learning. From this leadership he derives his claim to rank among those who have inaugurated new eras and changed the current of the world's intellectual history. It is not pretended that he was the sole scholar of his day. He had predecessors in the so-called Dark Ages, whose enthusiasm for the classical authors known to them was as great as his own; in every country that he

visited he found contemporaries zealous for learning; he had devoted pupils and fellow-workers who
shared his high aims and rivalled even his indefatigable industry.   What distinguishes him from all the
rest is the wonderful power of his influence.   Preceding scholars had been quite unable to make
scholarship a power in the world; men did not
change their modes of thought in the twelfth
century because John of Salisbury wrote good
Latin, or in the early fourteenth because Richard
de Bury composed *Philobiblon*.   But with Petrarch,
and because of him, the classical spirit resumed its
sway; people without the least pretensions to
scholarship began to think and talk in the ways
approved by scholars; the leaven of "the human-
ities" leavened the whole lump of society.

It is not possible precisely to define the quality of
temperament which enabled Petrarch to communicate the spirit which others had only been able to
possess; "charm" affords the only explanation, and
charm defies analysis.   It is evident from his whole
career that he possessed both intellectual and
personal charm to a rare degree; he fascinated
men's imagination and fired their hearts.   Entire
strangers came as pilgrims aglow with enthusiasm
to Vaucluse, and having seen the poet, they went
back to spread the fame of him through all lands.
So his reputation grew, and his influence became
more potent every day; and the studies that he
loved, from being the monopoly of a handful of
scholars, became the inspiration of the world's
culture.

The triumph was far more than a mere intellectual success; it was a triumph of personality and character, and like all great spiritual triumphs, it was hardly won. Petrarch enjoyed moments of intense happiness, but he was not a happy man; his life was one of storm and stress, of anxious self-questioning, and of severe emotional conflict. The very humanity, by virtue of which he quickened the souls of others, gave his own soul for a prey to warring passions; only by such spiritual pangs could the new birth be accomplished.

Surely it is precisely this human sensitiveness, this intensity of nature, which most endears him to us. He had his faults; who cares to remember them? or rather who would do this glorious man the disservice of caring to conceal them? and who shall stand in the judgment if this man falls? As a consummate artist he wins our admiration; as father of the new learning he claims our filial piety; but most of all we love and cherish in him the eager student, the passionate devotee of high ideals, the incomparable friend.

INDEX

Acciaiuoli, Angelo, Bishop of Florence, 156-7, 169

Acciaiuoli, Niccolò, Grand Seneschal of Naples, 168-9, 175, 192, 203, 214

Accursio, Mainardo : his character and friendship with P., 50-1 ; his visit to Parma and murder by brigands, 143-4

Africa, P.'s epic poem : begun at Vaucluse, 90 ; resumed in the Silva Plana and finished at Parma, 104 ; its history and appreciation of it, 224-7 ; lines falsely supposed to have been taken from Silius, *ib.*

Aix-la-Chapelle, 58

Albanzani, Donato degli, 260-1, 262

Alberti, *v.* Innocent VI

Albizzi, Francesco degli, 137

Albornoz, Cardinal, 182, 194, 248

Aldus, his cursive type not copied from P.'s handwriting, 86

Ammirato, Scipione, 250

Ancestors of P., 2

Andrew of Hungary, 111, 113, 120

Anguillara, Orso dell', 75 ; as Senator crowns P., 97-9

Anna, Empress, 198

Annibaldi, Paolo, 78, 98

Apology in answer to a Frenchman, 286

Ardennes, forest, 60

Arezzo, P.'s birthplace, 7, 8 ; P.'s visit, 152

Aristotle, 265

Arquà : P.'s first visit, 282 ; household expenses, 287-8 ; description of, 288-9 ; P. forced to leave, 291 ; his death and burial there, 302-3

Astrologer interrupts P.'s harangue at Milan, 184

Augustine, St. : the *De Civitate Dei* and the *Confessions*, 56 ; P.'s enthusiasm for him, 56-7 ; "Sors" taken on Mont Ventoux, 70-1 ; Commentary on Psalms given to P. by Boccaccio, 210 ; P. gives *Confessions* to Marsili, 267-8

Averroists, 265-6

Avignon : Petracco goes there, 13 ; seat of Papacy, 14 ; lack of accommodation, 15 ; P.'s hatred of, 28 ; advantages of residence there, 28-30 ; society there, 30-1 ; papal palace begun, 79 ; P.'s flight from, 89 ; his return from Italy, 107 ; P. leaves in 1343, 111 ; returns in 1345, 117 ; leaves again in 1347, 131 ; ravages of the plague, 140 ; revisited, 156, 164 ; P.'s last visit, 176 ; Nelli visited there by Giovanni, 213

Azzo da Correggio, *v.* Correggio

Baiani, Ghilberto, 136

Bailiff's wife at Vaucluse, 159-60

Bâle, earthquake, 196-7

Banditti, 97, 102, 114, 143-4, 174

Barbato, Marco : P.'s intimacy with, 96-7, 113 ; the *Poetical Letters* dedicated to him, 216 ; his death, 243

Bardi, Roberto de', Chancellor of Paris University, 93

Barili, Giovanni, 96, 97, 113, 203

Barlaam, Abbot : meets P., 89 ; Boccaccio's description of him, *ib.* ; his mission to Avignon, 90 ; revisits Avignon and begins to

309

teach P. Greek and learn Latin from him, 108 ; Bishop of Geraci, *ib.*

Beaume, Ste., 88

Beccaria, the, of Pavia, 195, 198-9, 252

Benedict XI, Pope, 6

Benedict XII, Pope : his election, 64 ; friendly to P., *ib.* ; P.'s first letter to him, 65 ; gives P. preferment, *ib.* ; P.'s second letter, 79, cf. 272 ; begins palace at Avignon, *ib.* ; sanctions the Correggi's schemes, 102-3 ; his death, 107

Benintendi de' Ravegnani, 246

Benvenuto da Imola, *v.* Imola

Bergamo, 207-8

Boccaccio : P.'s letter to him on culture and religion, 57 ; his description of the Plague, 135 ; character, genius, and friendship with P., 148-50 ; date of their first meeting and earliest extant correspondence, 151-2 ; brings P. decree revoking his banishment, 153 ; his remonstrance in form of a pastoral dialogue, 179-80 ; admired P.'s *Invectiva*, 193 ; visits P. in Milan, 209-11 ; their commerce of books, 210 ; letters to him, *ib.* ; Boccaccio's grievance, *ib.* ; sends P. the *Divina Commedia*, 211 ; his enthusiasm for P.'s Letters, 219 ; also for the *Africa* and for P.'s treatises, 225-7 ; eulogy of P., 229 ; his description of Fr. da Brossano, 235 ; frightened by a supposed revelation ; P.'s noble letter thereon, 236-41 ; visit to Venice, 242-3 ; P.'s cry of anguish in letter to him, 243 ; letters to him, 253-7 ; his rank as poet, *ib.* ; visits Avignon, *ib.* ; anxious about P.'s independence, 259 ; visits Venice, but misses P., 280-1 ; P. rejects B.'s advice to cease work, 294-300 ; the *Tale of Griselda*, 300-1 ; P., B., and Chaucer, *ib.* ; B.'s grief at P.'s death and eulogy of him, 304-5

Bohemia, John, King of, *v.* John

Bologna : P. at University, 21-3 ; P. leaves, 24 ; papal castle built, 63-4, 115 ; state after war, 248 ; Pope Urban's funeral, 284

Bolsena, 152

Boniface VIII, Pope, 4

Book-hunting, 43

Borromeo, Cardinal, 87

Boulogne, Cardinal Gui de, 164

Bretigny, Peace of, 230

Brossano, Francesco da, P.'s son-in-law, 235, 264, 281, 303, 304

Bruno, Francesco, 244, 251, 261, 269, 287

Bucolicum Carmen, *v.* Eclogues

Buonconvento, 13

Bury, Richard de, 53, 306

Bussolari, Fra Jacopo : his revolution in Pavia, 198-9 ; P.'s shameful letter to him, *ib.* ; his heroism and surrender, 251-3

Cabassoles, Philip de, Bishop of Cavaillon : lineage, character, and friendship with P., 83-4 ; at Naples, 112 ; at Cavaillon and Vaucluse, 119-20 ; the *De Vita Sol.* dedicated to him, *ib.*, cf. 256 ; P. and Socrates visit him, 120-1 ; P.'s last visit to Cavaillon, 174-5 ; letters, 245 ; his promotion, *ib.* ; meets Boccaccio, 256 ; Cardinal and Bishop of Sabina, 281-2 ; Legate in Umbria, and death, 291

Cæsars, medals of, 191

Caloria, Tommaso, 22-3, 106

Canigiani, *v.* Eletta

Canzoniere : special characteristics, 38-9 ; Italian and Provençal influences, 40 ; reflects P.'s individuality, *ib.* ; its imitators, *ib.* ; its contents, 40-2 ; tone of the second part, 139 ; place in literary history, 222

Capitol, *v.* Rome

Capra, Enrico, 207-8

Capranica, 74-7

Cardinals, Commission on Roman affairs, 169

Carpentras: P. taken to live there, 15; death of Clement V there, *ib.*; P. goes to school, 16; canonry, 250

Carpi, 141

Carrara, Francesco da, lord of Padua: friendship with P., 65, cf. 292; Vicar Imperial, 189–90; defeated by Venice, 291–2; attends P.'s funeral, 303

Carrara, Francesco Novello da, 292

Carrara, Jacopo II da: friendship with P., 65, 141–2; character, *ib.*; procures P. canonry at Padua, *ib.*; death and P.'s grief, 154; epitaph, 155

Castiglionchio, *v.* Lapo

Cavaillon, Bishop of, *v.* Cabassoles

Cavaillon, city, 83, 174

Celso, Giulio, 229

Celso, Lorenzo, Doge, 248–50

Charles, Duke of Normandy, afterwards Dauphin, 231

Charles IV, Emperor: as Prince of Bohemia commands his father's troops in Italy, 54; his election as King of the Romans, 187; P.'s letters to him, 189; invites P. to his Court, *ib.*; his compact with the Pope, *ib.*; arrival in Italy and disappointments, coronation in Milan and Rome, and return to Germany, 189–93; P.'s visit and exhortations to him, 190–1; crowns Zanobi, 192; secret hostility to the Visconti, 195; P.'s embassy to him, 196–7; his Golden Bull, 197; embellishment of Prague, *ib.*; creates P. Count Palatine, 198; gift of drinking-cup with invitation, 232; P.'s reply, *ib.*; P. invited again, starts, but is forced to turn back, 236; Charles visits Rome and makes mischief in Tuscany, 284

Charles of Valois, his mission to Florence and treachery, 4–5

Chaucer, 300–1

Church: P. enters, 27; his attacks on and loyalty to, 271–2

Ciano, 104

Cicero: MSS. of the *Laws* and *De Gloria* lost, 17, 27; P.'s boyish admiration, 18; MS. of the *Rhetoric* spared by Petracco, 20; MSS. at Liège, 43–4; P. finds his *Letters* at Verona, 115–16; P.'s enthusiasm for C., *ib.*, and his two letters to him, *ib.*; MSS. lent by Lapo, 151; episode of a Ciceronian enthusiast, 155–6; P.'s MS. of C.'s *Letters* injures his leg, 205–6; MSS. copied for P. by Boccaccio, 210; P.'s master and pattern, 221, cf. 227

Cino da Pistoia: never P.'s tutor, 22; exchange of poems and influence on P., 22, 40

Clarence, Lionel, Duke of, 279–80

Classics and classical literature, *v.* Revival of learning

Clement V, Pope, 11, 12; removes Papacy to Avignon, 13; dies, 15

Clement VI, Pope; election and character, 107; favours P. and confers many benefices on him, 108, cf. 117; offers him papal secretaryship, 117; attitude to Rienzi, 127, 129; tries to reconcile Venice and Genoa, 167–8; mediates in troubles at Naples, 168; buys countship of Provence, *ib.*; appoints Commission on Roman affairs, 169; imprisons and releases Rienzi, 170; his death, 171–2; P.'s poetical letter to him, 272

Cola di Rienzo, *v.* Rienzi

Cologne, 58–60

Colonna, the: formerly Ghibellins, rallied to the Pope, 45; their feud with the Orsini, 61; their misgovernment of Rome, 127; slaughtered by Rienzi, 131, 133

Colonna, Agapito, Bishop of Luni, 50

Colonna, Agapito the Younger, 269

Colonna, Agnese, 75, 77

Colonna, Giacomo: publishes Bull of excommunication against Lewis of Bavaria, 45; Bishop of Lombez, *ib.*; takes P. there, 46; their friendship, *ib.*; presents P. to his brother, 48; his return to Rome, 60-1; P.'s ode to him, 63; his bantering letter of invitation to P., 72-3; takes P. to Rome, 77; poetical Latin letter to, 79; his death and apparition to P., 106

Colonna, Giovanni, Cardinal: his pleasantry with Convennole, 16; receives P. into his household, 48; character and friendship for P., 48-50; P.'s letter to him from Capranica, 75; introduces P. to Dauphin Humbert, 87; invited to sup at Vaucluse, 91; P. consults him about his coronation, 93-4; probably recalled P. to Avignon, 107; P.'s letters to him from Naples, 112; strained relations and separation, 129-31; his death, 140

Colonna, Giovanni di San Vito, 52, 77

Colonna, Stefano il Giovane: defeats the Orsini, 61; escorts P., 77; Senator, 78; expelled from Rome by Rienzi, 128; killed in battle with many of his House, 131

Colonna, Stefano il Vecchio: character and affection for P., 51-2; eulogises P., 99; takes P. to Praeneste, 112; survives all his sons, 131, 140; P.'s letter of condolence to him, *ib.*

Colonna, Stefano, great-grandson of old Stefano, 268-9

Coluccio, *v.* Salutati

Company, *v.* Great Company

Convennole, of Prato: P.'s schoolmaster, 16; his affection for P., *ib.*; helped by Petracco and P., *ib.*; loses Cicero's *De Gloria*, 17, 27; his return to Prato and death there, 17

Copyists, *v.* Revival of learning

Corio, 252

Coronation, *v.* Laurel

Correggio, Azzo da: friendship with P., 65; meets him at Avignon, 66; P. pleads his cause, 67; revisits Avignon, 88-9; goes with P. to Naples, 95, and Rome, 97; regains Parma, 102-3; his quarrels and intrigues, 114-15; a refugee at Verona, 116; his unhappy career and death, 235-6

Corvara, Abbey and Abbot of, 156-8

Crete, 248-9

Cristiano, Luca, of Piacenza: character and friendship with P., 50-1; letter from P. to him, 142; visit to Parma and adventure with brigands, 143-4; P. renounces Canonry in his favour, 171

Crown of Song, *v.* Laurel

Dandolo, Andrea, Doge, 183, 246

Dante: of the White Guelf party, 3; eulogy of Henry VII, 12; refuses to recant, 13; view of Rome in the *De Monarchiâ*, 74, cf. 123; desired laurel crown, 92, cf. 211; *Divina Commedia* sent to P. by Boccaccio; P.'s letter thereon, 211-12; P.'s supposed jealousy of him, *ib.*; construction of the *De Monarchiâ*, 227

Dauphin, *v.* Charles, Humbert

Decameron, v. Boccaccio

De Contemptu Mundi: quotations relating to Laura, 37, 139; composition and nature of the dialogues, 109-10

De Otio Religiosorum, 120

De Remediis Utriusque Fortunæ: its importance, 227; dedicated to Azzo da Correggio, 235

De Republica optime administranda, 188, 292-3

De sui ipsius et multorum ignorantia, 266

De Viris Illustribus: P.'s great history, probably begun in early years at Vaucluse, 90; probable allusion to, 158; still unfinished in 1354, 191; its importance, 228-9

De Vita Solitaria: its dedication, 84, and composition, 119-20; its importance, 227; finally copied, 256

Despots, Italian, general characteristics, 66-7

Dionigi da Borgo San Sepolcro, Fra: intimate relations with P. and influence, 55-6; letter to him with account of ascent of Mont Ventoux, 67-71; his death, 106-7, cf. 207-8

Domitian, Emperor, 92

Dondi dell' Orologio, 193-4

Doria, Paganino, 183

Eclogues, P.'s Latin: composed at Vaucluse, 90; the *Divortium*, 130; appreciation of them and their place in literary history, 223-4

Eletta Canigiani, P.'s mother: her marriage, 3; lives at Arezzo, 6; gives birth to P., 7; lives at Incisa, 8-9; accompanies Petracco to Pisa, 11, Avignon, 13, and Carpentras, 15; "best of all mothers," 18; her death and P.'s eulogy of her, 24-5

Eletta, granddaughter of P., 25, 235

Empire, *v.* Rome

Enza, River, 104

Epistolæ, v. Letters

Epitome of the *Lives of Illustrious Men*, 228, 260, 302

Faliero, Marino, Doge, 247

Ferrara, battle, 55; P.'s illness, 283

Ferrara, Marquis of, 114, 141

Flanders, P.'s travels in, 58

Florence: native city of P.'s family, 2; party politics of, 3-7; opposes Henry VII, 13, Lewis of Bavaria, 44, and John of Bohemia, 54; claims Lucca, 88; P.'s visits in 1350, 148, 152; votes P.'s recall from exile and restoration of his property,

153; antagonism to Milan, 179-80; plan to get P. a Canonry, 250

Fournier, Jacques, *v.* Benedict XII

Fracassetti, 114, 177, 189, 251, 262

France, state after war, 232

Francesca: daughter of P., 84, 110; her marriage, 235; lives with P., *ib.*; "Tullia," 281, cf. 304

Francesco, grandson of P., 235, 281

Francesco da Brossano, *v.* Brossano

Francesco da Carrara, *v.* Carrara

Frignano, Tommaso da, 282-3

Gabrini, *v.* Rienzi

Garda, Lago di, p. 116

Garzo, Ser, P.'s great-grand-father, 2

Genèvre, Mont, 156, 176

Genoa, 14, 132; war with Venice and P.'s letter thereon, 167-8; defeat, submission to Milan, and victory, 82-4; P. gradually estranged from, 246

Ghent, 58

Gherardo, P.'s brother: born at Incisa, 9; goes to Bologna, 21; leaves it with P., 23; lives with him at Avignon, 31; ascends Mont Ventoux with him, 67-71; visits the Ste. Beaume and Montrieu, 88; visited by P. at Montrieu, 120; P.'s second visit to him there, 174-5; his heroic conduct, *ib.*

Ghibellin: general tendency of the party, 4; the name becomes a mere badge, 44

Giovanni, son of Petrarch: birth, character, and unhappy relations with P., 84-6; at school in Verona, 116, and at Parma, 136; leaves Padua with P., 155; appointed Canon of Verona, sent there, expelled, and returns to P.'s home, 184-5; expelled for misconduct, 212-13; death, P.'s lamentation, and note in the Virgil, 233-4

Giovanni Andrea, Professor of Law and P.'s tutor, 21–2
Giovanni da Firenze gives P. advice, 32
Gladiatorial games at Naples, 112
Gonzaga, the, of Mantua, 147–8, 190
Great Company, 135, 177, 275
Greek, P.'s attempt to learn, 108–9
Gregory XI, Pope, 286–7
Grimoard, Cardinal, 279
Grimoard, Guillaume, v. Urban V
Grosseteste, Robert, 100, 220
Guelf: general tendency of the party, 4; its supremacy in Florence, ib.; feud of White and Black Guelfs, ib.; the White Guelf political creed, 123, 188, 270
Guido, Don, 157–8
Guido Settimo, v. Settimo
Gulielmo da Pastrengo, v. Pastrengo

Henry VII, Emperor, expedition to Italy, and death, 11–13
Homer: P.'s MS. and delight in its possession, 185-6; translation made for him, 257–8
Humanism, v. Revival of learning
Humbert II, Dauphin of Vienne, 87–8
Hungary, v. Andrew, Lewis

Imola, Benvenuto da, 294, 305
Incisa, P.'s home in childhood, 8–11
Innocent VI, Pope: election and character, 172–3; threatens to excommunicate P. as wizard, ib.; offers P. the papal secretaryship, 204; death, 242
Isabelle de Valois, 230
Italy: P.'s passion for, v. Odes; Rome: his salutation from Mont Genèvre, 176; rumoured project of invasion, 195–6

Jacopo II da Carrara, v. Carrara
Joanna, Queen of Naples, 83, 111–13, 120, 168

John, King of Bohemia: his invasion of Italy, 53–5; death at Crécy, ib., cf. 187
John, King of France, 172, 230–1
John XXII, Pope: secretly encourages John of Bohemia, 54–5; his Bull against Roman family feuds, 61; feigns intention of returning to Italy, 62–3; death and character, 64
Jongleurs, Provençal, 253

Lælius: his real name Lello Stefani, 46; lineage, character, and friendship with P., ib.; sends P. bad news of Rienzi, 132; P.'s answer, 133; letters to, 148, 191, 198; waits on Charles IV, 192; quarrel and reconciliation with Socrates, 201–3; death, 243
Lapo da Castiglionchio: his great erudition, 150–1; exchanges books with P., ib.; his copy of P.'s letters, ib.
Laura: P.'s first sight of her, 33; not known who she was, 33–6; allegorical theory combated, 34–5, cf. 72, 86; effect on P. of his love for her, 36–9; at Avignon, 53; progress and episodes of P.'s love, 80, 81, 89, 118; death of L. and P.'s entry on the Virgil fly-leaf, 137–8; tone of his later poems, 138–9
Laurel Crown of Song: object of P.'s ambition, 72, cf. 92; its traditions, 92; offered from Rome and Paris, ib.; conferred, 97–101; stimulates P. to work, 104; v. also Dante
Law: P. compelled to study, 18–22; abandons the study, 27
Learning, v. Revival of learning
Lello Stefani, v. Lælius
Letter to Posterity, 138; its composition and significance, 293
Letters, P.'s Latin Poetical: various allusions to, 53, 65, 79, 119, 136, 184, 272; arranged in 1359 and dedicated to Barbato, 216; appreciation of them, 222–3

Letters, P.'s Latin Prose, quoted *passim:* many written in 1351-3, 158; many burnt, 216; arrangement of the rest and dedication of the *Familiar Letters* to Socrates, 216-18, cf. 263; appreciation of their value, 218, cf. 222; *Ep. Seniles,* 217, 244-5; *Ep. Sine Titulo,* 218, 271

Lewis of Bavaria, Emperor: invasion of Italy and coronation by an anti-pope, 44; retreats from Rome and Italy, *ib.*; encourages and then opposes John of Bohemia, 53-4; hostility to the Papacy, excommunication and death, 187

Lewis the Fleming, *v.* Socrates

Lewis of Hungary, 120, 135, 168, 195-6

Lewis of Tarentum, 120, 168

Library, P.'s: "his adopted daughter," 165-6; intention to leave it to Venice never fulfilled, 241; its dispersal, 242

Liège: P.'s first visit, discovery of MSS. and penury of ink, 43-4; his second visit, 58

Literature, *v.* Revival of learning

Liternum, or Linternum, P.'s villa near Milan, 213

Lives of Illustrious Men, v. De Viris, etc.

Loiera, battle, 182-3

Lombardo della Sete, or da Serico, 260, 288, 302

Lombez: P.'s first visit, 45-8; P. obtains Canonry there, 65

Luca Cristiano, *v.* Cristiano

Luzzera, Castle, 148

Lyons, 60

Macchiavelli, 188, 293

Mainardo Accursio, *v.* Accursio

Malatesta, the, of Rimini, 194

Malatesta, Carlo, 262

Malatesta, Pandolfo, 194-5, 289

Mantua, 114, 136, 141, 147, 190

Marsili, Luigi, 266-8

Martini, Simone, commonly called Memmi, 29

Milan (*v.* also Visconti): though Ghibellin, opposes Lewis of Bavaria, 44, and John of Bohemia, 54; P.'s Virgil there, 86-7; leagued with Mantua against Ferrara and Parma, 114; P.'s house near Church of St. Ambrose, 179; antagonism to Florence, 179-80; long exempt from plague, 181; Charles IV receives Iron Crown, 191-2; Boccaccio visits P., 209-11; P.'s house robbed, 213; P. migrates to monastery of San Simpliciano, 213-14; P. returns from France, 232; his connection becomes less intimate, 246; marriage of Duke of Clarence, 279-80

Miliarino, Priory of S. Nicholas, 108

Minstrels, wandering Italian, 253-4

Modena, 115; Canonry there, 171

Monet, Raymond: P.'s bailiff at Vaucluse, 162; his death and eulogy, 164-7

Montferrat, Marquis of, 195, 252

Montpellier, P. studies law, 18

Montrieu, Monastery, *v.* Gherardo

Naples, P.'s first visit, 94-7; title of its king, *ib.*; anarchy and corruption after Robert's death, 110-13; pacification of, 167-8, *v.* also Robert

Napoleon, 8, 87

Nelli, Francesco, Prior of the Church of the Holy Apostles at Florence, called Simonides by P.: their meeting and close friendship, 150, cf. 209; favours Don Ubertino, 156-7; letters to him, 159, 196, 210, 233, 235; remonstrates with P., 179-80; young Giovanni visits him, 213; his death, 243

Oczko, Johann, Bishop of Olmutz, 197

Odes: *Che debb' io far,* 140; *Italia Mia,* 42, 54, 176-7; *O aspettata,* 63; *Spirto Gentil,* 42, 126

Olympius, 51
Orsini, the, 61, 74, 127
Orso, *v.* Anguillara
Otio Religiosorum, De, v. De Otio Religiosorum

Padua, 136, 141–2 ; P.'s Canonry there, *ib.* ; translation of St. Anthony's body, 147 ; P. leaves in 1351, 154 ; Charles IV visits, 189 ; P. in residence there, 209, 236, 248, 278, 291 ; defeat by Venice, 291–2
Paganino Bizozero, 144–5
Paleologo, *v.* Montferrat
Papacy, *v.* Avignon, Guelf, Rome
Pardowitz, Ernest von, Archbishop of Prague, 197
Parenzo, Ser, P.'s grandfather, 2
Paris : P.'s first visit, 55, 58 ; offers P. the laurel, 93 ; P.'s visit as Ambassador to King John, 230–1 ; Marsili's repute there, 267
Parma : feud of Correggi and Rossi, 66 ; expulsion of Veronese and entry of Correggi, 102–4 ; P. settles there, 104 ; his second stay and escape during siege, 113–15 ; P. made Canon and Archdeacon, 117 ; P.'s home in 1348–9, 136, 142 ; subsequent residence there, 147
Pastrengo, Gulielmo da, 66–7, 89, 116, 148, 185
Patras, Archbishop of, 249
Pavia, 198–200, 251–3, 278
Peschiera, 116
Pestilence, *v.* Plague
Peter of Poitiers, *v.* Poitiers
Peter of Siena, his supposed vision, 237
Petracco, Ser, P.'s father, 2 ; position, marriage, condemnation, and banishment, 3, 5 ; envoy for his party, 6 ; visits Incisa by stealth, 9 ; goes to Pisa, 12 ; leaves Italy and settles in Provence, 13–15 ; talent for literature, 18 ; first encourages, then prohibits P.'s classical studies, 18–19 ; burns P.'s books,

19–20 ; death and character, 24 ; his fortune stolen by the trustees, 26
Philip VI, King of France : in league with John of Bohemia, 54 ; promises to lead Crusade, 62 ; drops project, 63
Philobiblon, 53, 306
Philosophy : badly taught at the Universities, 21 ; P.'s conception of, 227 ; mediæval conception, *ib.* ; the Averroists, 265–6
Physicians : P.'s feud with, 171–2 ; his *Invectiva contra Medicum,* 193 ; fortunate disobedience to, 289–90
Piacenza, 156, 192
Pilato, Leonzio, 243, 257–9
Pirro, Antonio, saved P.'s Virgil, 87
Pisa, 11–13, 102, 135, 190, 192
Pistoia, origin of the White and Black Guelf feud, 4
Pistoia, Cino da, *v.* Cino
Plague, the Great, 135–7, 140, 181, 233–6, 243
Po, P.'s voyage in time of war, 280
Poetry : P.'s vocation, 27 ; mediæval doctrine of, 223 ; "most glorious of the arts," 294
Poetry, Provençal, 29, 39, 253
Poggetto, Cardinal, Papal Legate, 61–2
Poitiers, Peter of : visits Vaucluse, 82 ; meets P. in Paris, 231–2
Pommières, de, *v.* Sagramor
Pontremoli, blind schoolmaster of, 105
Porto Lungo, 183
Prague, P. visits, 197
Prato, Convennole da, *v.* Convennole
Prato Magno, 9, 10
Prato, Niccolò da, Cardinal, Legate in Tuscany, 6, 7

Quintilian, his *Institutions* and P.'s letter to him, 152

Ravenna, Giovanni da, 262
Ravennas, Adolescens, 262–4
Razzolini, Luigi, 229

Reggio, 104, 114

Renaissance, *v.* Revival of learning

Reports of P.'s death, false, 250

Revival of learning : P. devotes himself to it, 27 ; literature as a profession, *ib.* ; P. diligent in collecting MSS., 43 ; his view of the right relation between culture and religion, 56-7, cf. 238-41 ; P.'s coronation marks important epoch in, 100-1 ; P.'s zeal and work for, 105, cf. 305 ; P. accepted as its prophet, 141 ; general spread of the movement, *ib.* ; P.'s industry in copying MSS. and generosity in employing copyists, 147 ; his complaints against copyists, *ib.*, cf. 151, 257, 287 ; his Greek MSS. of Homer and Plato, 185-6 ; importance of P.'s Latin writings in furthering the movement, 219-27 ; sense in which P. is rightly called the Founder of Humanism, 219-20, cf. 229, 305-6 ; his valuable conception of continuity of history, 221 ; his revival of the critical spirit, *ib.* ; P. took men back to the Ciceronian standpoint, *ib.*, cf. 227 ; and to that of the classical historians, 228

Rhine, the ; riverside ceremony 58 ; earthquake throughout the valley, 196

Rhone, the, "windiest of rivers," 28 ; P.'s joy at sight of, 60

Rienzi, 122-34 (chap. VII.) *passim;* prisoner at Avignon, 170

Rime, *v. Canzoniere*

Rinaldo da Villafranca, 116, 185

Rinucci, *v.* Nelli

Robert, Friar, 112

Robert, King of Naples, 83 ; P.'s admiration for him, 93-4 ; character, 94-5 ; honours P., 95-6 ; his robe, 96, 98, 303 ; favours the Correggi, 102-3

Roche, Cardinal Androuin de la, 248

Roger, Pierre, *v.* Clement VI, Gregory XI

Rome : P. jealous for her rights, 28 ; Lewis of Bavaria's coronation and retreat, 44 ; P.'s enthusiasm for Rome and Italy, his view of the continuity of her history, his political idealism centred in her supremacy, 73-4, 122-5, 188-9, 191, 220-1, 226, 270-8, 285-6 ; P.'s first visit, 77-9 ; offers the laurel, 93 ; P. accepts, 94 ; his coronation, 97-101 ; P. made a citizen, 99 ; P.'s third visit, 111 ; Roman embassy to Clement VI, 125-6; Rienzi's revolution, 126-34 ; P.'s last visit in year of Jubilee, 152 ; Commission of Cardinals on Roman affairs ; P.'s advice, 169 ; Charles IV crowned, 192; temporary return of Papacy, 276-83 ; P.'s answer to a Frenchman, 285-6

Rossetti, Domenico, 228, 272

Rossi, of Parma, 66-7

Sade, Abbé de, 36, 38, 177

Sade, Hugo de, 36

Sagramor de Pommières, 189, 196-7

Salisbury, John of, 100, 220, 306

Salutati, Coluccio, 150-1, 261, 262, 267, 305

San Simpliciano, 213-14

Scala, Bartolommeo della, Bishop of Verona, 88

Scala, Can II, della, 185, 190

Scala, Mastino della, 66-7, 88-9, 102-3

Scandiano, 115

Scipio Africanus the Elder, P.'s ideal Roman and hero of his *Africa*, 90, 225

Scott, Michael, 265

Secretaryship, papal, 117, 170-1, 203-4, 242

Secretum, v. De Contemptu Mundi

Selvapiana, or Silva Plana, 104

Seneca, quoted, 73, 160

Serico, da, or Sete, della, *v.* Lombardo

Settimo, Guido : P.'s lifelong friend, 14 ; his companion at home, school, and University,

14–20; taken with P. to Vaucluse, 17; letters to him, 118,
245, 246; death, 281
Sicily, the Two Sicilies, *v.*
Naples
Silius Italicus, 225
Simonides, *v.* Nelli
Socrates: his real name Lewis,
47; origin, character, and friendship with P., 47–8; lives with
him in Cardinal Colonna's
house, 50; visit to Cavaillon,
120; P.'s letter to him narrating
deaths of friends, 144, 158;
other letters to him, 151, 156;
quarrel and reconciliation with
Lælius, 201–3; the *Familiar
Letters* dedicated to him, 216–
17; his death and P.'s grief,
and entry on the Virgil fly-
leaf, 234–5
Sonnets, allusions to: *Chiare,
fresche*, 139; *Il successor*, 63;
Mille piagge, 60; *Perch' io*,
77; *Per mezzi*, 60; *Per mirar*,
29; *Quando giunse, ib.*; *Vago
augelletto*, 139; *Vergognando*,
58–9; *Vinse Annibal*, 62
Soranzio, Raimondo, 32
Sorgue, source of, *v.* Vaucluse
Spirto Gentil, v. Odes
Statius crowned with the laurel,
92
Strada, *v.* Zanobi
Style, literary: P.'s instinct for it,
218; his demand in respect of
it, 228
Sygerus, Nicholas, sends P. a MS.
of Homer, 185–6

Talleyrand, Cardinal, 164, 173
Tolomei, Enea, of Siena; P.'s
Latin poetical letter to him,
53
Travel: P.'s love of and first
tour, 43; visits Paris, Flanders,
and the Rhine, 58–60; visits
Rome, 77–9, and probably
Morocco and the English
Channel, 79–80
Tribune, *v.* Rienzi
Triumphs, *v. Canzoniere*
Tuscan popular poetry, 11

Ubertino, Don, *v.* Corvara
Urban V, Pope: offered P. the
papal secretaryship, 204, cf.
242; election and character,
242; believes rumour of P.'s
death and confers his benefices
on others, 250–1; P.'s admiration for him, *ib.*; his return to
Rome and back again to Avignon, 270–84 (chap. XVII.) *passim;* P.'s letters to him, 272–6,
277–8; invites P. to Rome, 278,
283; death and funeral, 284

Vallombrosa, Abbot and Abbey
of, 156–8
Varro; MSS. copied for P. by
Boccaccio, 210
Vaucluse: P.'s first visit, 17, 18;
settles there, 80–1; life and
work there, 81, 82, 90, 109–10,
117–20; description of, 118–19;
the last sojourn, 156–76; his
bailiff's wife, 159–61; his rude
victual, 161–2; his house and
two gardens, 162–4; his bailiff's
death and eulogy, 164–7; his
library there, 165–6; P. leaves,
returns, and leaves again for
the last time, 174–6; his wish
to return in 1362 frustrated, 236
Venice: war with Genoa, 167–8;
P.'s letter thereon, *ib.*; victory
and defeat, 182–4; P.'s embassy, *ib.*; sues for peace, *ib.*;
visited by P., 209; P. takes
refuge from the plague, 236;
assigns P. a house in return for
the intended reversion of his
library, 241; the books never
claimed; real origin of the Marcian library, *ib.*; Boccaccio's
visit to P., 242–3; congenial to
P., 246–7; his eulogy of her, *ib.*;
Cretan victory, 248–50; four
young men's judgment, 266;
war with Padua, 291–2; P.'s
embassy, *ib.*
Ventoux, Mont, P.'s ascent, 67–71
Verme, Luchino del, 248–9
Verona (*v.* also Scala), 66, 115,
116, 136, 156, 184–5, 190
Vicenza, 155

Villafranca, *v.* Rinaldo

Villani, Giovanni and Matteo, 54-5, 61, 123-4, 178, 214, 242

Virgil: MS. spared by Petracco, 20; the Codex of the Ambrosian Library and its fly-leaf, 86-7; P.'s poetical letter to Virgil, 136; notes on the fly-leaf, 137-8, 233-5; P.'s belief about the Eclogues, 224

Visconti, the, of Milan: worst of the despots, 177; their relations with Charles IV, 190, 192, 195-7; their wars with their neighbours and with the Church, 195, 199, 278-80; denounced by Bussolari, 198

Visconti, Azzo, 55

Visconti, Bernabò, 179, 184, 194, 252

Visconti, Galeazzo: saves P., 182; accession to power, 184; suspected of killing his brother, 194; engages Pand. Malatesta, *ib.*; instigates P.'s letter to

Bussolari, 199; his royal alliances, 230, 279; P.'s friendship and visits, 247, 251, 259, 278-9; enslaves Pavia and builds castle, 252

Visconti, Gian - Galeazzo, possessed P.'s Virgil, 87; married in childhood, 230; possessed many of P.'s books, 242

Visconti, Giovanni, Archbishop of Milan: persuades P. to settle in Milan, 177-9; his character, *ib.*; dominates and honours P., 180-2; assumes sovereignty over Genoa, 183; death, 184

Visconti, Luchino, 102-3, 144, 178

Visconti, Marco, P.'s godson, 184

Visconti, Matteo, 184, 194

Visconti, Violante, 279-80

Vita Solitaria, De, v. De Vita Solitaria

Viterbo, 276, 277

Zanobi da Strada, 175, 192, 204